Massachusetts
People and Politics
1919–1933

MASSACHUSETTS
PEOPLE and POLITICS
1919-1933

J. Joseph Huthmacher

———◆●◆———

*Originally published by The Belknap Press of
Harvard University Press*

ATHENEUM   1969   NEW YORK

Published by Atheneum
Reprinted by arrangement with Harvard University Press
Copyright © 1959 by the President and Fellows of Harvard College
All rights reserved
Library of Congress Catalog Card Number 59-9276
Manufactured in the United States of America by
The Murray Printing Company
Forge Village, Massachusetts
Published in Canada by McClelland and Stewart Ltd.
First Atheneum Edition

For

MY MOTHER AND FATHER

Preface

After the First World War interest in America's political past declined among historians. The more enterprising preferred to explore other phases of the nation's experience, and the result has been our increasing knowledge of economic, social, and cultural history. The pervasive influence of government in the lives of our people since 1933, however, has redirected attention to political history and begun a reassessment of our political development — a reassessment which necessarily relies heavily on the information and analytical tools supplied by economic, social, and cultural historians, political scientists, sociologists, and other co-workers in the social sciences. For political history can no longer be viewed as the unfolding of a "manifest destiny," nor as the product of the doings of "great men" exclusively. Moreover, in the course of this reintegration of our political tradition it has become evident that valid generalizations concerning national political eras as a whole can be based only on a firm understanding and thorough exploration of the diverse conditions which govern the conduct of politics in the United States. Hence, the individual state has been accepted as a useful focus for research.

Materials necessary for re-evaluating the nation's political past are most abundant for the current century, and present-day political historians have devoted their primary attention to the two periods of the century during which popular interest in government — and government itself — were most active: the Progressive era of 1900–1917, and the New Deal era of the 1930's and 1940's. The period in between, the era of "Only Yesterday," has been thought devoid of political significance and left largely to social historians probing the manners of the flappers. But surely the Progressive movement did not disappear in an instant, nor did the New Deal spring into existence freshborn at the moment the last ballots were counted on election day. Both phenomena, in part, were closely connected with the political emergence of what has been termed "the new frontier" of American life — the urbanized, industrialized, immigrantized Newer American civilization which has become so characteristic of a large segment of the nation in the twentieth century. The 1920's was the period in which the political effects of that Newer American culture became most evident — and set the stage for much that is important in comprehending the course of current politics in the United States. Certainly that transitional era deserves more attention than it has yet received from political historians.

Several considerations make Massachusetts a particularly appropriate area for investigation of the forces affecting the voting behavior of Americans in the 1920's. Her Democratic United States senator — the first in the Commonwealth's post–Civil War history — was also one of the first prominent members of his party to break with President Wilson over the League of Nations. In 1924 the Massachusetts delegation to the Democratic convention was one of the most tenacious in voting through more than a hundred ballots for Alfred E. Smith in his battle with William G. McAdoo. In 1928, despite her reputation as a Republican stronghold since before the Civil War, Massachusetts was one of the two states outside the South in the Democratic presidential column. Moreover, early in the century Massachusetts compiled an impressive record of Progressive legislation, and in the 1930's and 1940's she was among the most enduring supporters of the New Deal. Finally, all of these circumstances are entwined with the fact that Massachusetts has stood in the forefront of the states most permeated by the Newer American culture of cities, factories, and new-stock citizens.

Examination of the Bay State's experience in the 1920's, then, will illuminate the sources and meanings of political developments along America's new frontier — a frontier which, as the 1950's give way to the 1960's, is still being extended and matured.

My research into the history of Massachusetts people and politics brought me in contact with numerous individuals whose patient helpfulness made the work much more pleasant than it might have been. Among those whom I wish to thank are the staffs of the Widener and Lamont Libraries of Harvard University, the Massachusetts State Library, the Boston Public Library, the New England Deposit Library, Holy Cross College Library, the Franklin D. Roosevelt Library at Hyde Park, the Reference Library of the Massachusetts Department of Labor and Industries, the Boston Board of Election Commissioners, and three Boston newspapers: the *Italian News*, the *Gazzetta del Massachusetts*, and the *Jewish Advocate*. John McMahon of the *Boston Herald* helped me select illustrations, while the task of readying the manuscript for publication was handled efficiently by Chase J. Duffy for Harvard University Press. A grant from the Georgetown University Publication Fund facilitated compilation of the book's index.

All of the interviewees whose names are listed in the Bibliography were extremely co-operative and cordial, and two of them in particular, Elijah Adlow and B. Loring Young, gave me more of their valuable time than might reasonably be expected.

In thinking through the questions and answers connected with this study I profited immensely from discussions with many friends, especially Raymond H. Robinson, James H. Timberlake, and Milton Viorst. Professors Arthur M. Schlesinger, Jr., Frederick Merk, V. O. Key, Jr., and Frank Freidel of Harvard University were ready with assistance whenever called on. My greatest debt of all is to Professor Oscar Handlin, not only for aid in this project, but for his wisdom and insight which have conveyed to me a fuller meaning of the study of American history.

In the final stages of the work I enjoyed the help of my wife, Marilyn Catana Huthmacher, whose encouragement grows all the more valuable as time goes by.

J. J. H.

December 14, 1958

Contents

Illustrations

(Photographs courtesy of the *Boston Herald*)

Massachusetts
People and Politics
1919–1933

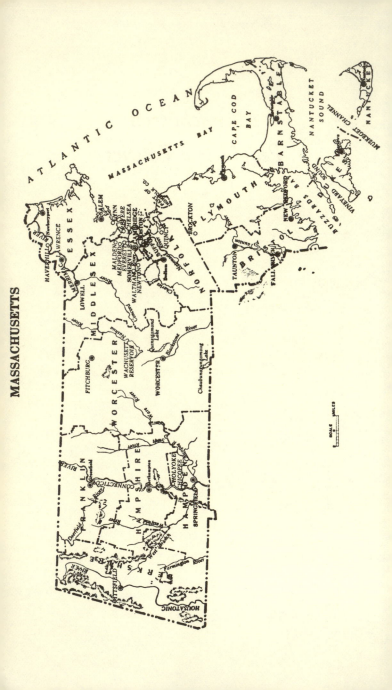

MASSACHUSETTS

Chapter One

A Modern Bay State and Her People

Massachusetts made her mark early and deep in American history; every schoolboy is familiar with the Puritans, the embattled farmers of the Revolutionary Era, the sea captains who ranged the oceans, and the abolitionists who helped free the nation from slavery. But the twentieth century Massachusetts that emerged from the First World War bore little resemblance to the Commonwealth of earlier days or of the history books. The state had changed radically between 1865 and 1919.

Manufacturing had long displaced agriculture, fishing, and commerce as the primary source of the Commonwealth's income.[1] True, approximately 120,000 people still lived on farms, in a total population of about 3,850,000. Moreover, fishermen setting out from Gloucester, Marblehead, and New Bedford continued to supply a considerable portion of the nation's sea food. And optimists still talked, at least, of restoring Boston's former position as one of the leading seaports of the world.

But in 1919 Massachusetts was first and foremost an industrial state. The value of products turned out in her factories was over four billion dollars, whereas the gross value of farm products was a mere $109,000,000. The average number of wage earners employed in manufacturing exceeded 700,000, nearly six times the total number of people living on farms. Textile and shoe manufacturing, the earliest sources of the

1

state's industrial expansion, continued to be the mainstay of her economy; other important branches of work were leather processing, foundry and machine-shop industries, and the production of paper, clothing, rubber goods, and electrical apparatus. In 1920 Massachusetts, with 3.6 per cent of the nation's population, produced 6.4 per cent of its manufactured goods, measured by value of product.

New England was the birthplace of the industrial revolution in America, and the factory's early displacement of the farm and the sea as the center of Massachusetts' economic life foreshadowed a transformation of the nation as a whole. Indeed, by the eve of the First World War industrial expansion in other parts of the country already threatened the Commonwealth's pre-eminence in the industrial world. Other sections enjoying natural and man-made advantages over New England succeeded in becoming the centers of new and strategic industries, like iron and steel. In addition, southern textile mills and middle-western shoe-manufacturing centers had begun to gnaw away at the Bay State's supremacy even in those lines. The outbreak of war, however, obscured the danger to Massachusetts' position, bringing record profits and wages to her entrepreneurs and workers, and inducing a vast expansion of her productive facilities. At war's end relative prosperity abounded in the state. But at the same time the menace of renewed intersectional rivalry loomed ahead.

One outgrowth of Massachusetts' industrialization was the extremely high degree of urbanization of her population by 1920. According to the census of that year 94.8 per cent of her people lived in areas classified as urban (incorporated places of 2,500 inhabitants or more). However, since all the territory of Massachusetts was included in incorporated cities or towns, contrary to the situation in most states, that figure was somewhat misleading. Many predominantly agricultural towns of 2,500 embraced a considerable area over which the population was spread, without having a central village of the requisite "urban" size. Nevertheless, even when allowance was made for that discrepancy, Massachusetts stood in the top rank of the nation's most urbanized commonwealths. In density of population to the square mile (479.2) she was second only to Rhode Island.[2]

Boston, with nearly 750,000 inhabitants, remained the Hub of the Commonwealth's economic and cultural life. Nestled about her were a number of important industrial cities like Quincy, Waltham, Cambridge, and Everett, and outlying cities where her workers lived, like Chelsea and Revere. North of Boston, in Essex and northern Middlesex counties, lay the great shoe and textile cities of Lynn, Haverhill, Lowell, and Lawrence, and a number of smaller manufacturing centers such as Peabody and Salem. South of Boston industry centered in Taunton and the shoe city of Brockton, and in the southeast corner of the state, in Bristol County, were the twin textile cities of Fall River and New Bedford.

Forty miles west of Boston lay Worcester, the Commonwealth's second largest city and a center of diversified industry. Worcester County also embraced several smaller manufacturing cities such as Fitchburg and Leominster and, especially in its southern reaches along the Rhode Island border, a number of textile mill towns like Southbridge, Webster, and Blackstone. Fifty miles southwest from Worcester was Massachusetts' third largest city, Springfield, another center of diversified industry situated in the valley of the Connecticut River. In that same area were the cities of Holyoke, Chicopee, and Northampton, and mill towns like Ludlow, Palmer, and Ware, devoted largely to the manufacture of paper and textiles. Finally, in the westernmost county of Berkshire, bordering on New York State, lay the industrial cities of Pittsfield and North Adams and several manufacturing towns.

Clustered about the industrial centers were the burgeoning suburban communities where those who were able to afford it could escape the noise and grime of the manufacturing city and lead their private lives in comparative quiet. Suburban development had progressed farthest by 1920 in the Boston area, giving rise to such residential cities and towns as Milton, Brookline, Newton, Wellesley, Belmont, Winthrop, and Melrose. Similarly, the chief beneficiaries of industrial prosperity in other manufacturing centers had begun transforming surrounding communities into suburban havens of repose.

Occupying the in-between territory, relatively untouched by industrialization and suburbanization, were the rural towns characteristic of old New England. In all parts of the state save the metropolitan Boston district one passed through them on the way from city to city. Within their borders doughty Yankees continued to gather in the central village to worship at the white-steepled Protestant church and to hold their periodic meeting in the white-painted town hall, earning their living tilling the rocky soil of the outlying farms or servicing the needs of those who did. This was the existence old New Englanders still wrote about, nostalgically, but by the end of the First World War the fate of Massachusetts clearly lay with her newer civilization of industrial cities and towns, and with her suburbia. In 1920, 81.6 per cent of the Bay State's people lived in places with a population of 10,000 or more, and fully 66.2 per cent lived in places having 25,000 or more inhabitants.

If the degree of industrialization and urbanization that characterized Massachusetts by the second decade of the twentieth century differentiated her from the Commonwealth of earlier days, so too did the composition of her population. The lure of economic opportunity that drew thousands of Yankees away from the soil to the mushrooming industrial centers during the nineteenth century also brought an influx of people from foreign lands, profoundly altering the make-up of the state's population. Old-stock Yankees, descendants of the typically English and Protestant original settlers of the Bay State, still clung to ancestral acres in the rural towns and dominated affairs there. Those in the industrial cities and mill towns were now usually the holders of "better" jobs — supervisory, white collar, and management positions — or followers of mercantile and professional pursuits, or coupon clippers.[3] As such they made their homes in the "better" residential areas of the manufacturing centers, or led the trek to the suburbs. But by 1920 authentic Yankees, whether rural or urban dwellers, had long ceased to predominate numerically in Massachusetts' population. In the census of that year only 31.9 per cent of the Commonwealth's people were classed as "native white of native parentage," and even a considerable but indeterminate proportion of those were merely the grandchildren of immigrants. Fully 66.8 per cent of the state's inhabitants were immigrants themselves, or the children of immigrants.[4]

Some types of newcomers assimilated rapidly with the descendants of the state's original inhabitants. This was the case especially with the hundreds of thousands of Englishmen from Great Britain and Canada who came to settle during the nineteenth century.[5] Like the natives in cultural traditions, they found adjustment to their new surroundings comparatively easy and soon felt at home whether in the rural towns or the industrial centers. By the First World War, moreover, they had advanced far up the economic scale. By that time, indeed, British and Canadian immigrants and their sons were hardly distinguishable from the remaining Yankees in social, occupational, or neighborhood status, and they were generally considered old-stock inhabitants of the Commonwealth.

The much smaller number of Scandinavians who came to Massachusetts found assimilation more difficult at first. There was the language barrier, for one thing. In addition the Swedes, Norwegians, and Danes (and the Protestant Germans, who can be included with them in this discussion) imported their own types of Protestantism, differing from that practiced by Yankees and Englishmen. Moreover, their ties were with homelands other than Britain and with somewhat different cultural traditions. Nonetheless, by the First World War the relatively small number of these immigrants and their long residence in the Bay State had gone far to ease the points of friction, especially among the second and later generations of immigrants. What differences remained after the twentieth century began yielded rapidly to the concept of "Anglo-Saxon" and Protestant unity, in the face of more marked differences accentuated by the growing numbers of "non-Nordic" and non-Protestant elements in the Commonwealth's population.

By 1919, then, Protestant native Yankees and Protestant British, Scandinavian, and German immigrants and their descendants made up the old-stock population of Massachusetts, and in that sense the term is used throughout this work.

The second great element of the Commonwealth's people were the Irish. Their immigration was well under way before the Civil War, and thereafter into the twentieth century they came in vast numbers.[6] Seeking relief from appalling conditions in their native land, the Irish entered the state's economic system at the lowest rung of the ladder, freeing old-stock wage earners from construction and dock work and other menial forms of labor. Gradually they were admitted to the ranks of industrial operatives as the old-stock inhabitants advanced to higher positions on the economic scale. Thereafter their number multiplied so rapidly through immigration and reproduction that they literally took over Boston and other industrial centers where they settled. Congregated at first in the worst neighborhoods vacated by the old-stock laborers whom they displaced, the more fortunate Irishmen eventually followed old-stock people into the residential districts of the manufacturing cities and towns, or joined in the march to the suburbs. By the First World War a substantial proportion of the Massachusetts Irish were in the ranks of higher-paid workingmen; many of them held supervisory, white collar, and mercantile jobs; a considerable number had made their way into management and the professional class; and a few had even become coupon clippers.[7]

Despite their economic advance, however, a wide gulf still separated the Irish from the Bay State old stock. The cleavage between Irish Catholicism and old-stock Protestantism marked off one important area of vexation. The Irishmen's traditional hatred for England — the "mother country," either recently or remotely, of the majority of the old-stock population — heightened their mutual antagonism. The appearance, accent, and manners of the Irish, and their mores in such matters as sobriety and observance of the sabbath, seemed strange and consequently "inferior" to native Americans in the nineteenth century, and continued to be so regarded by many old-stock people in the twentieth. Their cultural traits, then, combined with their status as economic competitors, resulted early in economic and social discrimination against them. This discrimination, and the hard feeling it engendered on the part of Irishmen, made satisfactory rapprochement impossible. The breach between the Irish and the old stock, clearly delineated before the Civil War, carried over through the second and later generations of immigrant children, and by the time of the First World War it was still very wide.

By then, however, the number and influence of the Irish had grown so strong that they were almost as typical of Massachusetts as the Yankee and the cod fish. In 1920 nearly one-sixth of the Commonwealth's population consisted of immigrants from Ireland and their children, and to them should be added a large but indeterminate number of the people classified as "native white of native parentage" — third- and fourth-generation descendants of immigrants whose consciousness of their Irish identity had hardly diminished at all.

The third element of the state's population in 1920 consisted of those groups which common parlance usually lumped together under the terms, "newer races" or "New Immigrants." They, too, generally came in search of economic opportunity. The French-Canadians settled in industrial cities and mill towns throughout the state, and especially in textile centers.[8] The same was true of Polish immigrants, though some of them became farmers in the Connecticut River Valley. Italians, on the other hand, concentrated more in Boston and the largest manufacturing cities. So did the Jews. Portuguese immigrants and those from the Atlantic Islands settled almost exclusively in southeastern Massachusetts, working in the textile mills of New Bedford and Fall River, or laboring in the cranberry bogs and the fishing industry. Minor groups — Lithuanians, Greeks, Armenians, Syrians — dispersed through Boston and other large industrial centers, working in factories or becoming active in trade. Finally, there was Massachusetts' relatively small number of Negroes who, though long resident in the United States, were by most standards one of the "newer races." In 1920 they constituted but 1.2 per cent of the state's population, most of them living in Boston and a few other cities, engaged primarily in domestic and personal services.

The newer arrivals who helped man Massachusetts' industrial expansion, like the Irish before them, entered the economic system at its lowest level. Displacing the Irishmen who held the worst jobs, the New Immigrants likewise displaced them in the poorest neighborhoods of the state's manufacturing cities and towns. Gradually, as the Irish like the old stock before them improved their economic status, the more fortunate of the New Immigrants also began to move up the occupational and neighborhood scales. By the time of the First World War each of the newer groups had seen some of its members advance to the ranks of better-paid workers and to higher types of employment.[9] Each group had produced a quota of lawyers, doctors, and other professional men, few of them widely known but all recognized as the natural leaders — the "prominenti" — of their particular ethnic element. As their incomes increased, the more successful New Immigrants in turn followed the old stock and the Irish to comparatively better housing districts. In Boston, for example, fortunate Italian immigrants or their sons moved from the teeming North End to somewhat better quarters at Orient Heights in East Boston, while their Jewish counterparts from the congested West End moved to the outlying Roxbury section of the city, a few even penetrating to suburban Brookline.

But just as cultural differences and economic competition brought old-stock discrimination against the Irish, so the same considerations brought discrimination against the New Immigrants on the part of both the old stock and the Irish, and served, at the same time, to keep the various component elements of the New Immigrants apart from one another. Language barriers constituted one important cultural cleavage, and religion was a second. The religion of the Jews and of those who adhered to various Eastern churches was different altogether from that of both old-stock Protestants and Irish

9

Catholics, while the brands of Catholicism imported by French-Canadians, Italians, Poles, and other groups differed in marked respects from the Irish Catholicism that had come to dominate the established Bay State Catholic community and its hierarchy. Appearance, manners, and mores also played a role, for if such considerations made Irishmen appear strange and inferior to old-stock people earlier, they now made New Immigrants seem strange to old stock and Irish alike. Finally, strong attachments to various mother countries proved a copious source of hostility among the diverse newer nationality groups and served to differentiate them further from the bulk of the population whose nationality ties ran back to the British Empire or the Emerald Isle.

The economic and social discrimination suffered by the New Immigrants evoked resentment on their part, and this resentment, often attended by feelings of inferiority, carried over almost unabated into the second and later generations. But by the First World War their increasing numbers — a product of continued immigration and a comparatively high birth rate — promised them an accretion of strength and influence in the affairs of the state. In 1920 at least one-quarter of the Commonwealth's people consisted of immigrants and their children who specified a New Immigrant language as their mother tongue.[10] To them, as in the case of the Irish, should be added an undetermined number of people classed as "native white of native parentage."

The social adjustment of the Irish and each of the component groups among the newer arrivals followed the pattern common to the experience of most American immigrants.[11] Invariably economic advancement was their first concern. There followed a process of assimilation, in matters not considered fundamental, to the dominant "native" American cultural traits and standards. The learning of English if necessary, the value of education, and changed modes of dress were generally accepted, at least after a while and for the second generation.

At the same time, however, there was a common tendency in each of the newer ethnic groups to perpetuate and justify what were regarded as the essential parts of its own cultural tradition — religion, knowledge of the mother tongue, and ties with the old country. Irish immigrants built their Catholic churches and their parochial schools, while Jews and adherents of Eastern rites erected places dedicated to their own forms of worship. When New Immigrant Catholics settled, they scrimped and saved in order to build churches of their own where sermons could be preached in Italian, French, or Polish, and where they could render homage to saints other than Patrick. Then they set up their own parochial schools where, under rules promulgated by the state Department of Education, certain portions of instruction could be carried on in languages other than English. Irishmen, Jews, and the other groups had their own newspapers and strove to keep alive interest in their native traditions of literature, drama, and music. Each group admonished its young to "marry your own kind," and each welcomed and aided fresh immigrants from its home country. Through visits, letters, and remittances members of these groups kept in touch with loved ones in the native land, and generally they were keenly interested in the political affairs and aspirations of the nation or would-be nation left behind.

The culture-preserving efforts of the Irish and other groups represented, on one hand, a natural human tendency to maintain what was familiar, and on the other, a reaction to the discrimination and condescension they suffered from the older inhabitants. Through such efforts the members of the group found companionship with like-minded people in the midst of an often hostile environment. Allegiance to the ethnic-centered neighborhood and "gang," formation of countless voluntary associations, and conformance with customary observances were other means of finding and retaining fellow-feeling. Involvement in these activities diminished somewhat as the first-generation immigrants of each group died out; for the second and later generations — their feet planted more firmly in the new environment — began to acquire new interests and attitudes. Yet their ethnic backgrounds conditioned the make-up of the immigrants' children and grandchildren, stamping them clearly as Irish-Americans, Italian-Americans, American Jews, and so on. In most cases the descendants of the immigrants acknowledged their antecedents, and knew they were therefore different from old-stock Americans.

Faced with the growing numerical strength of the Irish and the "newer races," who together might be designated the "Newer Americans," the old-stock people themselves in the closing years of the nineteenth century and the first decades of the twentieth became aware of their own special position in the population and of the threat which seemingly alien cultural traditions posed to the supremacy of their own traits and standards.[12] One difficulty lay in defining just what the native cultural tradition was. Some spoke of an "English" tradition dating back to the nation's forefathers, but this concept was soon expanded to embrace an "Anglo-Saxon" or "Nordic" tradition so that Protestant Scandinavians and Germans might be included in it. In the end the quest for definition boiled down to the assertion that the cultural characteristics of the native Yankees, and of the immigrants who had assimilated most readily with them, constituted the truly "American way of life."

A belief that the newer groups would eventually assimilate

to this American tradition persisted among some old-stock people, but to many the Newer Americans appeared to be undermining that tradition more rapidly than they were fusing with it. Protestantism was now on the defensive, it seemed to them, and so were the public schools and the principle of separation of church and state. In some areas the English language was threatened with submergence in a babble of foreign tongues. Protestant old-stock or "American" standards of mores and morals in such matters as observance of the sabbath and the use of liquor seemed about to be extinguished by foreign modes of behavior. Confronting those fears, old-stock citizens too sought the solace of fellow-feeling among their "own kind" through the agency of the neighborhood and the voluntary association, and emphasized their ties with the English or "Anglo-Saxon" forbears of America. Gradually a growing number concluded that alleviation of the problems they faced would come only with the restriction of immigration through government regulation.

By the outbreak of the First World War, then, the social structure of Massachusetts embraced three levels marked off by criteria of economic advancement and cultural similarity to the standards of the oldest inhabitants in the Commonwealth. The old-stock inhabitants discriminated against both the Irish and the New Immigrants, while the Irish looked with condescension on the New Immigrants. Irishmen bore their grudge against the old stock, while the various newer nationality groups were resentful of both the Irish and the old stock and regarded one another with suspicion.

The common war effort of 1917–18 temporarily diverted attention from the strains engendered by the evolution of Massachusetts' population and social systems. Old-stock, Irish, and New Immigrant homes alike knew their share of sacrifice and casualties. Nevertheless, at war's end, the prospect of renewed immigration and discrepancies in birth rates promised a revival of ethnic contention. The situation pointed toward a continued relative decline of the old stock in the face of Irish influence, and increasing impingement on the position of both by the rising "newer races."

By the beginning of the twentieth century political alignment within Massachusetts was primarily a function of the state's ethnic and social structure.[18] The Republican Party of the Civil War era was controlled by old-stock citizens, and consequently the Irish made the Democratic Party the outlet for their growing political consciousness. Boston, with its heavy concentration of Irishmen, soon became the center of the party's strength in Massachusetts. No single "boss" arose to weld the Irish Democrats of the Hub into a smooth-running machine like New York's Tammany Hall. Instead a number of leaders with ward or personal followings, men such as Martin Lomasney, John F. Fitzgerald, and James Michael Curley, vied with one another for supremacy. Through alliances formed at election time, however, the Irish Democrats came to dominate the city's political fortunes. At the same time, Irishmen gained control of municipal politics in other industrial cities where their numbers were preponderant. Gradually they were elected to the state legislature, and then to Congress, from districts they controlled. But in the first years of the twentieth century Irish politicians were interested primarily in local affairs, and few were widely known beyond their own bailiwicks. Hence in state-wide elections for the governorship the Democrats still usually put forth old-stock candidates — Yankees who, for economic reasons or out of sheer habit, refused to convert to the Grand Old Party.

The Democratic Party's identification with the Irish, however, did convert most Yankees to the Republican standard.

Protestant British, Scandinavian, and German immigrants, becoming accepted as members of the old stock, also joined the Republicans. And the gradual introduction of the New Immigrants into Bay State political life furnished still more recruits for the G.O.P.

Since the New Immigrants' first concern was economic advancement, politics long remained a matter of secondary importance with them. But increased naturalization, and especially the second generation's reaching voting age, added to their importance in the Bay State political situation. Irish Democrats, having just recently won for themselves the fruits of political success on the local level, were generally loathe to share them with still later arrivals. On the other hand old-stock Republicans, whose power in the state as a whole was much greater and longer established, were in a better position to court the votes of the newer groups with minor appointments and offices. In some cases New Immigrant resentment of the Irish Democrats' political selfishness was buttressed by hard feeling engendered by cultural disputes, such as the French-Canadian Catholics' periodic quarrels with the Irish hierarchy over control of churches and parochial schools.[14] Finally, the New Immigrants' heavy dependence on manufacturing industries for a livelihood made the G.O.P.'s high-tariff and sound-money doctrines attractive. (So alluring were those doctrines, in fact, that even Irish Democrats were not immune in national elections. In 1896 Boston itself had gone Republican, owing largely to the Irish workingmen's suspicion of Bryan's "agrarian radicalism.")

In some instances, under the stress of circumstances, Irish Democratic leaders accommodated the newer immigrant elements and secured their allegiance. In Boston, for example, Martin Lomasney and John F. Fitzgerald found their formerly Irish wards transformed into Italian and Jewish neighborhoods as Irishmen moved to better quarters. In order to insure their own supremacy Lomasney and "Honey Fitz" shared a minimum of rewards with their new constituents, and consequently their districts continued to return Democratic majorities. Usually, however, New Immigrants' ties with Irish Democratic chieftains were strongest in local elections. In state-wide and national contests their votes were more susceptible to change on the basis of economic and personal considerations.

Outside of certain areas in Boston and a few other large cities, then, the Republicans won the bulk of the New Immigrant vote in the early years. In the first decade of the twentieth century the effectiveness of that alliance gave old-stock Republicans fair hope of limiting the Irish Democrats to purely local victories and of blocking their march to any wider success in state or national elections.

The G.O.P.'s prospects were somewhat dimmed, however, by complications of politics in the Progressive era and the war period which disturbed party alignments and gave the Democrats a series of narrow victories. In 1910 and again in 1911 an old-stock Democratic candidate, Eugene Foss, managed to win the governorship.[15] A split in Republican ranks in 1912 that divided the party's vote between the regular nominee and an independent Bull Moose candidate enabled Foss to win a third term. Moreover, in the national election that year the Bay State's electoral votes went to the Democratic presidential aspirant for the first time in history, even though Taft and Roosevelt together got 61.2 per cent of the total popular vote compared to Woodrow Wilson's mere 35.5 per cent.[16] Continuation of the Republican schism in 1913 and 1914 allowed the Democrats to win the gubernatorial contests in those years, too, with David I. Walsh as their nominee. Walsh was the first Irish Catholic elected to state-wide office in the Commonwealth's history, and his victories insured that thereafter the Irish would not only constitute the Democratic Party's main source of strength, but also its main source of candidates.

But Wilson in 1912 and Foss and Walsh in 1912, 1913, and 1914 won only by minority votes, owing their success to internal strife in the opposition party. More disconcerting from the Republican point of view was Wilson's performance in the 1916 election. Then the G.O.P. was reunited, and though it carried the state for Hughes, Wilson secured 46.7 per cent of the total presidential vote, a vast improvement over his showing four years earlier. Next, in 1918, David I. Walsh actually defeated incumbent Senator John W. Weeks by a small margin, to become Massachusetts' first Democratic United States senator since before the Civil War.

Issues of domestic progressivism and war policy, and the prevalence of war-boom prosperity, influenced the outcome of the 1916 and 1918 elections. On the basis of those considerations Wilson and Walsh not only mobilized the full strength of the Irish Democrats, but also increased their party's vote among both the old stock and the New Immigrants. In light of the returns, Democrats looked forward to further conquests.

On the other hand, G.O.P. leaders maintained their faith in the basic Republicanism of the Commonwealth's voters. No Democratic presidential candidate had yet captured a majority of the state's popular vote. Even in his 1918 victory over Weeks, Walsh failed to secure a clear majority of the total senatorial vote. In that election the Republicans retained control of the governorship and the other executive offices on the state-wide ballot (lieutenant governor, secretary of state, attorney general, treasurer, and auditor). Both branches of the state legislature were heavily weighted in their favor, as in the past. The state's congressional delegation consisted of twelve Republicans and but four Democrats. In each of the Commonwealth's sixteen counties except Suffolk (Boston), long-entrenched G.O.P. "county rings" continued their customary control of county offices. In the rural towns and suburban cities, almost uniformly, Republicans were the managers of municipal government. Even in industrial cities the G.O.P. frequently controlled city hall, except in those centers where Irish Democrats were concentrated most heavily or had forged an effective alliance with the New Immigrants. Surveying the extent of their power, Massachusetts Republicans were not overly perturbed by their opponents' recent advances, though it seemed likely that future political encounters would be livelier and somewhat more evenly matched.

At the end of the First World War the people of Massachusetts faced a variety of problems. One was the matter of the state's position in the national industrial economy. Another was the process of urbanization. Still a third was the changing composition of the Commonwealth's population and the cultural, social, and political tensions accompanying that development. But in the fall of 1918 troublesome problems were temporarily obscured for all Americans by the haze of optimism produced by wartime idealism. Among the most optimistic in those days were the Massachusetts Democrats, who saw in the recent achievements of President Wilson and Senator-elect Walsh a prospect of shortly displacing the G.O.P. as the Commonwealth's majority party. Few then anticipated that the postwar decade would, in fact, render the state's economic and social problems more difficult of solution than ever. Few Democrats perceived that the war's aftermath would destroy their advances and reduce the party to the status of an almost hopeless minority.

Chapter Two

The Politics of Postwar Disillusion

Pʀᴇsɪᴅᴇɴᴛ Wilson expressed America's war aims in idealistic phrases, and when the armistice came many Americans agreed with him that it had been a war to make the world safe for democracy, to guarantee the right of self-determination for all people, and to inaugurate a new regime of righteousness in international affairs. When the President published the draft covenant of the League of Nations in February 1919, most Americans acclaimed it, or at least, tentatively acquiesced.

Yet, by 1920 the Massachusetts Democrats had repudiated Wilson, and in the election that November the Commonwealth's voters overwhelmingly rejected the candidates who espoused his League project. To some extent the change in public opinion was due to Senator Lodge's "educational campaign" against the League, a campaign motivated by intense nationalism and a zealous hatred of things Democratic.[1] Economic conditions, and popular resentment of wartime inconveniences, also played a significant role in Wilson's undoing.

In largest part, however, the President's failure in Massachusetts stemmed from shortcomings in his own performance as idealistic peacemaker. Nowhere were those shortcomings more pronounced than in the realm of self-determination.

19

That point of Wilson's reconstruction program had heightened the war effort of millions of Irishmen and New Immigrants, who saw in it a promise of justice for homelands suffering oppression under the prewar arrangement of the map. But once at the conference table and in the map room, Wilson discovered the immensity of the task he had set himself. His inability to placate the desires of ethnic groups began a process of alienation among them.

That fact, above all others, accounted for the thoroughness of the defeat of James M. Cox and the League of Nations in Massachusetts. It accounted, too, for the virtual disintegration of the Bay State Democratic coalition of voting elements which had functioned so promisingly in 1916 and 1918. Moreover, Irish and New Immigrant agitation on behalf of foreign lands rearoused the old stock's fears regarding the basic Americanism of the newcomers. Consequently, the social unity promoted by common wartime objectives ended, and when the period of peacemaking was over, the cultural gaps dividing the population were wider than ever.

One group whose enthusiasm for Wilson's objectives early turned to disillusion were the Italian-Americans. They fully expected the principle of self-determination to increase immensely the territorial possessions and prestige of their homeland at the expense of the Austrian Empire. With that in mind, Italian-American spokesmen hailed the new year 1919 as one "radiating hope for the vision of a new era . . . for the welfare and peace of all humanity," and the affectionate demonstration which greeted President Wilson on his visit to Rome early in January seemed to indicate that Italy's aspirations would be fulfilled.[2]

At Paris, however, Wilson came to regard the demands of the Italian diplomats as extravagant and in conflict with his other plans for handling the tangled Balkan situation. The port of Fiume was the main stumbling block; for while Orlando and the people of the city itself regarded it as Italian territory, Wilson saw it as an outlet to the sea for the newly created state of Yugoslavia.[3] Landing at Boston late in February 1919 for a brief stay in the United States, the President spoke in glowing terms of the aspirations of the Yugoslavs but failed to mention the claims of Italy, and the formerly cordial attitude of Italian-Americans turned to suspicion. In its next issue the *Gazzetta del Massachusetts* declared that "the Italians of Boston, of the United States, of the whole world, have now just one thing to do . . . to arouse themselves, to agitate, and to cry out in a loud voice: We are disappointed, Mr. President!"[4]

Italian-American agitation soon extended beyond the editorial column into politics, and in May 1919 the Massachusetts legislature, with but one dissenting vote, adopted a resolution asking President Wilson to support Italy's position. Senator Lodge, sensing the value of the situation for his campaign against the League of Nations, announced his belief that Fiume rightfully belonged to Italy. The Republican state convention went on record in October as deprecating "the action of our peace commissioners in Paris in opposing the wishes of the Italian people with regard to Fiume."[5]

But Republicans were not the only ones sensitive to Italian-American pressure. Early in May 1919 Senator David I. Walsh addressed a combined Liberty Loan and pro-Fiume rally sponsored by Boston Italians on the Common. In the course of his remarks he stressed the necessity for all who came to the United States to forget their country of origin and think strictly as Americans. Before Walsh had even left the platform, however, Italian speakers were on their feet denouncing his "insidious words" and urging that the audience never forget

"Roma Alma Mater." [6] Thereafter Walsh received numerous resolutions from organizations in the state demanding that he "support the Hon. Henry Cabot Lodge in his attitude toward the Italian question regarding Fiume." [7]

As Italian resentment against Wilson mounted during 1919, Republicans were not long in resurrecting a skeleton in the closet which, to many minds, served to explain this old-stock President's inability to appreciate Italy's claims. During his academic career Wilson had written *A History of the American People*, and in early editions such comments on the New Immigration as the following could be found:

> But now there came multitudes of men of the lowest class from the south of Italy and men of the meanest sort out of Hungary and Poland, men out of the ranks where there was neither skill nor energy nor any initiative of quick intelligence; and they came in numbers that increased from year to year, as if the countries of the South of Europe were disburdening themselves of the more sordid and hapless elements of the population.[8]

When quoted in Italian newspapers such passages required little editorial comment, but at times it was suggested that Italian-American readers "would do well to clip out this extract and keep it as a remembrance from Professor Woodrow Wilson of Princeton University." [9]

Two smaller groups whose optimism foundered on the rocks of self-determination were the Armenian- and Syrian-Americans whose homelands, formerly parts of the Ottoman Empire, craved independence. Instead of achieving autonomy each nation became entangled in the mandate system evolved at Versailles, with results that sorely disappointed patriots both at home and in the United States. Early in March 1919 the Armenian enclaves in Massachusetts secured from the state legislature a resolution asking independence for their mother country.[10] But shortly thereafter meetings were being held in protest against the Peace Conference's mandate scheme, which would "divide up most of historic Armenia between foreign powers . . . contrary to the sublime principles for the triumph of which the last great war was waged." [11]

Syria became a French mandate and by February 1920 Dr. Abraham Rihbany, a Bostonian who served as a representative of Syrian interests at Paris, was back in Massachusetts declaring that President Wilson had proved no match for the diplomats of Europe "and they fooled him in everything." In later speeches Dr. Rihbany advised that America not enter the League of Nations. [12]

The largest and most potent of all the disillusioned ethnic groups were the Irish, and with their desertion of the Wilsonian standard went also the regular Democratic Party organization in Massachusetts.

Sons of Erin showed little enthusiasm for the declaration of war in April 1917, following hard on the heels of England's suppression of the 1916 Easter Rebellion in Ireland. But as the war and Wilson's oratory continued, many Irish-Americans embraced self-determination as the remedy for their homeland. The Friends of Irish Freedom, the chief organization of Irish patriots in the United States, designated December 3–10, 1918, as Self-Determination Week, observed with appropriate meetings across the country. The climax came at a great rally in Madison Square Garden on December 10, when William Cardinal O'Connell of Boston told the throng, and inferentially the American peacemakers: "Ireland, like every other country, must be free, one united Ireland, indivisable, unseparated, now and forever. . . Let the test of sincerity be Ireland. Then we will be convinced that truth still lives." A month later, with the peace negotiations under way, the message was reiterated in the official organ of the Boston archdiocese, *The Pilot*: "Can the Peace Conference refuse to hear that heartrending cry? If the deliberations . . . close without mention of Ireland and the application to her of the principle of self-determination can the world expect uninterrupted peace?" But such would not be the outcome, *The Pilot* believed, for surely the leaders of the Allies had "begotten a unanimity of purpose and a clearness of vision on mighty questions that make certain the fulfillment of the peace articles so beautifully conceived and so eloquently preached." [13]

Meanwhile, President Wilson made *sub rosa* attempts to impress British statesmen with the necessity for a prompt solution of the Irish problem, but he had achieved nothing by the time of his return to the United States in February 1919. His arrival in Boston coincided with the closing session of an Irish Race Congress, which had assembled in Philadelphia at the call of the Friends of Irish Freedom. The five thousand Irish-Americans who attended not only applauded the familiar calls for self-determination, but also appointed a delegation to carry Ireland's claims directly to the President. The delegates saw Wilson but the interview proved stormy, for the President refused to make any public commitment on the Irish question. Actually Wilson, following his return to the Peace Conference later in March, continued urging settlement in private conversations with British leaders, but with little effect.[14]

By then, however, the postponement of self-determination had grossly altered Irish-America's estimate of Wilson, his idealistic principles, and his League of Nations. Coupling of the Irish issue with the question of American participation in the League was symptomatic of the change that took place in the Irishmen's attitude toward postwar reconstruction. In Massachusetts one of the first examples of such action came on March 12, 1919, when the Lawrence Central Labor Union resolved that "a League of Nations without Ireland included would be a failure." [15] A few days later the Reverend Gerald Treacy of Boston College "caused a sensation" at a self-determination rally by declaring that "the present draft of the League of Nations is not a concert of free peoples, such as President Wilson always advocated, but a league of defense for England. . . I am in favor of a real concert of free peoples, but don't forget the accent on the 'free.' " By the end of March such talk no longer caused sensations, and on the thirtieth a mass meeting in Faneuil Hall resolved:

> That we demand of President Wilson that he make good his pledged word that nations must be permitted to choose their own form of government. Notwithstanding President Wilson's fine words, Ireland is still chained to her British oppressor.
> That we are unalterably opposed to any League of Nations . . . which does not provide for the freedom of Ireland.[16]

In Ireland itself the parliamentary elections of December 1918 had resulted in overwhelming victory for Sinn Fein, the radical faction of patriots that rejected everything short of complete independence. The elected representatives refused to go to London but instead established their own Irish parliament (Dail Eireann), and on January 21, 1919, issued a Declaration of Independence. Thereafter Eamonn De Valera, chosen to head the Dail, styled himself "President of the Irish Republic." [17]

In June De Valera arrived in New York City and toured the United States on behalf of his country's cause. At Boston forty thousand people gathered in Fenway Park on June 29 to applaud the hero. De Valera expressed approval of a league of nations that would be democratic and guarantee self-determination for small nations, but suggested that a new attempt be made to draw up a satisfactory covenant. His secretary was less circumspect and stated bluntly: "We come . . . to ask you . . . not to set your hand to a document which will mean the perpetual slavery of our country." In the issue following De Valera's visit *The Pilot* reversed its pro-League position and concluded that "if this League, in its present form, is endorsed by America, Britain gains her point at the expense of the civilized world. This is preposterous." [18]

The political implications of Irish dissatisfaction became unmistakably clear by the end of 1919. David I. Walsh, elected to the Senate a year earlier while promising to support President Wilson's postwar plans, abided by his pledge well after his constituents' ardor for Wilsonian ideas had begun to cool. In a speech on March 16, 1919, Walsh not only defended the President's position on the League of Nations, but went on to urge that "Americans of Irish blood be patient. . . Let us remember to be Americans first." Such "un-Irish" utterances brought a flood of abusive letters, however, and meetings throughout the state denounced the Senator as a straddler on the Irish question.[19] Chastened, Walsh now strove to make clear that he strongly favored independence for Ireland, and in June played a prominent part in securing passage of a pro-Irish resolution in the Senate. The culmination of Walsh's conversion came on October 9, 1919, when he parted ways with his party's President, denounced the League covenant, and in a detailed analysis of the document sought to explode Wilson's claim that it constituted the salvation of the small nations of the world. At about the same time the Democratic state convention in Massachusetts adopted a League plank more hostile to President Wilson's position than that approved by its Republican counterpart.[20]

Old-stock reaction to Irish nationalism was not long in coming. Anglophiles viewed Irish-American agitation as a threat to Anglo-American cordiality. To others it seemed to introduce, as a controlling factor in the conduct of American international and domestic affairs, considerations which were foreign or even "un-American." Shortly after Irish-American dissatisfaction became pronounced in mid-1919, expressions appeared to the effect that "if the people who come here from Ireland cannot become completely American citizens, we should take some measures to keep them from coming in large numbers, for we cannot run a democratic country in which large groups are chiefly animated by politics in a land three thousand miles away. . ." [21]

Early in 1920 an "Ulster delegation" from loyalist northern Ireland visited the United States to offset the effects of De Valera's tour. Entering boldly into the lion's den, the loyalists conducted a rally in Boston's Symphony Hall the evening of February 16. Irish nationalists packed the galleries and hissed the king, but the Ulstermen made their points in attacks on Sinn Fein, De Valera, and the Roman Catholic hierarchy of Ireland.[22] After their departure the *ad hoc* reception committee resolved to establish a permanent organization — the Loyal Coalition — to combat Irish propaganda in Massachusetts and elsewhere. The charter membership roll, a roster of prominent old-stock Bostonians, included Dr. Charles Eliot, Moorfield Storey, Methodist Bishop Edwin Hughes, William Roscoe Thayer and the Reverend Paul Revere Frothingham. A series of Coalition-sponsored public meetings approved resolutions declaring "the so-called Irish question . . . not the proper concern of any department of the Government of the United States." Newspaper advertisements solicited new members, "if you are a good American, desire good government, and propose to keep the hyphenates out of American public affairs. . ." [23]

Denunciation merely fed Irish-American intransigence, and to the objects of their wrath Irish speakers now added the "Tories and English propagandists" who belonged to the Loyal Coalition and similar organizations.[24] One result of

27

efforts at postwar peacemaking, then, was that relations between the Irish and the old stock in Massachusetts became more strained than ever.

By the end of 1919 the Massachusetts Democrats held little in common with the Democratic Administration in Washington. President Wilson insisted that the League of Nations covenant be approved as he brought it from Paris, and in January of 1920 he declared that the presidential election should constitute "a great and solemn referendum" on the matter.[25] On the other hand, Bay State party spokesmen, reflecting the resentment of their Newer American constituents, were intent on thwarting the President as the one means of averting disaster in November. In the preliminaries to the campaign they seemed to achieve a measure of success. In the end, however, Wilson's program remained the program of the Democratic national ticket, and with that revelation the party's prospects for success in Massachusetts dimmed to the point of disappearance.

The outcome of the national convention that met in San Francisco late in June encouraged the anti-Wilson Democrats. True, Massachusetts and the other delegations in her camp made scant headway against the Administration-controlled resolutions committee as far as the platform was concerned. The convention adopted a League plank that met with Wilson's approval, and rejected an attempt to insert a strong pro-Irish statement in the platform. The Bay State delegates suffered another defeat when the convention rejected a proposal for modification of the new national Prohibition law. But balloting for nomination of the presidential candidate seemed to make amends for those setbacks. The votes of Wilson's supporters were split among the President's former Secretary of the Treasury, William G. McAdoo, Attorney General

A. Mitchell Palmer, and a number of dark-horse candidates. A deadlock ensued until, after forty-four ballots, Governor James M. Cox of Ohio emerged the winner.[26]

Political observers viewed Cox's nomination as a blow to the President. Cox's manager, Edmond H. Moore, had often worked hand-in-glove with Tammany and other organizations in the anti-Wilson element of the party, and the Ohio governor was expected to show little zeal for the League of Nations in his campaign.[27] The Loyal Coalition charged that he was "avowedly Sinn Fein," and he supposedly had no liking for the Prohibition experiment. Senator Walsh had supported Cox on all forty-four ballots, and on the last roll call all but one of the Bay State votes were in his column. Arrived back in Boston, the Massachusetts delegates pronounced it "a great convention." [28]

Their celebration was short lived, however. Within two weeks of his nomination Cox, after a moving visit with Wilson, made the League of Nations the chief issue of his campaign.[29] For a while Senator Walsh issued reassuring statements to his constituents. But as Cox toured the country damning the Lodge reservations (which Walsh had voted for), the meaning of what had transpired at the White House meeting became unmistakably clear. The Massachusetts Democracy was completely disordered — its Irish leadership immobilized, many of its New Immigrant allies of 1916 and 1918 repelled.

Cox realized the effect of his course on the Irish Democrats, and as the campaign progressed he put more emphasis on arguments designed to win back the disaffected party stalwarts. Self-determination again became an undying principle. The League of Nations constituted Ireland's best way out. Cox himself, if elected, would bring her case to the League's attention under Article Eleven, for it was an international peace-disturbing issue subject to League review. Article Ten, on the other hand, did not preclude Ireland's right to separate from England, even by force if necessary, for this would be an internal dispute *not* subject to League action. Nor could Article Ten prevent American recognition of a successful Irish revolutionary government. In fact, Cox declared, the same article would then obligate the United States and the other covenanting powers to guarantee the integrity of the new regime.[30] So the arguments ran, at times resembling a circle.

Before long, Republicans were poking holes in Cox's claims, citing sometimes Senator Walsh's speech of October 9, 1919.[31] Moreover, as the campaign progressed the severity of Britain's repressive measures in Ireland increased, which only made Cox's task among Irish-Americans more difficult. Public meetings in Boston and elsewhere protested British atrocities, demanded immediate recognition of the Irish Republic, and repudiated "any . . . League of Nations that would make liberty-loving, democratic America an associate of England in her crimes against the people of Ireland." In August the Massachusetts American Federation of Labor convention demanded that the government take steps "to end the further crucifixion of the Irish nation" by the "British invaders," and announced itself "bitterly opposed" to Wilson's League covenant, thus repudiating the stand of the national A.F. of L. convention.[32] A steady flow of statements from Irish-American spokesmen condemned the League as "the greatest menace, the most insidious effort against American institutions and American principles that has occurred since the Civil War," and "a super-government controlled by the imperialistic powers of Europe and Asia in whose councils England would have a controlling voice. . ."[33] The national council of the Friends of Irish Freedom denounced "the misleading and wholly unfounded statements . . . made . . . by Governor Cox" and urged opposition to "any candidate for national or

30

State office who favors the League of Nations." The Reverend Jones Corrigan of Boston College summed it all up as "a great moral issue before the American electorate. The United States of America, or the British League of Nations? Our country — that is the issue." [34]

If Cox attempted to pacify the Irish, his patience was shorter with other disaffected Newer Americans — Italian, Armenian, and Syrian — whose postwar reactions have been described earlier. By mid-1920, moreover, those elements had been joined by additional nationality groups whose initial satisfaction with the Peace Conference's work turned to disillusion. Aggrieved New Immigrants sought redress from the Wilson Administration, whose wartime propaganda had inspired their hopes in the first place. But the President, by 1920, could not help them, and their resentment grew. The Republicans found it easy to sympathize with them in words, and cultivated their discontent.

Thus Greek-Americans, whose homeland gained much territory at Paris, by 1920 thought it should have more. In March, at their request, Senator Lodge introduced a resolution in the Senate urging compliance with their desires. [35] American Jews were at first ecstatic over incorporation of the British Palestine mandate and the Balfour Declaration in the peace treaty with Turkey, and the inclusion of provisions guaranteeing ethnic minorities' rights in treaties establishing the new states of middle and eastern Europe. But their spirit dampened in view of the almost instant revival of anti-Semitism in Poland and elsewhere, making the treaty guarantees mere scraps of paper. Wilson's minister to Warsaw in a declaration made public by the State Department denied the existence of pogroms in Poland; American Jewish leaders characterized his statement as "astounding" and absurd. [36]

Poland found her new independence threatened by Russia, and in August 1920 a group of Fall River Polish-Americans petitioned Senator Lodge for assistance in getting the government to aid their homeland in the crisis. Lodge replied that only President Wilson could help Poland by summoning a special session of Congress, "if he feels that the situation demands action." [37] Independent Lithuania, another product of self-determination applied, was menaced in turn by an invading Polish army under Marshal Pilsudski. Lithuanian-Americans turned to Washington for help, and when it did not come, regretted their former "extravagant believing in Mr. Wilson's saying that 'might shall not triumph over right!' " [38]

Dismayed by the rising clamor of demands from ethnic groups, candidate Cox forsook the quest for their votes and instead condemned their "hyphenism," contrasting it with pure Americanism. In a bitter speech at Columbus, Ohio, in the middle of October, Cox attacked explicitly the Italian, Greek, and other ethnic "parties" backing Harding, picturing them as a "motley array of questionable groups and influences . . . an array that to survey brings the crimson blush of humiliation to an American." He carefully refrained from mentioning the Irish-Americans in his indictment, but did include "the Afro-American party, whose hyphenated activity has attempted to stir up troubles among Negroes upon false claims that it can bring social equality." [39] Thereafter the people of the "newer races," many of whom helped swell the Massachusetts vote for Wilson in 1916, could not be expected to support happily the Democratic candidate at the ballot boxes in November.

Under the circumstances, the Democratic campaign in the Bay State languished. September's primary election, which selected the state ticket, brought out five thousand fewer Democratic voters than the 1916 primary, despite the doubling of the potential electorate through the adoption of woman suffrage.[40] There was no "organization candidate" for the gubernatorial nomination, and the choice fell almost by default to an unknown but pro-Wilson state senator, John Jackson Walsh of Boston. Few competed for the secondary posts on the ticket, and no names appeared at all on the primary ballot for nomination as lieutenant governor and secretary of state.[41] The unusual hesitancy of Democratic politicians to run for office in 1920 was reflected further in the fact that the party nominated no candidates in two of the state's sixteen congressional districts, and seventeen of the forty state senatorial districts. In nine of the fourteen counties the Democrats presented no nominees for county commissioner, and no candidates for sheriff in eleven. Some who did run publicly repudiated the head of the party's national ticket.[42]

The Massachusetts Irish, the backbone of the party, had literally gone on strike. The voices of their spellbinders — Walsh, Curley, Fitzgerald, and the rest — were silent. All the Irish "big names" boycotted the state convention, which met in Springfield September 19, and only 250 of the 2,081 accredited delegates attended. When Governor Cox carried his campaign into Massachusetts, the Worcester Democratic city chairman urged that he make no more than a whistle-stop appearance in that city, for an extended talk on the League of Nations would only damage the chances of local candidates. And a former Democratic lieutenant governor frankly told the crowd awaiting Cox's appearance in Lynn that the party did not expect victory in November.[43]

The brunt of the Democrats' campaign, then, was carried by the Massachusetts contingent of League of Nations devotees among whom Yankees, college professors, and intellectuals were especially prominent. They dominated the state convention and adopted planks endorsing the national platform's position on the League, Ireland, and Prohibition, squelching the protests of the few Irish Democrats who bothered to attend.[44] As best they could they carried the Cox line to the people. In promoting the League they were helped by groups like the Massachusetts League of Nations Club, headed by Dr. Charles Eliot, but too many of its members belonged to the Loyal Coalition. The climax of the Wilson Democrats' efforts came when Cox himself toured the state on October 19, ending in Boston. But Senator Walsh had refused the honor of introducing the Democratic presidential nominee on Boston Common.[45]

The result was an ineffective campaign. Rallies were sparsely attended. Funds were lacking, for the Democratic national committee had written off Massachusetts as a poor investment.[46] While thousands of old-stock women took advantage of the Nineteenth Amendment by registering to vote, many of their Irish and New Immigrant counterparts in Democratic strongholds stayed home. The Newer American women, less accustomed to civic life to begin with, were predisposed to hold back from exercising the suffrage so readily. In the absence of attractive Democratic candidates and of prodding from the Irish Democratic organization leaders, there was little incentive for them to overcome their reticence in 1920. As registration totals mounted in Republican areas and the Democrats lagged behind, many in both parties prepared for the rare event of seeing not only Massachusetts — but Boston itself — go Republican in a presidential election.

Factional disputes marked the Republican pre-convention campaign in Massachusetts, but the outcome of the national meeting in Chicago temporarily glossed over intraparty differences and restored unity. The financial sinews essential to an extensive campaign were available. And the variety of issues at hand assured the party an easy victory in November.

A split between the two men who controlled Bay State Republicanism, Senator Lodge and former Senator Winthrop Murray Crane, was the source of dissension within the organization. Crane's espousal of the League of Nations opened the breach, and Lodge's lukewarmness toward the presidential aspirations of Crane's protégé, Governor Calvin Coolidge, widened it. As a result of Crane's exertions, the Republican state convention in October 1919 adopted a plank more favorable to the League than that of the Bay State Democrats. On the other hand, Lodge's dislike for the Governor deprived Coolidge of the full support of the Massachusetts delegation at the national convention — a circumstance which, according to Coolidge's supporters, alone prevented his winning the presidential nomination.[47]

In the end, however, the national convention gave both factions something to soothe their wounds. The platform, though vague, sufficiently damned the Wilson League to satisfy Senator Lodge. Then, in revolt against dictation, the convention chose Calvin Coolidge as Harding's running mate.[48] Crane was unhappy with the League plank, and the last-minute nomination of Coolidge unnerved Lodge. But both factions, having achieved partial victories, drew together to work for party success in November.

In its quest for votes during the fall of 1920, the national Republican organization and its Massachusetts counterpart appealed to all sides on the foreign affairs issue — encouraging the drift toward isolationism and reiterating calls for one hundred per cent Americanism, cultivating the discontent of Newer American ethnic groups and yet holding out hope to those who clung to the concept of an international peace-preserving agency. The Republican approach to the League

35

issue created complete confusion. To the ambiguities of the Chicago platform were added the conflicting statements of Harding and other party leaders in the months that followed. There was something for everyone in those declarations.[49]

In Massachusetts, however, the majority seemed to be against the League by the last quarter of 1920. Senator Lodge's educational campaign had an effect. In addition, disillusion with the peacemaking, first pronounced among the various Newer American groups, had by then infected other elements of the population. As the arrangements made at Versailles seemed to tumble down and Europe returned to its old bickering, while new threats like Communism emerged on the world scene, most people succumbed to the desire that America return to tending its own garden. The League of Nations "would only mean more wars." [50]

The mounting fear of "hyphenism" was another influence at work, turning old-stock Americans against international involvement and the League. Like Cox, Warren Harding also became a devotee of one hundred per cent Americanism in his campaign. In a statement even prior to Cox's speech at Columbus, Harding frankly characterized the Irish issue as an internal English problem and "not a question for official America." On September 18 he denounced our "meddling abroad" for its tendency to divide the American household, and "to drive into groups seeking to make themselves felt in our political life men and women whose hearts are led away from 'America first' to 'hyphen first.'" He dreaded the day when an organized "hyphen" vote would have the balance of power in American political life.[51]

With both presidential candidates and the Loyal Coalition sounding the alarm against hyphenate agitation, many old-stock people found it easy to conclude that this new trouble at home had arisen from Wilson's attempt to play peacemaker to the world. If such was the result, then better to avoid further entanglements and keep out of the League of Nations. Thus, in their reaction to Newer American agitation, native elements of the population developed an aversion to that attitude of international responsibility which the League's supporters sought to implant in their minds.

At the same time, those promoting Harding's cause in Massachusetts were not reluctant to appeal to the hyphen vote, even while their candidate denounced it. An insinuation here (only President Wilson can help Poland), or a Senate resolution there (Northern Epirus should belong to the Kingdom of Greece) — it was too easy to resist. Speakers at Republican rallies for voters of Italian extraction stressed again the manner in which Italy had been "used" by the President in the Fiume affair. Nor did the G.O.P. forget Lithuanian and Armenian centers in its campaign schedule. "What did England get from the war?" a Republican orator asked an Irish-American audience in Springfield. "Everything in sight as usual," was the answer he supplied.[52]

Nevertheless, an internationalist minority in Massachusetts still favored a League of some sort in the fall of 1920, especially in the western part of the state where the influence of Winthrop Murray Crane and the pro-League *Springfield Republican* was strong. Republican campaigners did not neglect those people, either. "It is not a question whether we will or will not have a league but whether we want the Wilson league," a prominent Berkshire County politician assured a Pittsfield rally. No less a personage than Congressman Frederick Gillett of the Second District, Speaker of the national House of Representatives, declared his belief that "under President Harding an agreement will be reached between the Senate and the President which will preserve for us the features of the treaty which will make for permanent peace. . ." Republican spokesmen in the Bay State truly worked all sides of the street concerning the foreign affairs issue in the election.[53]

The domestic situation provided more campaign material for the G.O.P. When the promised new world order failed to materialize, Americans quickly tired of the restrictions and sacrifices that the effort to create it had entailed. Congressman Gillett's speech nominating Coolidge for the presidency at Chicago was symptomatic: "We have been fed long enough on glittering rhetoric and extravagant novelties and rainbow-tinted dreams. We need an era of hard sense and old freedom. We need to re-invigorate the homely orderly virtues which have made America great." [54]

Demobilization and "normalcy" could not come too quickly, then. The war-nourished bureaucracy at Washington became in many quarters symbolic of Wilsonian "autocracy." Continued incarceration of "political prisoners" and Attorney General Palmer's Red raids alienated the advanced liberals who read the *Nation* and the *New Republic*, and labor leaders.[55] Republicans pointed to the doubling of the number of federal civilian employees between 1916 and 1920 as evidence of Wilson's extravagance, and taxes, as ever, were too high. The exorbitant prices of sugar and cotton and "the high cost of living" in general were due to the Administration's failure to prosecute the "trusts." "Scandals" involving the ordering of "too many" army uniforms were paraded before the voters. Even Wilson's "excursion" to Paris at an alleged cost of $1,500,000 was cited as demonstrating the President's penchant for wasting the people's substance — "and the cable bill was about $1,000,000 more." [56]

Massachusetts Republicans nursed additional, local grievances. The northern states, they said, paid an undue proportion of the cost of the war. The pro-South Wilson Administration had also discriminated against New England in allotting wartime draft quotas. As a final insult the War Department had transferred General Clarence Edwards, commander of the famed Yankee Division, to an insignificant southern post. The election of a Massachusetts man as Vice-President would atone for these slights. And, according to Republican gubernatorial candidate Channing Cox, the new Republican administration would bring General Edwards back north "and give him another star." [57]

Most potent of all the domestic issues for Republican purposes was the economic situation, which deteriorated rapidly during the summer and fall preceding the election.[58] The prosperity of the war years was interrupted by only a few months of uncertainty immediately following the armistice, and then gave way to an unprecedented boom during 1919 with the unleashing of the pent-up demand for civilian goods. But by February 1920 evidence had accumulated of the approaching satiation of consumer demand. Another disquieting factor was the drop in American exports as other parts of the world recovered from the war. In June the underlying faults in the situation came to the surface, and the economic hardship that ensued affected both industrial workers and farmers.[59] Thereafter G.O.P. spokesmen preached Republican economic doctrine with renewed urgency, bolstering their appeal for votes among significant elements of the Bay State electorate.

Those who worked in the factories received most attention from Republican campaigners. For here, in addition to exploiting the natural dissatisfaction that accompanied the turn of economic events, the G.O.P. had ready at hand its time-honored remedy for the troubles of industrial America, the protective tariff. That imports were rising was affirmed already in March 1920 by the Federal Reserve Bank of Boston.[60] The "free trade" ideas of the southern-dominated Democrats embodied in the Underwood Tariff, according to Republicans, provided no curb for this menace. Soon a flood of cheap goods not only from Europe but also from the Orient — where workers live "on rat tails and rice" — would inundate the American market and bring even greater distress to New England's economy. Republicans, armed with their protective policies, must be returned to the helm.[61]

That the days of Mark Hanna were not so far in the past was also evident as speakers told crowds that large orders, contingent on the election of a Republican President, had been received by mills in their locality, but if the Democrats were returned to power those mills would be without work and their employees idle. Moreover, charges that specific companies stuffed their pay envelopes with Republican circulars seem to have gone unanswered.[62]

Democratic campaigners abroad in Massachusetts offered nothing to counteract the Republicans on the economic issue. Intent on but one thing — Woodrow Wilson's League of Nations — they seemed oblivious to the worsening economic situation and its accompanying tide of hardship and discontent.

The Republican campaign moved steadily forward in the summer and fall of 1920, encountering little opposition from the Wilsonians who had taken control of the state's Democratic organization. Only in the last week before the election did the Democrats' camp show increased activity as some of the Irish old hands, heretofore silent, made a gesture toward saving the party from total perdition. At a rally in Symphony Hall the evening of October 26, sincere Wilsonites, like Mayor Andrew Peters of Boston and John Jackson Walsh, were joined by very recent converts like James Michael Curley in urging the election of Governor Cox and backing his League of Nations stand. Consequently some observers saw a last-minute "swing toward Cox" in the Bay State, and experts re-

40

vised downward their estimates of the size of Harding's margin. Talk of Boston going Republican was discounted to some extent.[63]

But the supposed Democratic renaissance was largely deceptive, and even though Curley and other Irish leaders finally came out for their party's national ticket, an event across the seas countered their efforts. On October 26 Lord Mayor Terrence MacSwiney of Cork, imprisoned by the English for his activities on behalf of Irish independence, died on the seventy-third day of a hunger strike.[64] The ordeal of the Irish patriot had attracted world-wide attention, and nowhere more than in Massachusetts. The news of MacSwiney's death seemed to sum up, in many minds, the galling frustrations that had replaced the dreams of a brave new order of things in the postwar world. The Sunday before election became MacSwiney Observance Day, and in cities across the Commonwealth memorial meetings voiced new resentment against the chief architect of the dreams, and against his work. "Every one of these [wartime] pledges has been broken so far as the Irish are concerned, and with the consent of the United States Government," the massed Irish-American community of Pittsfield was told. "Irrespective of creed and irrespective of party," urged the speaker at the Lawrence gathering, "it is your duty as Irishmen and Americans to vote against anyone who favors a covenant that will not grant to Ireland her freedom." [65]

So the campaign ended. In his traditional Sunday-before-election "instructions" to the voters of his ward Martin Lomasney, dean of Boston's Democratic politicians, declared that "this is our most important election since the Civil War. The great issue is 'Will the United States enter the League of Nations?' " Significantly, he did not endorse the Democratic presidential candidate. In its pre-election issue the *Gazzetta del Massachusetts* proclaimed in bold letters: "Finally the day

41

has arrived. The day of reckoning for the administration of President Wilson and his proconsuls." Pressed for a prediction, pro-Wilson Democratic State Chairman Michael O'Leary commented only: "The first hundred years are the hardest. Martin Lomasney will be elected to the House from Ward Five." [66]

The balloting on November 2 produced the anticipated Republican victory, and only the magnitude of Harding's sweep caused surprise. Led by Irishmen and New Immigrants, voters among all segments of the Massachusetts electorate who had supported Wilson in 1916 deserted the Democratic standard. Particularly significant was the failure of Democratic strongholds populated by Newer Americans to keep up with old-stock Republican areas in the matter of registration and voter participation.

Harding carried the Bay State by 681,153 to 276,691, a margin of 404,462 votes, far exceeding the fondest hopes of Republican leaders. Cox's total represented only 28.9 per cent of the two-party vote for President, a decline of 19.1 points from Wilson's mark of 48.0 per cent in 1916. The Democratic nominee carried but two communities in the entire state, the towns of Blackstone and Milford in Worcester County.[67]

Boston, the seat of Irish power, went Republican by a vote of 95,034 to 62,513, and Cox's 39.7 per cent of the two-party vote in the Hub represented a decrease of 20.5 points from Wilson's 60.2 per cent in 1916. The Democratic percentage of the aggregate two-party vote of Boston's fifteen strongest Democratic wards, characterized by large Irish and Italian populations, declined by 19.8 points; while in the remaining eleven Republican or doubtful wards — the old-stock, Negro, and outlying Jewish wards — the figure was 18.0.

The Democrats' percentage of the aggregate two-party vote of the thirty-eight cities outside Boston declined from 48.3 in 1916 to 29.0 in 1920, or 19.3 points. Here also traditionally Democratic Irish wards, and New Immigrant wards which in many instances had gone to Wilson in 1916, generally showed the greatest losses in Democratic strength. But in most cases old-stock Republican wards were not far behind in that respect. Finally, the Democratic percentage of the aggregate two-party vote of the Commonwealth's towns declined from Wilson's 40.7 to Cox's mere 23.3, or 17.4 points.

The relative falling off in the Democratic presidential vote between 1916 and 1920 in the state's Irish and New Immigrant strongholds, when compared to old-stock Republican areas, does not seem so striking as might be expected in view of the large-scale revolt supposedly affecting those ethnic elements. On the basis of similar evidence some authorities have concluded that these groups did not desert the Democratic Party in 1920 in any greater proportion than the population as a whole.[68] But this conclusion overlooks the vitally important matter of the relative degree of voter participation on the part of the various segments of the population.

Though the potential electorate more than doubled between 1916 and 1920 owing to adoption of woman suffrage and the natural increase in population, Massachusetts' two-party presidential vote of 957,844 in the latter year showed an increase of only 85.4 per cent over the 1916 figure of 516,669. Obviously a considerable proportion of the state's potential electors had not registered or taken the trouble to vote, and analysis indicates that inhabitants of Democratic strongholds were particularly lax in that respect. The percentage increases in the two-party presidential vote for Boston, for the thirty-eight other cities, and for the Commonwealth's towns were 68.5, 86.9, and 92.1, respectively. The predominantly old-stock Republican towns, then, outdid the more cosmopolitan and Democratically inclined cities, and especially Boston, in increasing the size of their electorates. In the cities themselves old-stock Republican wards invariably showed much larger percentages of increase than Irish and New Immigrant Democratic wards.

A concrete example demonstrates what this meant in terms of political effectiveness. In Boston the city's three strongest Republican wards, where the women took full advantage of their new right to vote, showed increases in 1920 of 102.1, 118.0, and 125.7 per cent over the 1916 two-party vote. Corresponding figures for the city's three strongest Democratic wards were 16.0, 51.9, and 50.0 per cent. Martin Lomasney's Ward Five constituency, composed largely of Italian and Jewish immigrants and their children, showed the smallest increase of all the city's twenty-six wards, a mere 12.8 per cent. Clearly large numbers of Irish and New Immigrant people in Democratic districts, especially the women, failed to register and vote, while old-stock Republicans flocked to the registration booths and the polls. When the chips were down, this indifference constituted party desertion, in a negative sense at least.

Defection from the Democrats in Massachusetts doomed not only the party's presidential nominee but most of its other candidates as well. In the gubernatorial contest Republican Channing Cox got 643,869 votes to John Jackson Walsh's 290,350. The Republicans retained control of all other state executive offices. Democratic representation on the Bay State's congressional delegation was reduced from four to two men as Michael Phelan of the Seventh District (who had supported President Wilson) and Richard Olney of the Fourteenth District went down to defeat. Only two representatives from Boston Irish districts were left. Democrats in the state House of Representatives (240 members) decreased from 59 to 45, and in the state Senate (40 members) from 6 to 5.

The Republican victory in Massachusetts was a product of many forces, and in any case was not unusual in view of the state's political tradition. The remarkable thing, however, was the almost complete disintegration of Democratic strength which this particular victory involved. Ironically, it owed most to the failure of a Democratic statesman-President to implement his aspirations for a better world, and the disappointment of those who had aspired with him.

The effects of the political upheaval of 1918–1920 were to span the following decade, and more. One was the boost given the spirit of isolationism — moribund when Wilson first sailed for Paris. A few weeks after the election, speakers at a non-partisan "America First" rally in Boston pronounced the League "dead forever." Said Senator Walsh: "There can never be a League of Nations because the imperialistic powers of Europe want, not peace through justice, but they want peace through force, and there can be no peace without justice." [69] Years later, even after another world war, that suspicion of foreign entanglements would still color the world outlook of the Irish and other significant parts of the Bay State's population.[70]

Another result of the politics of postwar disillusion was the increased self-consciousness and political assertiveness of the various American nationality groups whose homelands had a stake in the peace negotiations. Thousands of Irishmen, Italians, Lithuanians, and other Newer Americans had attended rallies, signed petitions, and passed resolutions on behalf of their home countries. On election night James M. Cox's campaign manager, Congressman George White of Ohio, declared that "in this election Republican propaganda has been shrewdly directed to induce the descendants of six European nations to vote as six European nations instead of as one American nation." [71] White misinterpreted the Newer Americans' motives, but indeed postwar events had taught those elements a new meaning of the American political system, of its relation to their own lives, and of the influence they could bring to bear on it. They would not forget those lessons in the years to come.

A third result, arising in reaction to the second, was the mounting fear of hyphenism and its alleged displacement of pure Americanism in the hearts of foreign-born and second-generation citizens. Aroused by the activity of the Irish and other ethnic elements, this fear had helped turn old-stock people against Wilsonian internationalism. At the same time it brought denunciation of those Newer Americans who also voted against Cox, but on supposedly "foreign" or hyphenate grounds. Governor Cox himself ascribed his defeat mainly to the defection of the Irish, the Italians, and other ethnic groups who deserted the Democrats on the basis of non-American considerations. Campaign Manager White felt that "our common task must be to coalesce these groups again." [72] Various approaches toward that task of "Americanizing" the "hyphenates" would account for much of the historical interest of the decade that followed in Massachusetts and the nation.

In addition, the Harding sweep indicated the Bay State's endorsement of the attitude which sought an end to "extravagant novelties and rainbow-tinted dreams," and a return to "the homely orderly virtues." That was one meaning the returns held for Vice-President-elect Calvin Coolidge — "the end of a period which has seemed to substitute words for things, and the beginning of a period of real patriotism. . ." [73] The craving for normalcy would be frustrated by the continuation of postwar problems in the Harding Administration, and "virtues" of any kind would scarcely find a home there. But after a while Coolidge would enter the White House and furnish the model of an administration based on few novelties, even fewer words, and hardly any dreams at all.

Another aspect of the 1920 campaign was its demonstration of the attraction which Republican economic doctrine held for the people of Massachusetts. The depression that accompanied the election campaign touched their vital pocketbook nerve, and the appeal of the protective tariff helped lure back to the G.O.P. many who had drifted from it in the prosperous year 1916. Republican leaders would count heavily on the continued effectiveness of that appeal in the years ahead.

The final result of the 1920 election, evident on the face of the returns, was the desperate situation of the Democratic Party in Massachusetts. Postwar developments had seriously undermined the traditional loyalty of the state's Irish-Americans, and had detached from the party many of its recent recruits among the New Immigrants and the old stock. The G.O.P., uniting the disaffected elements with the bulk of the old stock, who had remained its major source of support, now constituted a seemingly impregnable majority coalition.

Chapter Three

Normalcy, In Nation and State

Two years of the Harding regime in Washington dissipated the tidal wave of votes that swept the Republicans to national power in 1920. The mid-term election of 1922 reduced their margin of control in the United States Senate from 22 to 6, and their House majority from 167 to 15. The Democratic Party, leaderless and lacking a coherent program, could claim little credit for that result. Rather it stemmed from a vague but politically effective dissatisfaction with the Administration's handling of a number of problems that refused to recede into normalcy.[1] Postwar demobilization did not go smoothly, and when President Harding vetoed the soldiers' bonus bill two months before the election, veterans' organizations felt betrayed. Secretary Mellon's method of reducing the wartime tax load aroused considerable opposition, as did the Fordney-McCumber Tariff Act, which raised protective duties with an indiscriminate vengeance. There were disputes over what to do with the railroads, the merchant marine, and other services which the government had conscripted during the war. Even the treaties negotiated at the Washington Conference, generally regarded as the major accomplishment of Harding's Administration, antagonized "big navy" enthusiasts.

48

More serious still was the nation-wide economic depression, which reached its lowest point in 1921 and persisted throughout most of 1922.[2] Wage reductions brought a series of strikes, as when textile companies in New England announced a decrease of 20 per cent early in 1922 to offset competition from southern concerns. The ensuing work stoppage lasted from January to September and affected 22,000 operatives in Massachusetts alone.[3] Other labor disputes were national in scope. Some people resented the government's "union-busting" tactics in the strike of railway shopmen in 1922, and others criticized its failure to act in the coal miners' strike the same year. And the continuing "high cost of living," in the midst of recession, helped to make consumers unhappy. In the third quarter of 1922 real signs of improved economic conditions appeared, but the long period of depression and industrial strife was remembered at election time.

The depression also stimulated the drive to restrict immigration. The threat of a flood of "cheap foreign labor," added to the rising fear of hyphenism and the Great Red Scare of the postwar years, gave the extra push required for abandonment of America's traditional open-gate policy.[4] In May 1921 Congress passed the stop-gap Emergency Quota Law. Until a permanent formula could be evolved, the measure limited annual immigration to 3 per cent of the number of foreign-born in the United States from each country in 1910. This limitation affected particularly the New Immigration, whose spokesmen registered vigorous opposition to the measure, to no avail.[5]

The assorted dissatisfactions throughout the land meant that national officeholders faced an upsurge of discontent in 1922, and Republican congressional candidates suffered accordingly. In Massachusetts, Senator Henry Cabot Lodge was the target. The ineptness of his Democratic opponents saved him from complete humiliation, however, and the aging Senator won another term by the narrowest of margins.

While the outcome of congressional elections across the country demonstrated that the Harding Administration had failed to achieve "normalcy" on the national level, the situation was different as far as state politics in Massachusetts was concerned. The Progressive spirit that disturbed the Commonwealth's domestic political waters during the second decade of the twentieth century had been stilled by 1922. In the new placidity of the times Governor Channing Cox and the Republican state team experienced little difficulty securing endorsement from the voters. Their accomplishment at the polls overshadowed Senator Lodge's discomfiture in the eyes of G.O.P. organization leaders and reassured them that the party was safe in the Bay State.

It was inevitable that Senator Lodge, a principal figure of the Republican Administration, should feel the brunt of the anti-incumbent impulse. In addition, the Senator's position was made even more precarious by circumstances that particularly affected the temper of his own constituency.

One such development was the rapid and almost complete return of the Irish to the party of their traditional allegiance following the repudiation of Wilson in 1920. In office Harding adhered to the interpretation of the Irish question he had advanced during the election campaign, and Irish-Americans soon learned that their homeland could expect little comfort from the new Administration. Demands for recognition of the Irish Republic were spurned, and Harding abandoned the *sub rosa* efforts that Wilson had initiated to bring about settlement of the problem.[6]

Other incidents indicated Harding's seeming lack of gratitude for the Irish votes of 1920. Just a few days after his in-

auguration the President refused to allow contingents of
federal armed forces to march in South Boston's annual St.
Patrick's Day parade. Then in June, when Admiral William
Sims told a London audience to pay no attention to the activities of Irish-American agitators, whom he characterized as
"asses," Secretary of the Navy Denby merely handed Sims an
official reprimand. Irish-American leaders had demanded
severer punishment of the outspoken admiral, and his insults
continued to rankle.[7] These were small items in the world of
larger affairs, yet they commanded front-page headlines in
the Boston press.

The Administration's naval limitation treaty, which Lodge
engineered through the Senate, also brought denunciation from
Irish sources. By its terms, the Friends of Irish Freedom alleged, "America would concede to Britain undisputed control
of the seas at the very moment when naval supremacy was
about to pass to the United States." In 1922, on the other hand,
it became evident that most Democratic leaders had abandoned
the League of Nations as a live issue, for David I. Walsh was
selected to head the Democratic senatorial campaign committee that year. In short, the Democratic Party again appeared
sounder than the G.O.P., from the Irish-American stand-
point.[8]

Equally disconcerting to Lodge was the opposition he en-
countered in his own party, from two sources. One element
opposed the Senator on his "reactionary" record, organized
the Liberal Republican League of Massachusetts in the summer
of 1922, and backed Joseph Walker, former Speaker of the
state House of Representatives during the Progressive era, in
his contest against Lodge for the nomination in the September
primary. Walker and his followers attacked Lodge on the
League of Nations issue, his lukewarmness toward Prohibition,
his siding with the "interests" in tariff and tax legislation, and

his record of opposition to labor reforms, woman suffrage, and popular election of senators. Lodge won in the primary, but the size of the defection was not encouraging. Thereafter some of Walker's adherents announced they would support the Democratic candidate on election day, while others backed John Nicholls, an independent candidate running under a Progressive-Prohibition Party label.[9]

The second intraparty threat to Lodge arose from the dominant position which the Crane-Coolidge forces had assumed in Massachusetts Republicanism by 1922. Winthrop Murray Crane died in October 1920, but Coolidge's election to the vice-presidency made him the leader of the faction formerly commanded by his mentor. Soon Bay State Republicans were being divided into a "Coolidge group" and a "Lodge group"; and the Coolidge faction would not forget that, but for Lodge, their idol would be President of the United States. Among the leaders of the new Coolidge organization were William M. Butler, a wealthy textile industrialist of New Bedford who had served as "eastern manager" for Senator Crane; Frank Stearns, a Boston merchant who was attracted to Coolidge's side early in the latter's political career and liberally financed his advancement; Charles Innes, lobbyist and Republican boss of Boston; and others who had served in Coolidge's gubernatorial administration.[10] When the state committee met early in 1921 this group elected Frank Foss of Fitchburg state chairman, and the displaced incumbent loudly denounced "the Coolidge machine" at the conclusion of the business.[11] The Coolidge men endorsed Lodge's bid for re-election as a matter of course, but obviously they would not go "all out" for the Senator in the election at hand.

In 1922, then, Lodge found himself in some degree of trouble with all three elements of the Massachusetts electorate — the Irish, certain old-stock Republican groups, and the New

Immigrants, who resented his support of the 1921 immigration restriction measure. His campaign consisted of fence-mending all along the line. Erasing his earlier coolness toward the veterans' bonus, the Senator promised to vote to override the presidential veto. To take the edge off economic discontent, Lodge pledged to work for a constitutional amendment empowering Congress to enact a national forty-eight-hour law for women and children, similar to the Massachusetts statute, as a way of stifling the unfair advantage enjoyed by southern mills competing with Bay State industry. He defended the Administration's tariff and tax policies as providing protection and incentive for American manufacturers, on whose prosperity the economic welfare of New England depended so heavily.[12]

With regard to Newer Americans, the Senator's tactics called for an appeal to gratitude. Irishmen were reminded of his role in saving the United States from entanglement in the English-dominated League of Nations scheme. Italian-Americans again read the story of Fiume in pro-Republican newspaper advertisements and editorials. Jewish Republican leaders praised Lodge's resolution, which Congress adopted in 1922, endorsing establishment of the Jewish national homeland in Palestine. Armenian, Lithuanian, Greek, and Polish Americans were reminded of similar favors on behalf of their mother countries.[13]

Turning to the disaffected old-stock elements in his own party, Lodge and his friends attempted to conciliate the Liberal Republicans by "clarifying" the Senator's record on the League of Nations issue, reciting again the tale of how Wilson, not Lodge, bore responsibility for America's absence from the organization. To appease the Liberals' sentiments on Prohibition, a pledge was made that regardless of his original opposition to the Eighteenth Amendment, Lodge now agreed that the measure must have a fair trial through strict enforcement.[14]

Finally, there was the claim that the Senator's reputation and long record of service should overcome all antagonisms, even those harbored by Coolidgeites, and merit one more term for the man who epitomized Bay State Republicanism. Could the voters repudiate Henry Cabot Lodge, "a Massachusetts institution?" [15] In the end that appeal became the keynote of his campaign. But even admirers acknowledged that he faced a hard fight.

That Senator Lodge won at all was due primarily to the debilitated condition of the Democratic Party in Massachusetts. The Republicans' movement toward centralization of control in these years found no counterpart in the Democratic organization. David I. Walsh, the party's strongman, showed little desire to assume command after achieving his ends in 1920. Instead, the squabbling of Boston leaders who controlled votes — Curley, Fitzgerald, Lomasney, and lesser lights — and the maneuvering of businessmen-politicians who controlled money went on unchecked. With the approach of the 1922 primary, plots thickened as prospective candidates announced themselves and coalitions were made and unmade. At the end of the free-for-all, John F. Fitzgerald emerged as the party's nominee for governor, and the senatorial nomination went to a prominent banker and industrialist, Colonel William A. Gaston. Then the customary endorsements of the ticket came from all sides.[16] But beneath the surface factionalism persisted throughout the campaign, and the Democrats' earlier denunciations of one another provided a favorite source of material for the Republicans.

Another cause of Democratic disunity in 1922 arose from a scandal involving at once the explosive subjects of corruption and religion.[17] Daniel Coakley was a well-known Boston lawyer and lobbyist whose influence extended to members of both parties. Nathan Tufts was the old-stock, Protestant, Republican district attorney of Middlesex County. The third player in the drama, Joseph Pelletier, was the Democratic district attorney of Suffolk County (Boston), having been elected to that office continuously since 1909. Pelletier was of French-Irish parentage, had held office as Supreme Advocate in the national Knights of Columbus for fifteen years, and in 1920 was made a Knight of St. Gregory by the Pope. For several years the trio indulged in a lucrative perversion of justice involving frame-ups, blackmail, and suppressed prosecutions. Then, early in 1921, the state's ambitious attorney general undertook to clean up the situation. By the middle of 1922 the three conspirators were disbarred, and the two district attorneys had been removed from office by the Supreme Judicial Court of Massachusetts. Nonetheless, the national head of the Knights of Columbus denounced the proceedings against Pelletier as being "inspired by religious prejudice," and *Columbia*, the organization's magazine, called his removal a victory for "the Massachusetts forces of bigotry. . ." [18] In September's Democratic primary Pelletier, stressing the religious "issue" for all it was worth, won nomination for the office from which he had just been removed.

The discredited candidate's presence on the ticket put the Democrats in a quandary. Martin Lomasney, disgusted with the disgrace Pelletier brought to his religion, had played an important undercover part in the Boston prosecutor's downfall. William A. Gaston, too, was rumored to favor repudiation of the disbarred attorney. But John F. Fitzgerald supposedly favored a policy of silence. And that was the tactic adopted by the Democratic state convention when it met later in September.[19]

So the disrupted Democracy and its warring factions lumbered through the campaign. Lomasney and Mayor Curley, who had supported another candidate in the senatorial primary, were not enthusiastic about endorsing Colonel Gaston. Nor, of course, was Pelletier. Rumors of a rift between Gaston and his running mate, Fitzgerald, over finances and tactics persisted throughout the fall. Senator Walsh, friendly with Lodge to begin with and loathe to entangle himself in a campaign so disjointed and tainted, postponed his appearance in Massachusetts until a few days before the election.[20]

Moreover, Colonel Gaston proved himself incapable of mobilizing the anti-Lodge elements of the electorate, for his background and ideology offered little contrast with those of the senior Senator. Advanced liberals and labor leaders could not enthuse over a man who declared, in keynoting his campaign:

> I believe that we all have a great business interest in the business of this country. We should select our candidates from this position, from a business standpoint. . . I have nothing to say against my opponent, Senator Lodge, as to his ability and integrity. But as a business representative of our business he has been a failure.[21]

Nor could workers warm to a candidate who was alleged to have spent two million dollars, as an official of the Boston Elevated Railway, in efforts to break the Carmen's Union.[22] Because of his labor record, and because he was an old-stock Yankee Democrat, the Colonel was no hero to the Irish. His efforts to cultivate the New Immigrants' resentment against Lodge's immigration views were not as effective as they might have been, for by no stretch of the imagination could Gaston be considered "one of them."

The Democratic standard-bearer flayed the exorbitant rates of the Fordney-McCumber Tariff Act, but it was known

that he favored ample protective tariffs. He received the endorsement of the national Association against the Prohibition
Amendment, but so did Senator Lodge. He urged federal
regulation of working hours for women and children, but his
opponent had suggested it earlier in the campaign. Senator
Walsh and other Democrats speaking in Gaston's behalf attacked Secretary Mellon's pro-rich tax policies and the "big
business" favoritism of the Administration in Washington.[23]
But even a vehemently anti-Lodge newspaper felt obliged to
comment that "Gaston . . . represents 'the interests' as much
as a man could." And in the heat of the Democratic primary
battle James Michael Curley had proclaimed of the Colonel:
"His whole public and professional career has been spent in
association with and in the futherance of the fortunes of
corporations and financial forces that have constantly antagonized the public good, betrayed the public interests and
plundered the people, ruthlessly." [24] No wonder Republicans
snickered when Democrats called the election a fight of "plain
people against Big Business."

Early in the campaign the *Springfield Republican* predicted
that Gaston would "go as far as his money, plus current dis-
contents, will carry him, but that far will probably land him
at a place considerably short of the nation's capital." [25] As it
turned out, the factors mentioned, along with Republican
defection from Senator Lodge, carried Gaston closer to his
goal than the Springfield journal surmised, but not quite to
success. The Colonel polled 49.5 per cent of the two-party
vote, and lost to Lodge by a mere 7,345 votes out of a two-
party total of nearly 821,000.[26] Given a little more unity and
organization among the Democrats, or a more attractive Democratic candidate, Senator Lodge would certainly have been
among the victims of the anti-incumbent upsurge of 1922. As

it was, the once mighty leader returned to Washington — his prestige on the national scene blemished by his narrow escape, his power reduced almost to the vanishing point in the councils of Bay State Republicanism, where the Coolidge machine now reigned.

Governor Channing Cox, Lodge's running mate, had an easier time securing re-election. He polled 50,000 votes more than the Senator and defeated his opponent, John F. Fitzgerald, by more than 60,000 votes. Cox benefited from the fact that national issues like the soldiers' bonus and immigration restriction did not count so heavily in the gubernatorial contest. Moreover, he enjoyed solid support in his own party. The Liberal Republicans had no bones to pick in this race, and Cox was as well a charter member of the Coolidge machine, having risen through the ranks of the Innes organization and served as lieutenant governor when Coolidge was governor.[27] In addition, Cox profited as much as anyone from the factionalism rampant in the opposition party.

But most significant of all was the absence of important issues on the state level. Normalcy, with its concomitant ideal of government inaction, had come to Massachusetts, if not yet to the national scene. In a message to the legislature in January 1920, Governor Coolidge had set the tone:

> In general, it is a time to conserve, to retrench rather than to reform, a time to stabilize the administration of the present laws rather than to seek new legislation. . . The greatest benefit you can confer is the speedy making of necessary appropriations, adjustment of some details, and adjournment. You can display no greater wisdom than by resisting proposals for needless legislation.[28]

The men to whom Coolidge gave that advice complied with it, and so did the governors and legislators who succeeded them throughout most of the 1920's.

The inactivity of Bay State lawmakers in the 1920's reflected the temper of their constituents and emphasized the fact that the innovating impulse of the previous decade — the Progressive era — was gone. That era had produced a plenitude of reforms in Massachusetts — in political machinery, business regulation, labor conditions, and education — as all segments of the state's population contributed to the demand for affirmative government action. But through the 1920's, at least to 1928, not one major reform measure appeared on the statute books.

A variety of circumstances fostered the retreat into normalcy. Massachusetts had enacted most of the popular Progressive measures of the prewar era, and the achievements of that decade reduced the number of projects left for reformers to promote. Moreover, the sustained activity necessary to compile that record "tired out" many crusaders in the Bay State, and, as elsewhere, disillusion with the First World War and its aftermath further dampened the spirit of those who had been intent on modernizing the world at home and abroad.[29] Also, experience with the actual working of some Progressive innovations, such as the direct primary, cast doubt on their effectiveness.

Another reason for the lack of reform legislation in the 1920's was the essentially conservative outlook of most labor leaders at the time. Union spokesmen had strongly backed measures in the Progressive era which seemed to confer many benefits and impose few restraints on the workingman. But the growth of government bureaucracy during the war, and the assumption of control over that bureaucracy by elements traditionally hostile to labor after 1920, brought a reassertion of the labor leaders' old philosophy of reliance on private bargaining and hostility to government intervention in their affairs. "The continuing clamor for extension of State regulatory powers under the guise of reform, can but lead to greater confusion and more hopeless entanglements," declared the 1923 national convention of the A.F. of L.[30] Such strictures applied to measures like compulsory unemployment insurance. Said President Gompers: "If we were to have [it] the working people would be subjected to rules and regulations and investigations and supervisions of almost every act of their lives. It would open the door to the Governmental agents and agencies who would spy and pry into the very innermost recesses of the home life." When legislation for unemployment insurance was introduced in the Massachusetts General Court during the depression in 1922, prominent labor spokesmen testified against it.[31] Those who favored such welfare acts could now expect little encouragement from the supposed leaders of the working masses.

But most important of all in stopping the flow of reform activity in Massachusetts was the breakup of the Progressive coalition of voting elements which had made possible the enactmert of liberal legislation. The secret of that coalition's effectiveness had been its success in partially bridging the economic and ethnic divisions among the Commonwealth's people. Consequently, its disruption involved those same two sets of dividing lines, and in the postwar decade economic and ethnic group hostility attained a new peak.

By 1920 co-operation among the Commonwealth's economic groups in the interest of Progressivism had ended. During the decade that followed, the leaders of the Massachusetts A.F. of L. did espouse some reform proposals which did not seem conducive to excessive government "spying and prying." They wanted, for example, a state system of noncontributory old-age pensions; the state's noncompulsory minimum wage law for women to be made mandatory; and the state to establish a workmen's compensation insurance fund to displace private companies in this kind of insurance. Year after year the A.F. of L.'s legislative agent lobbied in vain for those bills. The same frustration greeted the welfare organizations that sponsored even more advanced social measures, like unemployment insurance. Democrats at the State House and those Republicans who represented mill districts often backed the labor and welfare reform proposals, as in the past.[32] But they no longer won support among middle-class Republican representatives from rural and suburban constituencies or among business interests — support that had been essential to the success of the Progressive coalition.

In the Progressive years, many among the latter elements of the population had been willing to redress the balance of power in the industrial world and to embark the state on social experiments. Government formerly had been too much on the side of "big business," and the time had come for the public to regulate the "interests" more strictly, while giving the "common people" a helping hand through humanitarian legislation. But the spread of unionization, the rash of strikes in the postwar years, and the increasingly "paternalistic" attitude of government convinced many that the redressing of power had gone too far in the opposite direction. The "neutral state" ideal must not be sacrificed to the interests of "big labor" and state bureaucracy.[33] Then, too, the Great Red Scare of 1920 further put the majority of the non-labor citizenry on guard against the aspirations of the working class and the trend toward centralization in government.

Fears thus engendered among the Commonwealth's traditionally more conservative economic groups mounted steadily in the early 1920's and turned against pending federal legislation backed by uplift organizations and endorsed by the A.F. of L.[34] The Towner-Sterling bill, providing for a national department of education and for federal aid to education, was denounced by the *Boston Transcript* as "a bill to Europeanize our public schools" by concentrating control in Washington.[35] That proposal never became law. However, another measure, the Sheppard-Towner bill providing federal grants-in-aid to the states to assist indigent mothers, was enacted by Congress in 1922. The *Boston Herald* warned against Massachusetts' acceptance of the act's provisions:

> It will be a hard blow at the men and women who are trying to neutralize the insidious trend toward socialism which is now sedulously working through Russian and German bolshevistic channels — and there is plenty of evidence [unspecified] that the Sheppard-Towner bill, with its intimations of birth control, was inspired originally by Russian propaganda.[36]

The state legislature subsequently rejected the proffered grant-in-aid, and instead directed the Commonwealth's attorney general to bring suit to have the law declared unconstitutional as an infringement on the reserved rights of the states. In 1924 the proposed national child labor amendment aroused similar opposition among economic conservatives in Massachusetts, and on the floor of Congress Representative A. Piatt Andrew of the Sixth District attacked it as another example of centralization and bureaucracy and impingement on states' rights.[37]

On the state level, liberals and labor leaders were forced to spend most of their time in the 1920's repelling attacks on the gains they had made in earlier, friendlier years. In this, at least, they succeeded quite well. Defeated rather handily in the Massachusetts legislature were measures which would have abolished all the labor laws of the state, authorized investigations of labor unions, limited the right to strike and to picket, and established compulsory arbitration of labor disputes. More serious were the annual attempts to repeal or weaken the workmen's compensation act, the forty-eight-hour law, the law forbidding night work for women and children in textile mills, and the noncompulsory minimum wage law for women; but these too were withstood. Labor's major defeat came in 1921 with passage of an act establishing a state police force, an act which union leaders vigorously fought as a strike-breaking measure.[38] They narrowly averted another setback when a bill that would allow unions to be sued, passed by the legislature, was defeated on referendum at the 1922 election by a vote of 301,205 to 300,260. Significantly, only the six counties of Berkshire, Bristol, Essex, Hampden, Suffolk, and Worcester, containing most of the state's industrial cities and towns, returned majorities against the "anti-union" measure. The rural and suburban areas favored it.[39]

Through almost a decade, then, economic reformers could hope for little more than to hold their own. What new proposals they did introduce at the State House met with suspicion and hostility. Muckraking and the social gospel were now things of the past; instead fears of "big labor," paternalism, and Bolshevism held considerable sway over the Republican inhabitants of the farms, the small towns, the suburban cities of Massachusetts, and Back Bay.

The breakup of the Progressive coalition along lines of economic division, traced thus far, was paralleled by a concurrent dissolution of the alliance along ethnic lines, which proved to be even more instrumental in bringing about the reign of normalcy in the Bay State. Despite insistence by some authorities on the basically Yankee-Protestant ethos of the Progressive movement,[40] in Massachusetts non-Protestant Newer Americans had supported many typically Progressive measures even more zealously than the old-stock inhabitants. A new sort of leader had begun to emerge among the urban immigrant masses after the turn of the century. Less addicted to viewing politics solely as a means of personal enrichment, the new leaders saw political power in its wider context as a means of securing ameliorative governmental action for their followers. On the municipal level, Newer American spokesmen of this type became leading exponents of public health and housing laws, sweat-shop restrictions, recreational improvements, and similar measures. In the state legislature, the Irish Democrats and those Republicans who represented New Immigrant districts became the staunchest supporters of labor, humanitarian, and even political machinery reforms.[41] Analysis of election returns in referendums on a number of Progressive bills shows that Newer American areas supported them just as strongly as old-stock districts. On the question of adopting the Initiative and Referendum Amendment to the state constitution in 1918, for example, the proposal generally secured a higher percentage of the vote in districts dominated by Irish and New Immigrant people.[42] Much of the state's liberal legislation of the Progressive era was recommended by Irish Catholic Governor David I. Walsh, and enacted in his administration. Indeed, Progressives across the country recognized Massachusetts as a leader among the states in adopting such legislation, notwithstanding the fact that she was second only to Rhode Island in proportion of foreign-born population.

The success of the liberal movement in the Bay State, then, depended on continued co-operation between old-stock social gospelers and reform-minded Newer Americans. United, they compiled a remarkable record during the Progressive decade. But even then, there were discrepancies in the motives and ideology of the two elements. In the end, intensification of those differences was the most important factor of all in bringing Massachusetts' Progresive era to a close.

The Irish and New Immigrant masses supported labor and humanitarian reforms as means of guarding against the insecurities of the industrial, urban civilization in which they lived. They supported political machinery reforms as a way of making their demands more effectively heard. Hence to these Newer Americans, Progressivism was a movement toward economic, social, and political _self_-improvement. On the other hand, to many old-stock inhabitants of Boston's Back Bay and the farms, small towns, and suburban cities of Massachusetts, the Progressive movement was largely aimed at uplifting _others_. It was a crusade to uplift the "inferior" cultural traditions of the Irish and New Immigrant masses, and preserve "American" ways of living. Alleviating the economic plight of the newer arrivals was one means to that end, and thus wage and hour laws merited support. Even more important to some old-stock elements, however, was the effort to "Americanize" those traits of the Newer Americans which ran contrary to the norms of the old settlers. The Sunday blue laws must be guarded and enforced to show non-Puritans the virtues of traditional New England sabbath observance. The coming of the movies demanded censorship to insure that none but pure American mores were depicted on the screen.[43] A careful watch must be kept over the parochial schools. And especially needed was Prohibition. To many old-stock reformers in the prewar decade such measures were as essential to Progressivism as workmen's compensation. To the Irish and the New Immigrants they were not.

The Newer Americans' resistance to old-stock attempts to improve their customs only redoubled the efforts of the up-lifters in the war and postwar period, for the growing specter of hyphenism, which helped bring immigration restriction, seemed to make more imperative than ever the need for Americanizing the strangers already in the land. By 1920 that had become the meaning of "reform" to many old-stock people. The time and effort formerly spent by the Protestant "church lobby" and women's organizations on behalf of labor and welfare measures were now largely devoted to legislation forbidding Sunday movies, to warding off attempts to legalize professional boxing in the state, and to pressuring the legislature for an act to make the state's liquor laws conform with the national Prohibition code.[44] Even when they did endorse social welfare measures in the 1920's, old-stock groups tended to emphasize their "Americanizing" features above all else.

The Irish and New Immigrant reaction to this sort of "reform" was equally disastrous for the Progressive spirit. The old stock's emphasis on using the government to alter forcibly the Newer Americans' "inferior" standards made them suspicious of reformers and reform measures in general. By the early 1920's the Newer Americans' interest, too, had been diverted away from the labor and welfare measures that occupied them in the previous decade. Their faith in the government as an agency of change had been suspended, to be revived again only when they could feel certain that "reform" would not involve interference with cherished aspects of their own cultures. For the time being, the Irish and New Immigrants focused their attention on withstanding further encroachment on their personal and group "rights," and on retrieving those already trod underfoot. In the process, their spokesmen took up the cry against centralization and "government meddling," and demanded a return to states' rights and "the Jeffersonian tradition." [45]

Prohibition became symbolic of ethnic divergence in the ranks of the Progressive coalition. Adopted early in 1919, the Eighteenth Amendment resulted from fears aroused in some parts of the country, especially in the South and West, by the growing influence of the "wicked" cities with their foreign populations and low moral standards.[46] In Massachusetts the experiment was backed by old-stock elements, particularly in rural and suburban areas, who regarded it as a victory for Americanization. To the Irish and New Immigrants, however, it was the most glaring example of unwarranted interference with their way of life.

The Eighteenth Amendment aroused some opposition also among the traditionally conservative higher echelons of the business community. Though of old-stock lineage, some in this group distrusted Prohibition as an example of that extension of government control which might one day threaten their own economic interests. Businessmen of this type constituted the bulk of such organizations as the national Sentinels of the Republic and the Massachusetts Constitutional Liberty League which proliferated in the early 1920's and opposed enforced temperance along with every other form of expanded government regulatory power.[47] These groups too talked of states' rights and decentralization. Happy were they to hear spokesmen for the Irish and New Immigrant masses speaking the same language of opposition to "big government," for with these recruits came an accession of popular support to its cause which the economic Old Guard itself could never hope to command. Thus Prohibition, and what it represented, not only forced a wedge into the ranks of the Progressive coalition, but also served to drive the Newer American element of that coalition into a tentative alliance with conservative men who had contributed least of all to the reform movement of the previous decade.

Similar to Prohibition in its disruptive effects on Progressive ethnic collaboration was the school issue. As hyphenism emerged as a matter for serious concern, the same elements that backed the Eighteenth Amendment showed increasing anxiety over the influence of the parochial school and its supposed threat to native American educational, lingual, and religious traditions. Anxiety led to action, and in 1920 the

67

people of Michigan voted on a proposed state constitutional amendment to abolish private schools. The measure was rejected, but two years later the voters of Oregon approved a similar ban after a strenuous campaign on its behalf by the Masons and other "patriotic" organizations, including the Ku Klux Klan.[48]

In Massachusetts improvement of the educational system was part of the reform program of the Progressive decade. A number of advances were made, in large part under the aegis of the Walsh administration.[49] But as the Americanization drive gained momentum, the old-stock component of the Progressive coalition focused its attention on the parochial school as a block to its effort to uplift the cultural standards of the Irish and other immigrant groups. A commission to investigate the whole problem of education in the Commonwealth, appointed by Republican Governor McCall and headed by state Senator George Chamberlain of Springfield, reported in 1919 in favor of strengthening the Department of Education's control over parochial schools. Especially significant was a recommendation that enforcement of the laws pertaining to compulsory use of English in the teaching of mandatory subjects in the parochial schools be transferred from local school committees to state officials. Allegedly, those laws were not being carried out in communities where the foreign-born predominated.[50]

New Immigrant and Irish Catholics reacted swiftly to the Chamberlain report. French-Canadian and Polish parishes adopted resolutions condemning the commission's proposals. The town meetings of Webster, Dudley, and other centers of immigrant population did likewise.[51] *The Pilot* characterized the report an insult to parochial schools and local school committees and termed its recommendations "unnecessary additions to our educational laws." The Bishop of Springfield in a letter to his clergy said: "It is our wish that you use every legitimate means to oppose and defeat any legislation which unnecessarily introduces State control over our private institutions." Members of the legislature were deluged with form letters signed by Catholic school children and their parents demanding rejection of Chamberlain's proposals.[52]

The commission also urged inauguration of a program of compulsory physical education in the public schools. Thousands of Catholic children still attended public institutions, and to many of their parents that proposal seemed to open the way to sex hygiene instruction and possible dissemination of birth control propaganda. Such was the claim, at least, of numerous Catholic spokesmen who appeared in opposition to the measure before the state legislature. Democratic candidates accused their old-stock Republican opponents of supporting the "Chamberlain Sex Hygiene Bill," and one aspirant for a seat in the legislature was able to charge that the Republican incumbent was "a Sexagenarian." [53]

A third among the Chamberlain commission's many proposals was the establishment of a state fund to help poorer communities improve their public school systems and raise teachers' salaries. Each improvement in facilities and standards in public education meant increased expenditures by church authorities for similar advances in parochial institutions, lest Catholic children be wooed over to "better" public schools. Perhaps with this factor in mind Cardinal O'Connell in June of 1919 declared: "The medical inspection of schools, the physical examination and treatment of school children, the supplying of food for the indigent pupil, free dispensary treatment for the defective, and other similar provisions which have been added to the educational program of the State, all are signs of the spirit of machine centralization and control," which should be abandoned.[54]

If consolidation of educational control at the state level was an example of unwarranted "centralization," even worse were the attempts by certain old-stock women's organizations, labor leaders, and others including the Ku Klux Klan to further consolidation at the national level. The Towner-Sterling federal aid to education bill, whose backers saw it as another desirable step in Americanization,[55] was bitterly denounced in Catholic circles. The Reverend Jones Corrigan of Boston College called it "the end of educational freedom and progress . . . an effort to put the schools of the nation as much under the power of Washington as is the postal service." The bill "gives to the state the absolute and exclusive control of education," declared *La Semaine Paroissiale*, official organ of St. Anne's parish in Fall River.[56]

Typically, the old stock's Americanizing reforms in the realm of education heightened the Newer Americans' suspicion of "reform" in general. "Let [the state] restore to its subjects in the field of education and in other pursuits the fullest freedom consistent with the public welfare. . ." said Cardinal O'Connell.[57] That attitude inhibited Catholic support of such measures as federal and state maternity aid, which would allegedly intrude the government's influence into the home and which seemed, moreover, to be supported most ardently by the same elements favoring Prohibition and educational tinkering. Then, in 1924, Cardinal O'Connell attacked the pending child labor amendment to the federal Constitution as a threat to the integrity of the private school system and a further interference with the rights of parents by an overcentralized state. The effect of his words on wary Irish and New Immigrant Catholic voters played a large part in the overwhelming defeat of the amendment in Massachusetts' referendum on ratification that year.[58]

Again, in their opposition to "centralization and control,"

Newer American Catholics found themselves aligned with ✓
economic conservatives who also deprecated expansion of
government power, though largely on different grounds.
Again the conservatives were glad to welcome the new recruits, and the *Boston Herald* was quick to allude to unspecified "intimations of birth control" which it found in the
federal maternity aid bill.

The significance of the school issue, then, like that of Prohibition and other "Americanizing" measures, lay in its dis-
integrating effect upon the ethnic co-operation vital to the
success of Massachusetts Progressivism. The legislative battle
over the Chamberlain bills which persisted for years after
1919, like the fight over the state Prohibition enforcement
act, deepened ethnic cleavages and distracted attention from
other matters. In that atmosphere of mutual distrust, economic
and welfare and political reform measures were all but forgotten by the old stock and Newer Americans alike.

The ending of the Progressive era left Massachusetts state
government in a condition of repose through most of the
1920's, and elections to choose its masters were conducted in
a vacuum. Dynamic leadership on the part of the executive
seemed unnecessary, and during the 1922 campaign Governor
Cox told audiences that the state had taken on too many jobs
in recent years.[59] The legislature, overwhelmingly Republican,
did little more than pigeonhole bills and authorize commissions
to study the more persistent problems. A strong demand
arose for biennial sessions in view of the lack of business at
the yearly meetings, but even this innovation was never effected.

"Economy and sound administration" became the criteria
by which the incumbent regime was judged, and in these
respects the Republican record appeared highly satisfactory.

At the end of his first two-year term in 1922, Governor Cox was able to claim a reduction of $2,000,000 in the direct state tax and erasure of $12,000,000 of the state debt. He stressed that the Commonwealth's program of institutional care for her wards did not suffer in the economy drive and that improvements were being made, all on a "pay-as-you-go" basis.[60] The size of the savings alone seemed to interest the citizenry most, however, and that became the core and substance of the Republican Party's state campaign strategy for the rest of the decade. "Re-elect Governor Cox. He has made a careful, conservative executive, obeying the mandate of the times to the letter by preaching, practising and enforcing economy. . ."[61]

The regime of normalcy left the Massachusetts Democrats without an effective state issue on which to campaign. Almost by habit the state convention in 1922 endorsed old-age pensions and other reform measures espoused by labor leaders and advanced liberals, but little was heard of such matters during the ensuing campaign. Fitzgerald promised the strike-weary workers of Lawrence that there would be no more wage cuts if he became governor, and told the people of the state he would foster establishment of new industries in the Commonwealth.[62] But the means of accomplishing those objectives were left unspecified, and Democratic campaigners presented no affirmative plan for meeting the social and economic needs of the people through the agency of government. On the contrary, they were hardly less vociferous than their opponents in denouncing the trend toward centralization. Fitzgerald belabored "paternalism" on both the state and national levels, citing as examples Prohibition and the pending proposals for federal education and maternity aid. "Unless we make a start and correct the situation," he declared, "the time will come when we will no longer determine what kind of a life we are going to lead, but our lives will be determined for us by men and women on the Government payroll. . ." [63] Thus he expressed the changed attitude toward reform and government activity that had come to characterize his Newer American followers in the early 1920's.

In the end, the Democrats offered little more than to outdo the Republicans in the realm of economy and sound administration. "My platform," declared a Democratic candidate for the legislature from the western part of the state, "is very simple. I believe in home rule, fewer laws, and lower taxes." A Democratic newspaper endorsing Fitzgerald promised only that "he will put a stop to state extravagance." [64] In view of the Republicans' economy record that was a tenuous basis for asking the voters to turn out the incumbents, and past actions of Fitzgerald himself further limited the effectiveness of such campaign tactics. His term as mayor of Boston in 1907–1908 was not remembered as a regime of austere purity in many quarters, and as recently as 1919 the national House of Representatives had voided his claim to a disputed congressional seat on the basis of improper election procedures. In the final two weeks of the 1922 campaign Governor Cox "opened up" on Honey Fitz's record to refresh the memories of those who might have forgotten the details. The result did not enhance Democratic chances of occupying the executive suite on Beacon Hill.[65]

In the election Channing Cox polled 464,873 votes to Fitzgerald's 404,192. Though he lost, Fitzgerald's 46.5 per cent of the two-party vote represented a sizable increase over James M. Cox's 28.9 per cent in the presidential contest two years earlier. Moreover, the number of registered voters had increased by nearly 70,000 since 1920, and most of the increase was in the cities, which were more likely to favor the

Democrats. At least a start had been made in catching up with the Republicans in the vital matter of registration.[66]

Analysis of ward returns in both the gubernatorial and senatorial elections shows that the Democrats increased their percentage of the vote among all segments of the electorate, but the relative size of the increase was least in old-stock Republican wards. Wards dominated by the New Immigrants showed much more improvement, from the Democratic point of view, while the increases were largest of all in the traditionally Democratic Irish wards. In general Fitzgerald made a better showing than Colonel Gaston among the Irish, but in many New Immigrant areas Gaston outran his partner on the ticket — a reflection of the sharp resentment felt against Senator Lodge on the immigration restriction issue.

While the increase in the Democratic percentage of the two-party vote in the gubernatorial election of 1922 compared to the presidential election of 1920 was 17.6 points for the state as a whole, the increase for Boston was 25.2 points. For the aggregate vote of the ten other Newer American cities over 25,000 (each having 70 per cent or more foreign-stock population), the figure was 19.3. On the other hand, for the aggregate vote of the thirteen old-stock cities over 25,000 (each having more than 30 per cent "native white of native parentage" population), the figure was only 15.9. For the twenty-nine old-stock towns of 2,500 to 10,000 (each having 50 per cent or more "native white of native parentage" population), the Democratic increase was a mere 8.3 points.

Clearly the Democrats had undermined the overwhelming Republican coalition of 1920 in two respects. Irish support of the party was back to normal, and impressive inroads had been made among the newer nationality groups, with both Fitzgerald and Gaston carrying a considerable number of wards where various New Immigrant elements predominated.

74

But the final outcome of the election, especially the gubernatorial race, indicated that even thus weakened the Republican coalition continued to hold sway in Massachusetts — its
basic strength among the old stock unimpaired and retaining
still the allegiance of a very significant proportion of the
state's "newer races." Another factor accounting for Republican optimism was the known tendency of off-year elections
to magnify Democratic strength by failing to call out the
full complement of Republican votes. While 74.8 per cent
of the registered voters in the cities voted in 1922, only 69.0
per cent of those in the towns did so. The total two-party
vote cast for governor in Boston that year was actually 5.4
per cent larger than the two-party vote cast for president
in 1920, and in the ten Newer American cities mentioned
above it was only 3.3 per cent less in the aggregate. In the
thirteen old-stock cities, however, the aggregate vote was 12.5
per cent less than in 1920, and in the twenty-nine old-stock
towns it was fully 20.8 per cent less. Voters in the Democratically inclined places came to the polls more regularly, in other
words, than those in Republican old-stock strongholds, many
of whom chose to stay at home in elections unenlivened by
a presidential contest. Had voters in old-stock districts gone
to the polls in the same proportion as Newer American Democrats, the size of the Republican margins of victory would
have been greater.

The election of 1922 left the Massachusetts Democrats in
a better condition than had the debacle of 1920.[67] But two
considerations had prevented them from making the most of
their advantages. The first was the party's lack of unity and
direction, which in turn affected the quality of the candidates
it was able to offer the electorate. The second was the inability
to find convincing issues on the state level with which to stir

the public, a situation reflecting the temper of the times, and more especially, the breakup of the old Progressive coalition. Consequently the Democrats dissipated their energies in internal squabbling. Their senatorial nominee, whose background and outlook offered no real alternative to his opponent's, was unable to exploit effectively the national issues at hand. Their candidate for governor, whose personal characteristics at least aroused the enthusiasm of Irish party stalwarts, conducted an essentially issueless campaign.

In the midst of it all, political interest and voter participation dropped to the lowest point in years.[68] With Gaston vying against Lodge to give "business" proper representation in the Senate and Fitzgerald competing with Cox to end "state extravagance," the belief became more widespread that "there really is no choice between the two big parties today." [69] Thousands, unconcerned, stayed home on election day. Others, desiring some form of affirmative government action, talked of the need for a new third party.

At the same time, however, the ethnic-cultural tensions which had played such a large part in splitting the Progressive coalition continued at work in the early 1920's. At first their main effect was seen in the ending of the reform movement of the previous decade. But those same tensions would command the political limelight — in a different way — in the next presidential year, 1924. Their eventual product would be a new set of political issues, leaders, and alignments, and a revival of popular interest in politics surpassing anything found even at the height of the bygone Progressive era.

Chapter Four

Ku Klux Years

THE inconsistencies of the American two-party system were more prominent than ever in the 1920's.[1] Clearly the Republicans were the national majority party, but the mainstays of that majority were two elements of the population with bitterly divergent economic interests: the conservative "business" Republicans in the East, and the "agrarian radical" insurgents in the West. Despite their economic differences, however, both elements were predominantly old stock, and hence were fairly united on measures designed to preserve native cultural standards against the onslaught of Newer Americans. Nonetheless — and complicating the situation further — the Republicans, as the party of "the full dinner pail," still laid hold to a large proportion of urban New Immigrant votes, especially in national elections.

The Democratic minority party was split internally as seriously as the G.O.P. The major cleavage was cultural, for the party embraced both a rural, old-stock, Protestant wing centering in the South and West, and an urban, Newer American, non-Protestant wing centering in the Northeast. To some extent the division carried over to the field of economic policy, for the rural Democrats of the South and West sided often with the agrarian radical Republicans, while the urban Democrats of the Northeast sometimes allied with the business Republicans who controlled that section economically.

A rational shuffling of party factions would have delineated at least three major elements in the political make-up of the country.[2] There were, first of all, the old-stock agrarian liberals of the West (Republicans and Democrats) and South (Democrats). Here lay support for measures aimed at relieving the plight of agriculture in the face of expanding industrialism — for tariff aid to farmers, for "surplus-handling" schemes, for farm credit facilities, for increased government regulation of transportation and power utilities, for an end to the Republican Administration's "pro-business" attitude. Here also was found the strongest support for measures to inhibit the growing influence of the new stock in American life — for Prohibition, for other Americanizing proposals like federal intervention in the field of education, and for drastic, permanent, and discriminatory restriction of immigration. Here were the main recruiting grounds for the Ku Klux Klan.

A second element consisted of the old-stock conservative business Republicans of the East, who reveled in the Administration's policies — on tariffs, on tax programs, on the function of government regulatory commissions. Less government in business — except for government aid and encouragement to "free enterprise" — was their watchword, and Harding and his successors complied. These Republicans opposed the demands of the agrarians, and their spokesman in the White House stood guard lest anything too drastic be accomplished by discontented farmers.

The business Republicans were the happiest element on the American political scene. But they too shared concern over the rising power of the Irish and New Immigrant masses and frequently sympathized with efforts to protect "American"

ways of life. Some proposals, like federal aid to education,
cost too much and involved excessive "government meddling":
their enthusiasm for Americanization did not extend that far.
But to most of the conservative Republicans Prohibition —
for others, if not for themselves — seemed a good thing, and
most of them went along with the noble experiment at least
until the latter half of the 1920's. Their acquiescence in re-
stricting immigration also reflected a determination to maintain old-stock dominance. President Coolidge told Congress
that "America must be kept American," and endorsed restriction.[3] The business Republicans apparently agreed with
their President, for they made little protest against the bars
which shut out the supply of "cheap labor" formerly
cherished.

The third element in the rationalized national political structure would be the Newer Americans — the Irish-dominated
Democratic machines in the Northeast; and the "newer races"
of the industrial cities and towns, split between both parties.
On the economic issues dividing the agrarians and the business
Republicans, the Newer Americans exhibited a dual person-
ality. Since the days of William Jennings Bryan and the inflationary free silver crusade, these city-dwellers had been
suspicious of farmer radicalism. At the same time, however,
the social welfare and labor reform measures which the Newer
Americans espoused during the Progressive era had made
them, in turn, seem "radical" in the eyes of conservative businessmen. In the 1920's, this dualism persisted. The Newer
Americans continued to oppose many of the agrarians' demands, such as higher tariffs on agricultural products and the
various "surplus-handling" schemes, for fear these measures
would increase the urban cost of living. Moreover, their dependence on industry for a livelihood aligned them with the
conservative Republicans in favor of adequate tariff protec-

tion for American manufactures. Resentment of government interference also made them allies of the conservatives for some purposes, in opposition to "government meddling," especially where measures like federal education and maternity aid were concerned. On the other hand, the mass of the new stock belonged to the working class and could not endorse all aspects of the Republican Administration's "pro-business" outlook in the postwar decade. Their spokesmen attacked the government's "exorbitant" tariff rates, its tax policy, and its lax regulation of big business, all of which fostered the growth of "monopoly" and threatened the workers' pocketbooks. So the Irish and New Immigrants seemed neither fish nor fowl. Conservative business Republicans often saw them as wild-eyed levelers. Agrarian liberals in the South and West, unfamiliar with the Newer Americans' urban type of liberalism, frequently counted them "reactionaries" of the worst sort.

But far more important than economic issues, in constituting the separateness of the Newer American element, were the social and cultural considerations involved. For these were the "foreign" masses whose personal behavior, languages, religions, schools, and political organizations were deemed strange, inferior, "hyphenated," or even un-American by the old-stock members of both parties.[4] Their ways of life were to be uplifted and Americanized and their strength reduced by immigration restriction. On the other hand, the Irish and New Immigrants, determined to maintain the integrity of their ways, resented the slurs of the old stock and hence felt politically isolated from both the agrarian liberals and the conservative Republicans.

In the early 1920's, then, business control of the Republican Party, agrarian insurgency, and the widening gulf between old-stock and Newer Americans made the traditional two-party structure less logical than ever. Nevertheless, party

Mayor Andrew J. Peters, President and Mrs. Woodrow Wilson, and Governor Calvin Coolidge, on Wilson's arrival at Boston, February 24, 1919.

Former Senator Winthrop Murray Crane and Senator Henry Cabot Lodge, Sr., at the Republican national convention, Chicago, June 1920.

Governor Channing Cox (right), running for re-election against John F. Fitzgerald, greets Charlie Bush, the oldest voter of Boston's Ward Seven, at the polls on Election Day, 1922.

Former Mayor John F. Fitzgerald, the Democratic candidate for governor, and Mrs. Fitzgerald cast their ballots on Election Day, 1922.

lines were not so easily erased in practice, and during the first four years of normalcy tensions were confined within the bounds of the old system. Senators from the East serving the interests of corporate wealth and insurgent senators from the West both called themselves Republicans. Representatives from the melting-pot districts of eastern cities and representatives from homogeneous old-stock areas in the South, some of them elected with the aid of the Ku Klux Klan, both called themselves Democrats.

Consequently, Congress conducted its business with little regard for party responsibility and with much crossing of party lines. A farm bloc emerged embracing agrarian representatives of both parties and succeeded in its demands for higher agricultural tariffs, expansion of rural credit facilities, and encouragement of the co-operative movement. But the farmers' most drastic proposal, for dealing with the problem of crop surpluses, met stiffer resistance from conservative business Republicans and urban Democrats, and the House defeated the first version of the McNary-Haugen bill in June of 1924. The conservative Republicans, backed by the Administration, eventually had their own way in most things. Nevertheless, coalitions of agrarian liberals and urban Democrats slowed down Secretary Mellon's tax program and persisted in investigations of the Administration's ties with corrupt business interests. Spokesmen for the Newer Americans in Congress — few as they were — staved off proposals for federal intervention in education and similar projects with the aid of "cost-conscious" conservative Republicans. In the face of overwhelming old-stock solidarity, however, the Newer Americans' representatives were incapable of undermining the Eighteenth Amendment and the Volstead Act, or of blocking efforts to raise immigration bars to an even higher and more discriminatory level. The Johnson Act of 1924, which only six senators opposed, lowered the annual number of immigrants admissible to 2 per cent of the number of foreign-born from each country resident in the United States in 1890. This reduced not only the total number who could come in, but also the proportion who would come from the homelands of the "undesirable" New Immigrants. The National Origins Clause, to become effective after further study and the working out of complicated formulas, promised even more drastic reductions along both lines.

Another result of the irrationality of the prevailing party alignment was the growing sentiment in favor of an independent third party. The Conference for Progressive Political Action, formed in 1922 at the call of a group of insurgent Republican agrarians, gained the support of a number of labor leaders, particularly from the railway brotherhoods, Socialists, and advanced liberals who read the *Nation* and the *New Republic*. Senator La Follette of Wisconsin was the most likely choice for a candidate should the group undertake an independent campaign, but among the disparate elements making up the C.P.P.A. many insisted that no action be taken until the nominees and platforms of the two major parties could be scrutinized. In February of 1924 they agreed to hold a national convention on July 4, after the Democrats and Republicans had met, to decide a course of action.[5]

Finally, it was evident that the approach of another presidential election would intensify the internal conflicts in both major parties. Between national election years the patchwork two-party alignment might hobble along, or at least give way to action-producing blocs and coalitions in Congress. But when Republicans from Iowa and New York and Democrats from Massachusetts and Georgia should attempt to gather under one tent for a presidential campaign, it would likely prove harder to side-step the strife brewing within each party.

The death of President Harding in the summer of 1923 put Calvin Coolidge of Northampton in the White House. Like Harding, Coolidge represented the conservative business Republicans, only more so. He desired nomination in his own right in 1924, but for a time it seemed possible that his ambition might be denied. Toward the end of 1923 an old Progressive, Senator Hiram Johnson of California, announced his candidacy, and some economic liberals hailed him as a savior. The gradual unearthing of the sordid story of corruption in the Harding regime also seemed to darken Coolidge's prospects.[6]

But the President deftly handled the scandal situation, and in the end little blame for the doings of former party leaders attached to this New England Puritan. Moreover, between the summer of 1923 and convention time in 1924 the President constructed a nation-wide Coolidge machine, with the New Bedford textile magnate, William M. Butler, as national chairman. Senator Johnson and other dissidents made little headway against Butler's tight-knit organization in the preconvention campaign, and on June 12 the Republican meeting in Cleveland gave Coolidge the nomination.[7]

Coolidge's rise to the pinnacle of national power also encompassed the complete ascendancy, in Massachusetts, of the machine he inherited from Winthrop Murray Crane. Even Senator Lodge now stoutly maintained his admiration for the President, although he had opposed him on a number of legislative issues in 1923 and 1924. But at the Cleveland convention the Coolidge men wrought their full measure of revenge on the Senator. Though given a place as delegate-at-large, Lodge was shut out from honors he had grown accustomed to in earlier days. He was neither keynoter nor permanent chairman of the convention. He was not selected to head the Massachusetts delegation, nor was he the state's representative on the platform committee — a post which had been his almost traditionally. He was just a lonely delegate, but conspicuously so. As a final insult the hotel room assigned for his use was so inadequate that his former secretary, Louis A. Coolidge, offered to trade quarters with him.[8] Back in Boston, Mayor Curley twitted the fallen leader of a bygone era, quoting to newspapermen the words of Cardinal Wolsey in *Henry VIII* as a fitting lamentation for the aged Senator:

> Had I but served my God with half the zeal
> I served my King, He would not in mine age
> have left me naked to mine enemies.[9]

The G.O.P. platform followed lines laid down by the President. The agrarian radicals presented their program as a substitute for the report of the resolutions committee, but it was rejected overwhelmingly. Neither the farmers nor other elements flirting with the Conference for Progressive Political Action found consolation in the planks endorsed by the delegates, nor did the Newer Americans. The approved document praised the recent immigration legislation, and pledged strict enforcement of Prohibition.[10]

For the time being, the dominant conservative wing had glossed over the internal economic split in the ranks of the G.O.P. The grumbling of western radicals and lingering doubt as to possible effects of the Harding scandals caused some uneasiness for a while. By the end of July, however, Coolidge, Butler, and other powers in the new regime were looking forward to a smooth campaign and an easy victory. For by that time the Democratic Party had committed hara-kiri.

At first it appeared that the Democratic convention of 1924 might be a cut-and-dried affair. By the fall of 1923 William G. McAdoo, Wilson's Secretary of the Treasury, was far and away the leading contender for the party's nomination. In January of the presidential year over half the members of the Democratic national committee were willing to endorse him. The main basis of his support lay with the rural, agrarian liberal wing of the party in the South and West, which saw in him the antithesis to Coolidge's pro-business views. McAdoo's espousal of Prohibition, which counted against him in the East, also added to his popularity with the old-stock elements of the Democratic Party.[11]

Of all the Democratic hopefuls, moreover, McAdoo held most appeal for C.P.P.A. supporters and sympathizers. His wartime administration of the railroads endeared him to the railway unions and to labor leaders in general. The *Nation* acknowledged on behalf of advanced liberals that "no Democratic nomination will so unloosen the purse-strings of the backers of the Republican party as would Mr. McAdoo's." [12] And with him as their candidate, the Democrats might hope to capture the most vocally discontented group in the nation, the agrarian radical wing of the Republican Party, which would provide the margin of victory. Such was the logic and strategy of the McAdoo candidacy.

Opposition to the former Secretary stemmed from the big-city bosses headed by Charles Murphy of Tammany Hall and George Brennan of Illinois, who still remembered McAdoo as a member of the Wilson coterie.[13] But in January of 1924 only one potential nominee appeared as a possible foil to McAdoo's success — Senator Oscar Underwood of Alabama. Except for his low-tariff views, Underwood was generally classed a conservative on economic matters. He was unsympathetic with Prohibition, too, and hence somewhat of an anomaly in his section. The Senator was not an intimate of the bosses, but his wetness found favor with them.[14] Only by encouraging the candidacies of Underwood and a large number of favorite sons, and thus tying up the necessary one-third of the delegates, could the anti-McAdoo cabal of urban leaders hope to block his nomination. As the year began their prospects of stopping the McAdoo drive were very dim.

But on February 1, 1924, the patness of the Democratic pre-convention campaign was upset. For days a congressional committee had heard E. L. Doheny unravel the story of the Teapot Dome oil scandal, while Democrats rubbed their hands with glee at the windfall of campaign material. Then, however, the oil magnate testified that McAdoo and his law firm had been on the Doheny pay roll since 1919. The ex-Secretary at once explained that his services were in no way connected with the oil land deals. Nonetheless, many economic liberals who had supported McAdoo's presidential aspirations now deserted "Mr. Doheny's lawyer" and looked toward the Fourth of July C.P.P.A. convention, or elsewhere.[15]

Doheny's revelations rearoused the hopes of the boss bloc within the Democratic Party, for McAdoo's goal of two-thirds of the convention delegates now seemed infinitely harder to attain. And McAdoo's own recognition of that fact gave rise to the final, most important result of the "exposure." Deprived to a large extent of his former backing among labor leaders and liberals, McAdoo thereafter relied increasingly on the support of the old-stock wing of his party, the Prohibition forces, and the Ku Klux Klan. That made all the difference in the world when the national convention met June 24 in New York City — the very heart of Newer America.

The rise of the Ku Klux Klan was the extreme result of the cultural split that rent the social fabric of the nation in the 1920's and separated the old-stock from the Newer Americans. Originating in the South as a white man's society during the First World War, the organization subsequently came under the control of a band of shrewd promoters who fostered its growth, exacting their "cut" with the initiation of each new member and the chartering of each local branch. With expansion, however, violence increased against Negroes and people who failed to live up to the local Kluxers' code of behavior. The organization's notoriety brought an intensive investigation of its activities by the *New York World* and demands for a congressional inquiry in 1921 and 1922. The results were twofold: free publicity for the Klan, and an internal shuffling of its leadership. Thereafter recruitment of new members proceeded at an even faster pace, the pecuniary interests of the Klan's new directors became a less obvious motive behind their efforts, and the "philosophical" objectives of the organization were given greater prominence.[16]

According to its new Emperor and Imperial Wizard, Dr. Hiram Evans, the Klan's main principle was "the fundamental instinct of race pride and loyalty — what Lothrop Stoddard calls 'the imperious urge of superior heredity'. . . There are three of these great racial instincts," he continued, ". . . loyalty to the white race, to the traditions of America, and to the spirit of Protestantism, which has been an essential part of Americanism ever since the days of Roanoke and Plymouth Rock. They are condensed into the Klan slogan: 'Native, white, Protestant supremacy!' "[17] A more earthy expression of its aims was contained in a K.K.K. newspaper advertisement:

This organization stands with positive emphasis for Americanism as opposed to foreign idealism; for the principles of the Christian religion as opposed to Roman Catholicism and infidelity; for the American public schools and for the placing of the Holy Bible in the schoolrooms of the nation; for the enforcement of the laws upon the statute books and for a wholesome respect for the Constitution of the United States; for the maintenance of virtue among American women, sobriety and honor among American men, and for the eradication of all influences and agencies that would threaten the character of our children.[18]

Riding the wave of postwar anti-hyphenism and one hundred per cent Americanism, the Ku Klux Klan in the early 1920's spread from the South to the West. By 1924 a number of western states were as strongly permeated by its influence as any below the Mason-Dixon line. Indeed, by that time Ku Kluxism had made considerable headway among old-stock elements even in those eastern states that were the strongholds of the Newer Americans. Late in 1922 small meetings of the white-robed men took place in Massachusetts. The first large-scale demonstration of Klan strength in the Bay State came in September of 1923, when 2,600 Kluxers gathered in Worcester and heard F. Eugene Farnsworth, King Kleagle of the Maine realm and ex-president of the Loyal Coalition, promise that "the future America is not going to put up with hyphenates." Farnsworth lauded the public schools, which developed "the highest type of mentality in the world, Protestant mentality." "Who is it who makes and handles the booze against the law?" he asked. "What nationality comprises the bartenders and the bootleggers? Not the real Americans." Sixty-two per cent of all elective and appointive offices in the government were filled with Catholics, according to his statistics. "The Ku Klux Klan has gone out to vote. . ." the King Kleagle proclaimed, and presumably that action would straighten out the unhappy situation he had just described. Afterwards Farnsworth told reporters that Boston itself was ripe for a Klan membership drive which would soon get underway, and then the organization would stage a parade right in the heart of the Irish-dominated Hub.[19] That parade never took place but the Ku Kluxers did make progress, at least in other parts of the Commonwealth. On a Saturday night in April 1924 crosses were set afire simultaneously in over a dozen communities across the state. Later in the year a "klonvocation" on the fair grounds near Worcester drew 15,000 Klansmen.[20]

That the Ku Klux Klan would resort to politics became evident in 1922 when Klan-backed candidates figured in election battles in Texas, Indiana, and Oregon. In 1923 it played a part in more municipal and state contests.[21] Its technique was that of the nonpartisan pressure group. That meant working through the Democratic primary in the South, and playing off each major party against the other in the West. In the East, where the Democratic Party was controlled largely by Irish Catholics, the Klan inevitably associated itself more closely with the Republicans. Pursuit of this strategy brought a considerable measure of success, and by 1924 a number of local and state administrations, and some members of Congress, owed their victories to the K.K.K. Speculation was rampant concerning the part the Klan would play in the presidential politics of the national election year.

Some Republicans felt that the party's platform should condemn the hooded order as a matter of principle, but in the end the question was passed over in silence at Cleveland.[22] The Klan was satisfied with Calvin Coolidge's Americanism and raised no rumpus at the convention, although Dr. Evans was there. No use for the G.O.P. to disturb calm waters, then!

With the Democrats it was different, for that party harbored the bulk of the Irish and an increasing proportion of the New Immigrants, and the Klan was determined to thwart the growing influence of the alien, wet "boss-ridden" new-stock wing. Moreover, the Klan disliked the wet Senator Underwood, and in the fall of 1923 made known its intention of actively opposing him in the primaries.[23] Since the favorite, William G. McAdoo, was the most available instrument for blocking the ambitions of both Underwood and the city bosses, the Klan attached itself to his candidacy. Though frequently heckled about the matter, McAdoo never repudiated the Ku Klux Klan by name, and in a number of primary contests it helped him defeat Underwood. In the minds of people who worried about such things the former Secretary of the Treasury was "the Klan candidate," if anybody was.[24]

The bluntness of the Klan's words, the violence which at times marked its actions, and the undemocratic overtones of "invisible government" that characterized its political activities evoked condemnation among all segments of the population. Even some of the one hundred per cent Americans who seemed to agree with much of the K.K.K.'s program denounced its abuses. Admiral Sims, whose salty deprecations of hyphenate activity have been mentioned earlier, attacked the Invisible Empire and its methods. The *Boston Transcript*, which had not hesitated in 1921 to label the activities of Irish-American patriots as treasonable, later called Ku Kluxism an "un-American thing." "The 'one hundred per cent' American should be a person devoid of such prejudices," it commented. The American Legion at its 1923 national convention condemned organizations that fostered racial and religious strife (though a resolution specifically attacking the K.K.K. was defeated). Various groups of Prohibition fanatics also dissociated themselves from the secret order.[25] No doubt Warren Harding and James M. Cox, whose preachments on one hundred per cent Americanism in 1920 did much to heighten distrust of the new stock, likewise had no stomach for the Klan's doings. Nevertheless, though they now rejected the organization's excesses, these elements were largely responsible for creating the atmosphere of postwar America which fostered the growth of the Ku Klux Klan.

More to the point was the criticism offered by those who had repudiated the one hundred per cent Americanism drive from the beginning. For even while most old-stock people were succumbing to ideas of immigration restriction and forced Americanization, some had continued to cherish the traditional melting-pot concept. Others adopted a newer view of America as a pluralistic society, in which ethnic and cultural diversity should be regarded as an asset rather than a defect. Dr. Horace Kallen, a leading exponent of that attitude, asked the question: "What do we *will* to make the United States — a unison, singing the old Anglo-Saxon theme 'America,' the America of the New England school; or a harmony, in which that theme shall be dominant, perhaps, among others, but one among many, not the only one?" [26] Recognizing the stifling implications of the old-stock drive to mold all elements of the population into a common standard of Americanism, defenders of diversity like the *Nation* and the *New Republic* opposed the movement. When the Ku Klux Klan emerged as a national problem, they attacked it as the logical culmination of the foolhardy cult of forced Americanization.[27] In effect, they became the intellectual spokesmen for the principle of ethnic tolerance and harmony — that is, for cultural liberalism.

Most important of all were the Klan's effects on the immediate objects of its hate campaign, the Irish and the "newer races." To these masses, too, the K.K.K. represented the culmination of the anti-hyphen Americanization mania of the postwar era which had maligned their beliefs, their institutions, and their very stature as desirable citizens. Told that they failed to measure up to the standards of true Americanism as defined by the dominant older inhabitants of the land, some Newer Americans — those most bitterly affected — renounced the values of their new homeland entirely and immersed themselves instead in the glories of real or imagined old countries. Italian-Americans of this type reveled in the triumph of Mussolini and joined the Fascist League of North America. Among Negroes, Marcus Garvey's "Back to Africa" movement met some success. Zionism gained new recruits in the American Jewish community. Others among the disillusioned newer arrivals adhered to the fledgling Communist movement in the United States. Some actually went back to Europe. Better to be one hundred per cent something else than half-baked, unaccepted Americans.[28]

The more common response, though, was a rejection of the old stock's contention that all true Americans must be of one cultural mold, and a determination to demonstrate that divergent ways of life were nonetheless capable of producing good citizens and enhancing the nation's welfare. In Massachusetts the *Jewish Advocate* assiduously reported the football exploits of Harvard student Arnold Horween, as if to prove that a boy who worshiped on Saturday could still be a terror between the goal-posts to old-stock youths who went to church on Sunday. Other ethnic journals similarly doted on the achievements of their group in colleges, in the sports and entertainment worlds, and in the professions. Nor was the realm of ideas neglected, and for weeks at a time in the 1920's the *Italian News* of Boston ran a cartoon strip depicting the close friendship between Thomas Jefferson and the Italian liberal, Fillippo Mazzei, pointing up Mazzei's supposed influence on the philosophy of the man who wrote the Declaration of Independence. Thus did Newer Americans attempt to make plain their ability to contribute something to the American "harmony" of ethnic influences envisioned by Dr. Kallen. They, too, were cultural liberals.

The increased self-consciousness of the newer ethnic groups also made them defend more aggressively their right to respect and equality. Their resentment against old-stock superciliousness, against attempts to forcibly Americanize their preferences, and against restricted immigration found expression in word and deed.[29] They also fought with new vigor the crasser offshoots of one hundred per cent Americanism reflected in racial and religious discrimination. Irish spokesmen decried the economic discrimination practiced in Boston (in the 1920's the word "Protestant" still frequently appeared as a required qualification in the "help wanted" section of the *Boston Transcript*). Negroes demanded and got from the legislature a law forbidding racial discrimination in the hiring of employees by public-controlled street railways. Jewish representatives secured an act authorizing removal from the Boston Public Library of a mural by John Singer Sargent allegedly offensive to their faith.[30]

Perhaps the most significant result of the drive for one hundred per cent Americanism was the manner in which it promoted a growing sense of unity among the ethnic segments comprising the Newer Americans. Racial, nationality, religious, and political differences had acted in the past to keep Irishmen, French-Canadians, Italians, Poles, Jews, and Negroes quite apart from one another. But now, sharing a common status as "inferior" citizens and enduring common attacks at the hands of the old stock, the different brands of newcomers, to some extent at least, overcame their mutual suspicions and pooled their efforts at fighting back. Thus the move to increase state control over parochial schools in Massachusetts joined Irish Catholics of Boston with French-Canadian and Polish Catholics of the hinterlands in an effort to preserve the "hands off" policy. When Harvard University in 1922 appeared to be succumbing to a plan for discrimination against Negroes and Jews, cultural liberals of all ethnic backgrounds joined in the chorus of protest.[31] In 1923 the Irish-dominated Knights of Columbus, taking cognizance of the "manifestations of racial intolerance . . . we have witnessed for the last few years," commissioned a series of historical monographs designed to point out "the great contributions of alien races to the development of the United States."[32]

When a federal judge addressing a public meeting in Boston lamented that the type of immigrant passing before his bench in naturalization proceedings "now . . . is not of a kind, generally speaking, to fit into our kind of life," the next speaker, Mayor Curley, proclaimed that "this is an immigrant nation . . . and thank God it is." [33] In his speech on the floor of the Senate opposing the Johnson Immigration Act, David I. Walsh enumerated each of the nationalities comprising the New Immigration, recited its virtues, and listed its contributions to American civilization.[34] Clearly then, although former hostilities were by no means eradicated, the pressure of the old-stock citizens taught the components of the Newer American population that, for the time being at least, their similarities outweighed their differences.

The emergence of the Ku Klux Klan provided the Newer Americans a focal point for their counterattack on cultural illiberalism. They followed closely Senator Underwood's campaign for the Democratic presidential nomination as he reiterated his attacks on the K.K.K. and demanded an anti-Klan plank in the party platform. In the spring of 1924 his prospects declined further, however, as McAdoo won several important primary battles. And by then the Newer American Democrats had turned to another champion, Alfred E. Smith.

Al Smith was first elected governor of New York in 1918.[35] In the Republican landslide two years later he was defeated, but while Harding carried the state by 1,088,000 votes, Smith lost by a mere 75,000. In 1922 he won his second term by an unprecedented majority of 400,000 ballots. Smith was the pride and joy of Tammany Hall, yet in spite of that fact he had won the support of labor leaders, advanced liberals, and even the "good government" people by his record of honesty, intimate knowledge of administration, and advocacy of social and welfare reform legislation. He represented, in its most mature form, the new and broader-visioned leadership that had begun to emerge among the urban masses at the turn of the century. A writer in the *New Republic* summed up the phenomenon: "Smith has been 'regular' with the organization and with the voter at the same time. That is little short of a miracle, in itself." [36]

When Underwood's effectiveness waned, Smith replaced him as the main hope of the anti-McAdoo "bosses." Moreover, the revelation of McAdoo's relations with Doheny had turned the attention of economic liberals to a consideration of Smith's qualifications. As one writer put it:

> I at least have never met any man, for or against Al Smith, who has more than the faintest idea of his thought on the economic questions that engage national attention. . . Nevertheless, there seems to be in the back of every head an unconscious appraisal of Al Smith as a man willing to take a chance for the underdog.[37]

Some even hinted that Smith's nomination by the Democrats might make unnecessary the launching of a third party at the Fourth of July C.P.P.A. convention.

It soon became evident, however, that the mainspring of the Smith movement was his appeal to the Newer Americans. He was one of them. An Irish Catholic, born and bred in New York City, he was forced to leave school at an early age and work in a fish market to help support his widowed mother. But he had made good, and was living proof to the one hundred per cent Americans that a product of the "inferior" new stock could so administer the affairs of the largest state in the nation as to merit re-election by the biggest plurality in history. In 1923 he signed a bill repealing the state's Prohibition enforcement act and another bill compelling secret societies to furnish membership lists to state officials. Prohibitionists and the Ku Klux Klan hated him. But by environment, instinct, and conviction he was a cultural liberal, and the Newer Americans revered him. As their fear that the Klan might dominate the Democratic convention increased, so did their zeal for Al Smith.

The situation in Massachusetts gave some indication of the spark the New York governor ignited in the strongholds of the Irish and the newer nationality groups. Certainly Senator Walsh, the kingpin of Bay State Democracy, recognized the mounting Smith sentiment in the Commonwealth. He preferred to have the convention delegation uncommitted to any one candidate, however, in order to placate all segments of the state party organization. Perhaps, as some said, the Senator did not want too many Irish Catholic names on the ballot in the fall, since he faced a battle for re-election himself. In any case, the "official" slate of eight unpledged candidates for delegate-at-large which he disclosed in the middle of March appeared to give no presidential aspirant an edge.[38]

Within a few days General Charles Cole filed as an independent candidate, pledging to support Smith at the convention and challenging his opponents to make similar commitments. Only one did so. When the primary ballots were counted on April 29, Cole had succeeded in displacing one of the members of the regular slate — an almost unprecedented accomplishment. Indeed, Cole placed second among the nine contestants, topped only by the invincible Walsh, and in Boston he received only a hundred votes fewer than the Senator. Third place in the field went to Joseph Ely, the other announced Smith man. In the district contests a large number of winners were men who had committed themselves to Smith following Cole's debut on the scene. A short time later, Senator Walsh announced that he favored the nomination of Al Smith for President.[39]

The upheaval did not stop there. When Walsh arrived in

...esident Calvin Coolidge and Republican Senators William M. Butler and ...ederick Gillett review a National Guard unit during the summer of 1925.

Herbert Hoover, Republican presidential candidate, makes a campaign speech on Boston Common, 1928.

John F. Fitzgerald and James Michael Curley wearing the brown derbies of the 1928 campaign.

Democratic Boss Martin Lomasney instructing the voters of Boston's Ward Three before the 1930 primary. Lomasney traditionally discarded collar, tie, and other encumbrances in the course of his pre-election harangues.

New York City for the convention in June and unveiled a proposed platform centering on economic issues, the document disappointed many in its failure to damn the Ku Klux Klan by name. Instead, one passage merely reaffirmed the civil liberties guaranteed in the Bill of Rights. Within a matter of hours the Senator received a flood of telegrams from Massachusetts constituents, demanding that he fight for an "out-and-out" Klan plank. When the Bay State delegation caucused the next day, it discarded Walsh's proposal and voted overwhelmingly to support the stronger position. Chastened again, Walsh now leaped wholeheartedly into the all-out fight on the Klan.[40]

Developments similar to those in Massachusetts took place in other states heavily populated with Newer Americans. By the eve of the convention Smith, with the pledged support of the 126 delegates from New York, Rhode Island, and Wisconsin, had become the popular hero of the northeast section of the country. But McAdoo, with 270 pledged votes from states in the South and West, was still in the lead; and a pitched battle appeared imminent.[41] Moreover, the squaring off of Smith against McAdoo had also defined the issue that would dominate the Democratic meeting, and as delegates poured into New York from all parts of the country, everything seemed to turn on whether or not three little words — Ku Klux Klan — should appear in the party platform.[42] The Democratic convention which met in Madison Square Garden on June 24, then, hardly resembled a consultation for plotting defeat of the political enemy in November. Foreign affairs, economic policy, Republican corruption, practically the Republican Party itself, were all but forgotten. Instead, with attention centered on McAdoo, Smith, and the Klan, the convention was a struggle to determine which of the party's two jarring wings would gain internal ascendancy.[43]

The result of the encounter was a draw. The fight over the

platform in the early days of the meeting, which demonstrated just how evenly the contending forces were divided, insured that outcome. A plank favored by a majority of the resolutions committee reaffirmed the civil liberties guaranteed in the Constitution and concluded: "We . . . deplore and condemn any effort to arouse religious or racial dissension." But thirteen members of the committee — the representatives of Maine, Vermont, Massachusetts, Rhode Island, New York, New Jersey, Pennsylvania, Maryland, Illinois, Minnesota, Alabama, the District of Columbia, and Alaska — sponsored an amendment pledging the Democratic Party "to oppose any effort on the part of the Ku Klux Klan or any organization to interfere with the religious liberty or political freedom of any citizen or body of citizens because of religion, birthplace, or racial origin." [44] For five hours spokesmen for the two wings of the party debated the issue on the floor, as twelve hundred policemen stood guard. Finally it was put to the ballot, and in a welter of cheers and groans the result was announced: $541\frac{3}{20}$ votes in favor of naming the Klan, $542\frac{3}{20}$ opposed. The session adjourned without the threatened bloodshed, but its effects permeated the remainder of the convention.

When balloting for a presidential nominee began, the McAdoo-Smith deadlock was soon apparent. Smith's vote never exceeded half the total, but he controlled enough delegates to keep his opponent from reaching the required two-thirds mark. The roll calls dragged on for a week until, after seventy-seven ballots, the convention adopted a resolution releasing all delegates from their pledges. Thereafter the strength of McAdoo and Smith dwindled. Several dark horses rose and then fell, for none who had been connected in any way with the Klan fight were able to win. Finally, on the one hundred and third roll call, the weary delegates selected John W. Davis of West Virginia.

In the course of the nation's longest political convention, the Democratic Party had all but wrecked itself in a momentous conflict of cultures. Its presidential candidate represented a meaningless compromise of the profound issues involved, and failed to arouse enthusiasm among either old-stock or Newer American Democrats. He therefore offered no prospect of party victory in the election.[45]

Midway through the Democratic debacle the Conference for Progressive Political Action assembled in Cleveland. Perceiving as little hope for economic liberalism in the deadlocked Democratic Party as in business-dominated Republicanism, the C.P.P.A. plunged into third-party politics, with La Follette and Senator Burton K. Wheeler of Montana heading its ticket.[46]

Economic issues dominated the election campaign that followed, although effects of the nation's cultural dichotomy played some part. Davis attacked Republican corruption and favoritism toward big business, but at the same time decried any extension of "special privilege" by the government to farmers or labor. His old-line Jeffersonian approach did not interest the nation's discontented economic groups. The nature of Davis' Wall Street law practice (he counseled J. P. Morgan, among others) also hurt him, particularly in the West. And although Davis denounced the Ku Klux Klan by name in August, he failed to satisfy the disgruntled Smithites in the East.[47]

Senator La Follette's campaign won the major share of attention. Speaking primarily for the insurgent agrarian wing of Republicanism, La Follette centered his attack around the time-honored theme of monopoly. The platform adopted by the C.P.P.A. demanded government ownership of the railroads and creation of a government marketing corporation for agriculture, but these more radical proposals figured little in the Senator's personal appeals. "La Follette's principal stand in 1924 is on the Sherman law of 1890," observed one of the more perceptive writers of the time. La Follette was "not only an individualist, but an intense and aggressive individualist." [48]

Nevertheless, to business Republicans in the East the third-party movement was a prelude to the sovietization of the United States. Seizing upon the platform proposals for government ownership, and especially on the demand for a method of overriding Supreme Court decisions, the conservatives denounced La Follette as an un-American revolutionary. "The issue of transcending importance in this campaign is Communism or Americanism," Governor Channing Cox told the Republican state convention in Massachusetts. [49]

In the eastern part of the country Senator La Follette's strength lay among usually Democratic elements of the electorate. Labor leaders spearheaded his campaign there. Advanced liberals, ever anxious for a rationalization of the nation's party system along economic lines, also hailed La Follette as the messiah who might finally unite workers of the farms and of the cities in opposition to the business interests. The agrarian bias of the Senator's brand of economic liberalism inhibited the forging of such an alliance, although his attack on the Administration's overweening pro-business favoritism made some impression among the industrial masses. [50] But considerations other than economic were more significant in accounting for La Follette's support in Newer American centers. For one thing the Senator, whose Wisconsin constituency included such melting-pot areas as Milwaukee, denounced the Ku Klux Klan in specific terms even earlier in the campaign than did John W. Davis. His record of agitation on behalf of Ireland in the postwar years was also well-known among the Irish-American inhabitants of the eastern cities. Moreover, La Follette had opposed American entry into the First World War, and in 1924 he endorsed proposals designed to avoid future European entanglements, including a demand for a national referendum prior to declaration of war. Those views recommended him to many Newer Americans, who now remembered America's world-saving experiment as a time of bitterness and disillusion.[51]

President Coolidge abstained from the contest and put into full practice his underlying political strategy — that a candidate can never be hurt by what he doesn't say. He never mentioned Davis or La Follette. Nor did he mention the Ku Klux Klan, although he made a point of personally addressing the Holy Name Society's national convention in September. He made no campaign tour and confined himself to a few "nonpolitical" speeches during the fall, barely mentioning his candidacy. "His only response to attacks . . . was complete silence," according to a favorable biographer, who concludes naïvely that the President did not care "to prostitute his high office in order to gain votes." [52]

The Republicans who did the President's campaigning for him all but ignored Davis, centered their attacks on La Follette, and sang the praises of Republican economic doctrine. Nineteen hundred twenty-three had been a boom year, marking the end of the postwar depression, but with 1924 another recession became noticeable across the nation. G.O.P. campaigners in the fall saw three essential solutions: full implementation of Secretary Mellon's tax-reduction plan which would release more capital for investment, continued immigration restriction, and even higher protective tariff rates. That program would restore the good times of 1923 and inaugurate an even more dazzling era of "Coolidge prosperity." [53]

As the campaign drew to a close, few doubted its result. Davis was left behind in the dust. La Follette could hope to win votes away from Coolidge in the West and from Davis in the East, but even his ardent supporters saw little more hope than a possibility of throwing the election into Congress.[54] Calvin Coolidge seemed secure in his tenure of the White House.

In Massachusetts, certainty of the outcome of the presidential race was even more marked. Davis received no more than lip-service support from party leaders. The Democratic national committee again "wrote off" the Bay State, and Davis canceled his expected appearance there.[55] La Follette's campaign cut into the ranks of the Democrats and some felt he might win second place, especially after he spoke in Boston on October 30. But Coolidge was the state's favorite son — the first Massachusetts man to occupy the presidency since John Quincy Adams. He was the idol of old-stock Republicans, and in his earlier state contests had always done well in New Immigrant areas and even among the Irish.[56] So it appeared that Boston might again go Republican.

Meanwhile, Bay Staters were more interested in other offices at stake. Leading the Democratic ticket were David I. Walsh, seeking a second term in the Senate, and James Michael Curley, who saw the time ripe for his first assault on the State House. Both were strong candidates. Curley has had few peers as a political orator in the twentieth century, and Walsh's spellbinding powers were only slightly less distinguished. The relations between the two men were far from friendly, but burying their hatchets for the time being, they seemed to pose a powerful threat to the Massachusetts G.O.P.

The Republican "escalator system" put Lieutenant Governor Alvan T. Fuller in line for the governorship in 1924.

Finding a fit opponent for Senator Walsh proved more difficult, however. At first National Chairman William M. Butler
was expected to take on the job, but Coolidge retained him
in charge of the presidential campaign. While the machine's
directors looked for another suitable contender, two unwanted candidates jumped into the breach. Louis A. Coolidge
was a close friend of Senator Lodge and, moreover, wanted
to make revision of the Volstead Act the main point of his
campaign. On both counts he was anathema to the regular
organization, which by now had aligned itself firmly with the
dry forces in the state. Congressman Frederick Dallinger of
Cambridge, on the other hand, enjoyed the endorsement of
the Anti-Saloon League but had aroused the President's ire
earlier in the year by voting to override several vetoes. Neither
aspirant satisfied the dominant machine, which finally chose
Congressman Frederick Gillett of Springfield, Speaker of the
House, as its man.[57] Gillett had opposed Prohibition at its in-
ception but now made known his conversion into an ardent
dry. Nevertheless, those who placed the sacredness of the
Eighteenth Amendment above everything else insisted on
loyalty to Dallinger, and it took all the ingenuity of the Calvin Coolidge organization to put Gillett across. Prohibition
had caused trouble for the first time — but not the last — in a
Republican state primary of the 1920's.[58]

The lineup of Curley and Walsh against Fuller and Gillett
presaged the disposition of Irish Democrat and old-stock Republican votes. The largest block of ballots left at stake were
those of the "newer races." Their increasing political importance in Massachusetts had become evident to all since 1920,
and both parties now angled for their support more earnestly
than ever. The membership of the committees for the Republican state convention which met in September included
representatives of the French-Canadians, Italians, Poles, Jews,

Portuguese, and Negroes, and the *Boston Transcript* was at pains to point out that fact. Those in charge of planning the Democratic convention countered with a similar move, though their list was not quite so cosmopolitan.[59] Walsh, Curley, and the state committee, however, did sponsor H. Oscar Rocheleau and Michael Eisner for the positions of secretary of state and state treasurer in the party primary. Hence the Democratic ticket embraced representatives of two New Immigrant groups, something of which the Republican slate could not boast. But in October Governor Cox made up lost ground by appointing a Jew, David Lourie, to the Superior Court bench, and then named Joseph Zottoli to occupy the judgeship Lourie vacated on the Municipal Court of Boston. Both honors were the highest ever accorded a member of the two ethnic groups involved, and Republican campaigners lost no time calling attention to them.[60]

In the matter of platform planks adopted by the parties' state conventions, the Democrats clearly outdid their opponents in appealing to the New Immigrants. The Republican platform urged "the enforcement of all laws," which meant Prohibition, while the Democratic version favored modification of the Volstead Act to permit light wines and beer. The Republicans rhetorically evaded the issue presented by the Johnson Immigration Act by voicing praise of it, "except wherein its provisions are discriminatory"; the Democrats condemned it outright. A Republican plank deplored "any organized effort to create racial or religious prejudice," but the resolutions committee rejected a proposal to insert those three little words — Ku Klux Klan. The Democrats denounced the organization by name.[61]

In the gubernatorial contest James Michael Curley focused on the Klan as his leading issue. To what extent Curley lieutenants themselves set fire to crosses, which seemed to burn more frequently as the campaign progressed, remains a disputed question. That the Klan was active in Massachusetts could not be denied; that Curley exaggerated its influence was also true. At any rate, throughout the fall Curley inveighed against the "protection" afforded the society by the Republican administration, which provided state policemen to patrol its convocations. He boasted that under his regime as mayor the Klan had never held a meeting within the confines of Boston and promised to make that condition state-wide if elected.[62] As a result, newspapers reported increasing signs of defection among Republican mill workers of foreign extraction in the industrial centers. In mid-October it was ordered that state police should no longer be present at Klan meetings. And when the Republican national committee booked Governor-elect Ralph Brewster of Maine — whose victory was allegedly tainted by Klan support — for an appearance in Massachusetts, the Bay State organization leaders turned him down.[63]

That the G.O.P. expected to receive and was willing to accept the votes of the Ku Kluxers was obvious. But Curley's attempt to make the Klan label stick to the Republicans of the state in general, and to his opponent for the governorship in particular, was a difficult task. The Republican-dominated legislature passed a resolution condemning the Klan in 1923, and some prominent party leaders denounced it in public thereafter. The sharp-tongued campaigning of Elijah Adlow, a Jewish member of the legislature, proved especially effective in dulling Curley's barbs. "Curley is trying to ride into the State House on the tail of the white hood," Adlow repeated up and down the Commonwealth. "Curley is the only man who sees the Klan. He's the only man who wants one." [64] Moreover, Alvan T. Fuller's wife was a Catholic, and his large donations to Catholic charities were no secret. Fuller claimed that the Klan had opposed him in the Republican primary, and felt sure that the people would recognize him for what he was — "just . . . a broadminded, liberal minded, plain American citizen." [65]

Fuller himself concentrated on the Republican record of "economy and sound administration." At the Republican state convention and thereafter he cited the achievements of his predecessor — reduction of the debt in four years from thirty-five million dollars to nineteen million, and of the direct state tax from fourteen million to ten million — and promised to do likewise. He endorsed the movement for biennial sessions of the legislature, and declared that the people's representatives should concentrate on repealing existing statutes. "We need less laws." [66]

After 1922 the Republican economy drive was spear-headed by a newly created Commission on Administration and Finance, which pared down the budget with ruthless efficiency. By 1924 even the *Boston Transcript* felt that the commission's zeal was impairing essential state services and demoralizing the spirit of public officials. This situation provided Curley with a second issue. He attacked the pre-eminence that Republicans gave to "cost" in the administration of state affairs and promised to substitute therefor Curleyism — "being another name for kindly, considerate and humane treatment of the poor, the sick and the unfortunate." [67] Curley's record as a spender as chief executive of Boston needed no substantiation, and all agreed that his liberality improved the city's appearance and its facilities. But there was always some question whether the citizens received a full return on their tax dollar under the Mayor's regime, and consequently Republicans denounced Curleyism as a graft-ridden spending spree. It was doubtful whether, in 1924, the economy-minded inhabitants of the Bay State would be ready to hand Curley a key to the state treasury.

Then, too, some of the Mayor's personal characteristics worked against him. Like Fitzgerald in 1922, Curley epitomized the traditional Boston Irish Democrat. As a result people of the hinterlands — including the New Immigrants of the manufacturing towns who applauded his sallies against the Ku Klux Klan — hesitated to ensconce him in the State House. Finally, the debacle which developed over the proposed federal child labor amendment, up for ratification on a referendum at the November election, hurt Curley's reputation in some quarters. Both Curley and Senator Walsh backed the measure early in the campaign, but on October 5 Cardinal O'Connell and the Catholic clergy denounced it and urged a "No" vote. Walsh, disappointed, remained silent on the matter in the following weeks. But Curley immediately reversed his position and proceeded to damn the amendment as a Bolshevist scheme spawned in Russia, "which has deluded many good people." The incident sustained the fears of those who saw demagogic tendencies in Curley's make-up. "Do you want a political jumping-jack for governor?" asked Representative Adlow.[68] As the election approached, Republicans felt that they had succeeded in extracting the sharpest teeth of the Boston Democratic tiger, and counted Fuller "safe." Curley, though colorful and dynamic, was not a flawless candidate — at least in a state-wide contest.

In the race for the senatorship, on the other hand, David I. Walsh was an almost faultless contender. As the only one of their number who had attained prominence on the national political stage, Walsh could count on the allegiance of the Massachusetts Irish. Yet, despite his similarity to Curley as an Irish Catholic Democrat, the Senator appeared "different" to people inclined to find fault with that breed.[69] He was not from Boston. He was not a "boss." His views were not so parochial as Curley's. And, though Walsh's stand on issues was slippery enough at times, he was not so subject to the accusations of demagoguery that were frequently hurled at Curley. Consequently, Walsh enjoyed more solid backing among the groups who distrusted his running-mate: the New Immigrants, the Yankee Democrats, and the advanced liberals. In addition, the Senator could garner votes even among "independent" or disaffected old-stock Republicans, a source of support virtually barred to Curley.

Moreover, Walsh's tactics were more effective than those of his partner on the ticket. The Senator was more moderate in his approach. Instead of concentrating on one or two issues, Walsh conducted a many-sided campaign aimed at winning support among all elements of the population. He stressed his independence of party ties, and promised to support President Coolidge "when he was right." An advertisement headed, "Partisanship Has Never Obscured His Vision," and signed by "fifty Cape Cod Republicans," solicited votes for him from members of the G.O.P. who desired to end "boss rule" within their party. The Association against the Prohibition Amendment, from its New York headquarters, urged bipartisan wet support for the junior Massachusetts senator.[70]

Walsh also stressed the economic liberalism of his congressional voting record. He attacked the Mellon tax program, "which benefits the twenty-five hundred multimillionaires and the twenty-five hundred great corporations of the country only." [71] He denounced the exorbitant rates of the Fordney-McCumber Tariff, which raised the prices of the things the common people ate and wore. The "Big Four" railway brotherhoods called his labor record "one hundred per cent favorable to the interests of the workers" and endorsed him for re-election. The national executive council of the C.P.P.A.

endorsed him too, acclaiming him as "one of the nation's greatest progressives." The Socialist Party put up no candidate for senator in Massachusetts, though it entered a full slate for the other posts on the state ticket. Finally, Senator La Follette himself devoted a large part of his Boston campaign speech to praise of his colleague. David I. Walsh, according to the third-party candidate, like Norris and Borah and Smith W. Brookhart, "stands for something more than party." [72]

At the same time, Senator Walsh always took pains to qualify his attacks on the economic "interests." What he opposed was "big business" — the monopolists, the multimillionaires, the "barons." For "little business" he was extremely solicitous. Democrats like himself, he claimed, were the champions of "little business" against the policies of the Republican Administration, which threatened to wipe out the little man.[73] The Senator's tariff views were similarly qualified. For while Walsh criticized the Fordney-McCumber Act, he did not hold to the historic low-tariff policy of his party. What he opposed, along with all other New England congressmen, were high rates on food and on raw materials, which that region must import from outside its bounds. With manufactured goods, which New England produced, the story was different. "I believe in tariffs which will protect American labor and develop American industries," Senator Walsh assured a rally in the factory town of Hudson, although he would add that the rates should not be exorbitant or foster monopoly.[74] His attitude on that issue was shaped by his section, not his party. Consequently, low-tariff ideologists, like the *Springfield Republican*, repudiated him. But the pro-Republican *New Bedford Times* editorialized that "New Bedford and New England need have no fear that their industrial security will be weakened with Walsh in the Senate." The

Times supported Coolidge and Fuller in 1924, but endorsed Walsh for senator.[75]

Friends of the Senator early advised him of unemployment in the Bay State's industrial cities and towns. In subsequent campaign appearances he dwelt on the "hard times" theme and attacked the federal government's neglect of the situation. Moreover, Walsh could claim that he had done something about it, for in May Congress had approved his resolution directing the Tariff Commission to investigate the depressed condition of the New England textile industry. The commission reported in June but no action was taken because, the Senator charged, the Administration failed to back him up. His allegations aroused the attention of businessmen and workers alike in the affected areas, and rallies in New Bedford, Fall River, Lowell, Holyoke, Chicopee, and similar places were well attended and enthusiastic.[76]

Finally, there was the matter of cultural liberalism. Walsh did not chase the Ku Klux Klan in his campaign, as did his running-mate. Instead he concentrated on the Johnson Immigration Act of 1924, which "closed America's door of opportunity" and constituted the "greatest insult" ever offered the foreign-born residents of the United States and their children. "I am opposed to the restriction of immigration which would make certain races undesirable as citizens. They did not ask the Jew, the Italian or the Pole their nationality during the war and I do not propose to do it now. . ." [77] Some complained about the Senator's bold appeal for the votes of ethnic groups. Would hyphenism never end? The New Immigrants, however, were grateful to the man who had defended their character on the floor of Congress against the onslaught of one hundred per cent Americanism. Walsh's stand on immigration restriction, the *Boston Transcript* commented ruefully, "has won him thousands of Republican votes in districts where there is a large foreign-born element." [78]

The Senator's opponent, Representative Frederick Gillett, was seventy-three years old and had never been noted for his ability as a public speaker. During the campaign a story circulated that Gillett avoided coffee in the morning "for fear it would keep him awake all day." [79] The *Transcript* felt that Gillett's active participation at Republican rallies lived down the joke. Nevertheless, he made a poor showing on the stump compared to the handsome bachelor, Walsh, whose appearance and suavity were not the least of his political assets in the new era of female suffrage.

Republican campaigners were hard pressed for effective issues to use against the incumbent, but they depended on the Coolidge tide to sweep Gillett into the Senate. Gillett promised to uphold the state's favorite son in all things, and rested his appeal to the electorate on that basis. Walsh's personal advantages, his well-rounded campaign, and the relative weakness of his opponent gave him a good chance of retaining his seat. But in the Bay State, as columnist David Lawrence reported, everything hinged on Calvin Coolidge.[80]

The balloting on November 4 produced a sweeping national victory for the President. Davis carried twelve states in the traditionally Democratic South. La Follette won in Wisconsin. All other electoral votes went to Coolidge. In Massachusetts, he carried every community, including Boston, except the little town of Blackstone. He polled 703,476 votes to 280,831 for Davis and 141,225 for La Follette. Alvan T. Fuller beat Curley for the governorship, 650,817 to 490,010. And Gillett defeated Senator Walsh by 18,588 votes — 566,188 to 547,600. The Republicans added slightly to their majorities in the state legislature, but the three Democratic congressmen held their places. On a referendum the voters finally approved a state Prohibition enforcement act by a narrow margin, 454,656 to 446,473.[81]

Coolidge's presence on the ballot brought out old-stock Republicans in full force. Though Mayor Curley's registration drive in Boston had increased the city's potential electorate by approximately 12 per cent over 1922, the Republicans were just as busy, and aggregate registration in the towns of the Commonwealth increased by almost 11 per cent. On election day over 86 per cent of the registrants in the towns took the trouble of going to the polls, while in the off-year 1922 election only 69 per cent had done so. Boston's total three-party vote for President in 1924, compared to the vote for governor in 1922, showed an increase of approximately 20 per cent. But the aggregate vote of the thirteen old-stock cities over 25,000 (each having more than 30 per cent "native white of native parentage" population), increased almost 34 per cent, while for the twenty-nine old-stock towns of 2,500 to 10,000 (each having 50 per cent or more "native white of native parentage" population), the figure was higher still — approximately 42 per cent. All this meant a swelling of Republican majorities over their 1922 volume.

Compared to 1920, however, the Republican presidential victory was <u>not</u> as overwhelming. True, Davis' percentage of the state's total three-party vote (24.9) was smaller than Cox's percentage of the two-party vote in 1920 (28.9). But analysis of the returns indicates that the votes for La Follette in 1924 came mainly from potential Democrats — from people who voted for Walsh and Curley, but not for Davis.[82] The combined vote for Davis and La Follette, then, represented 37.5 per cent of the three-party total. Hence Coolidge received only 62.5 per cent of that total, whereas Harding won 71.1 per cent of the two-party vote in 1920.

Further analysis of ward, town, and city returns indicates the source of the relative falling-off in the Republican vote. For example, while Coolidge's percentage of the three-party vote in Boston was fully 14 points less than Harding's proportion of the two-party vote in 1920, for the aggregate vote of the twenty-nine old-stock towns mentioned above it was only about 2 points less. In the aggregate vote of the ten other Newer American cities over 25,000 outside Boston (each having 70 per cent or more foreign-stock population), the Republican decrease was 11 points, while in the thirteen old-stock cities of that class it was only 8 points.[83] Clearly the Irish and the newer ethnic groups accounted for most of the slip in the Republican performance.

Nevertheless, it was also clear that many Newer Americans still maintained their loyalty to the G.O.P. when it came to choosing a president, as evidenced by the substantial gap between the combined Davis–La Follette percentage of the presidential vote, and the percentages received by the Democratic candidates in the senatorial and gubernatorial contests. Curley got 42.9 per cent of the two-party vote for governor, while Walsh won 49.2 per cent of the two-party senatorial vote. The Senator's percentage led the Mayor's in almost every locale, be it old-stock or Newer American, and including each of the twenty-six wards of Curley's bailiwick, Boston. Curley's performance, in fact, was considerably poorer than that of Fitzgerald in 1922, for the latter had won 46.5 per cent of the vote. In Republican wards and places the Mayor's percentage was almost invariably less than Fitzgerald's. The same was true, to a lesser extent, in many Irish wards also. Practically the only wards in which Curley was able to improve on Honey Fitz's record were certain ones dominated by New Immigrant people. The Mayor's crusade against the Ku Klux Klan helped him in those instances, but was not enough to offset the other factors handicapping his campaign.

Senator Walsh received about the same percentage of the state-wide senatorial vote as had William A. Gaston in 1922, despite the great outpouring of Republicans in the presidential year. Places where the Senator's percentage fell behind Gaston's were generally old-stock Republican strongholds. But those losses were made up by Walsh's improvement over Gaston's showing in the Irish wards, and especially in localities where the newer immigrant elements predominated. For example, while Walsh bettered Gaston's percentage of the vote in every one of Boston's twenty-six wards except the old stock's Back Bay, the largest increases were in the two Jewish wards (11 points in each case) and in Martin Lomasney's melting-pot ward of Italians and Jews (8 points). In the neighboring city of Chelsea, the increases in Walsh's percentage over Gaston's in the two Jewish wards (16 points in each case) outstripped even the increase in the Irish ward (6 points). In Haverhill the Senator's proportion of the vote in the city's strongest Republican ward was less than Gaston's had been, but in Ward Five, with a population four-fifths foreign stock, it showed an increase of nearly 19 points. The same thing happened in Leominster where the Democratic percentage of the senatorial vote decreased by 2 points in the strongest Republican ward, and increased by 12 points in the French-Canadian ward.

Nevertheless, despite Walsh's good showing in old-stock places, despite his hold on the Irish vote, and despite his recruitment of new supporters among the newer ethnic elements, the Coolidge landslide was too much for him. Speaker Gillett rode into the Senate on the President's coat-tails.

The year 1924 saw a culmination of the intraparty tensions

that wracked both the Republicans and the Democrats. The economic split in the G.O.P. led to a definite break in the ranks of the party as its agrarian radical wing embarked on a third-party venture. That venture failed to produce any lasting results, but it did provide most of the excitement in an otherwise apathetic national election. Moreover, La Follette's experience demonstrated two things: that agricultural depression was not yet stringent enough to sever effectively the western farmers' traditional ties to the Grand Old Party; and that a liberal movement, based primarily on old-fashioned agrarian discontent, stood little chance of creating a political upheaval in a nation so permeated by industrialization and urbanization as was the United States in the 1920's.

The Democrats at first expected to capitalize on Republican agrarian insurgency. But the embarrassments which befell the principle aspirant for the party's nomination thwarted that strategy. Even more significant was the festering of the Democrats' own sore-spot, the cultural split between the Old and Newer American factions. The result was a deadlocked convention, a colorless presidential nominee, and a lethargic campaign. The outcome of the election indicated the necessity for breaking the party's internal stalemate, if the party was to survive as a meaningful political instrument.

In Massachusetts the vote polled by Calvin Coolidge seemed only to reaffirm the Commonwealth's traditional Republicanism. His presence on the ballot, together with the handicaps surrounding the Democratic gubernatorial nominee, produced a resounding vote of confidence in continued Republican control of the state government. Finally, the outpouring of votes for the President unseated the state's leading Democratic vote-getter, Senator Walsh. Bay State Republicanism was at the peak of its power.

At the same time, however, those Republicans who stopped

to look could find cause for concern in the decreased percentage of the Massachusetts vote won by Coolidge, compared to Harding's performance in 1920. Even more disconcerting were the remarkable vote polled by Senator Walsh in the midst of the Republican avalanche and the sources of his support.

Two weeks after the 1924 election Senator Henry Cabot Lodge died. Governor Cox, acting at President Coolidge's behest, appointed Republican National Chairman William M. Butler to fill the vacancy until the next election.[84] The Coolidge organization now controlled all. But Lodge's death promised David I. Walsh an opportunity for a comeback in short order. His campaign for the 1926 senatorial election got under way immediately.

Chapter Five

The Walsh Coalition

THE inauguration of Calvin Coolidge in his own right on March 4, 1925, began a distinctive interval in American life. Prosperity reigned, it was said. People seemed complacent and content to leave things as they were. Conspicuous consumption, a succession of fads, and cultivation of the art of "ballyhoo" by a circulation-hungry press diverted popular attention from weightier matters. Interest in politics ebbed in the face of general satisfaction with the fruits of "Coolidge prosperity." Old issues like the tariff or "monopoly" were stale, and after La Follette passed from the scene, no political leader was capable of dramatizing them. Apathy seemed to engulf the electorate.[1]

But in Massachusetts, at least, the situation in the Coolidge years differed a great deal from the stereotype. True, the Bay State had its share of "high living" in some quarters, and its share of fads and ballyhoo. Even the staid *Boston Transcript* opened its columns to crossword puzzles and contract bridge lessons, enlarged its headlines, and devoted much space to the Scopes affair, the Hall-Mills murder trial, and of course, Charles Lindbergh. Nonetheless, certain forces were at work in Massachusetts promoting discontent which, finding expression in the senatorial election of 1926, demonstrated that apathy was by no means the hallmark of the Bay State electorate. One source of discontent was ethnic in nature. Another was the Commonwealth's economic plight. A third was Prohibition. Their aggregate effect indicated, too, that Republican hegemony in Massachusetts rested on insecure foundations.

In 1926 appeared a book, *The Conquest of New England by the Immigrant*, written by an old-stock inhabitant of Massachusetts named Daniel Chauncey Brewer. The seeds of the conquest, according to the author, were sown by the post-Civil War generation of New Englanders who, having eyes for nothing but money and markets, imported large quantities of alien labor to man the section's industrial expansion. Thereafter the natives' birth rate declined but that of the immigrants, "not yet restrained by the artificialities of sophisticated society," did not. The result was evident by 1926: the remaining Yankees, most of whom were among the elderly portion of the population, were a "waning factor" and "will soon be only a memory"; whereas "the foreigners. . . are either youthful or in the period of vigorous maturity, and are a *waxing factor*." Naturalization and voting had become increasingly common among those "foreigners," to whose number should be added the "so-called native voters who are of foreign parentage, and who have a European lilt to their minds." "So constituted, [this electorate] controls the political destinies of New England. . . It is undoubtedly true that no military incursion could have more profoundly affected the political future of the Puritan Commonwealths. . ." [2]

When Brewer published his book, the direction in which the political destiny of Massachusetts was moving had already become clear. The identification of Prohibition, one hundred per cent Americanism, and Ku Kluxism with the Re-

publican Party in the Bay State threatened to create an upheaval among the newer immigrant elements that would end
the G.O.P.'s control of the state's politics. Republican leaders
were aware of the danger and took steps to head it off, but
at the same time their efforts were countered by another — in
some ways more materialistic — consideration affecting the
votes of the state's newer inhabitants. That was the matter
of "recognition."

The Republicans were the old-stock party of Massachusetts,
as the Democrats were the Irish party. When the G.O.P. was
in power most of the political plums went to Yankees, and
the same element controlled the party's state-wide primary.
Nevertheless, the Republicans claimed a large share of the
votes of the "newer races." Some rewards in the form of
jobs had indeed gone to French-Canadians, Jews, Italians,
Negroes, and representatives of other elements, but in most
cases only relatively minor positions were involved. Moreover, no member of the newer groups had ever succeeded in
winning a place on the Republican ballot for a state-wide
office.

As the various New Immigrant groups became more aware
of themselves and their political power in the postwar era,
however, and as their desire to be counted equally "American"
with the older elements of the population intensified, the dis-
proportion between their service to the Republicans and the
rewards they received seemed ever more striking. The common remedy for all these groups was sounded for one of them
by the *Italian News* of Boston: "Organize, you men of the
Italian race, and receive the recognition that should be
yours." [3] "Recognition" was the key word. It meant the
usual recognition of past loyalty in the form of patronage, and
yet in the 1920's it meant something more. It meant acknowl-
edgment that the ethnic group involved was capable and

worthy of sharing in running the government — as first-class American citizens — just as it was capable of producing first-class American football players, college students, and entertainers.

At the same time more impetuous spokesmen for the newer elements were emerging to press their demands. An increasing number of second-generation New Immigrants had been attending colleges and graduate schools and entering the professional class. Many of them — especially the lawyers — had political aspirations. Often they viewed themselves as the natural leaders of their ethnic groups, with an obligation to mobilize their parents and their second-generation cousins to a fuller appreciation and exercise of their political power. Each was a spokesman for "his people," able and willing to demand "just" recognition for them. "Our fathers organized and yet, for how long? They failed to bring respect and recognition to their people in this section," lamented the *Italian News*. "But there is hope. . . And that hope lies in the second generation. . ."[4] These newer and younger spokesmen, apparently, would not be satisfied with the modest rewards that had served to keep the older generation of leaders — the "prominenti" — content.

As the percentage of the vote won by Democrats in New Immigrant strongholds mounted after 1920, the leaders of Bay State Republicanism tried to placate ethnic demands for recognition. Soon after the election of 1924 the newly appointed Senator William M. Butler unveiled the "Butler idea" to save the party: "We must emphasize . . . that we know neither class nor creed nor nationality . . . that the open door is an actuality, and not a mere figure of speech."[5]

But recognition was a tricky business, sometimes fraught with dangers that threatened a loss of more votes than could be gained. Great care, for example, had to be taken in selecting a proper representative of the group to be rewarded. Governor Cox's choice for a place on the Municipal Court of Boston in 1924 happened to be a "left-handed Italian" (i.e., one who was not a Catholic). Consequently, some Italian-Americans regarded the appointment as an insult rather than a compliment.[6]

Recognition of one element often meant offending another. When Governor Cox appointed a Jew to the Municipal Court in 1922, some Italian-American leaders claimed that he had broken a pledge to appoint one of their group to the post. In the ensuing election the usually Republican *Gazzetta del Massachusetts* opposed Cox and supported Fitzgerald, although it endorsed Senator Lodge.[7] Again, when a vacancy opened on the Superior Court in 1926, French-Canadian Republicans urged Governor Fuller to appoint Raoul Beaudreau. The Governor, for his own reasons, appointed an Irishman. The disappointed element voiced its resentment shortly thereafter at a Republican outing near Fall River, when a speaker urged those present to join the new Franco-American Civic League of Massachusetts "so that [we] may stand as one for the proper recognition of the Franco element in the state by the Republican Party. . . God grant that we may hold on to whatever small influence we are now enjoying within the party, if for any reason we should not be able to get more." [8]

Beaudreau remained a loyal Republican (and eventually became a judge). But sometimes the disappointed aspirant broke with the party, and he then became a recruiting agent for the Democrats among his ethnic group. Such was the case with Julian D. Rainey, a Negro from Carolina who came north just prior to the First World War. After attending college and serving as an officer overseas during the war, Rainey was admitted to the bar and began practicing in Boston. Like most Negroes at the time he was a Republican, and when a position as assistant United States attorney at Boston became vacant in 1922, Rainey sought the job with the endorsement of a number of Negro organizations. He also secured the support of William Lewis, another Negro attorney who had held the position in question under the last Republican president, Taft. Lewis went to Washington to tell Senator Lodge of Rainey's qualifications, but the Senator's secretary informed him that the position would go to an Italian. Back in Boston colored voters held a protest meeting, and Rainey began inducing his friends to change their party registration. Soon Lodge's secretary was on the phone offering Rainey the assistant United States attorneyship. But by now Rainey was allied with Colonel Gaston, and in the 1922 election he campaigned for the Democratic senatorial nominee. In 1924 he worked for John W. Davis. By 1926 he had organized the Colored Democracy of Massachusetts, and his efforts among his people were beginning to bear fruit. Prior to 1922, then, Bay State Democrats had no spokesman among the Commonwealth's Negro inhabitants. Republican policy on the matter of recognition gave them one.[9]

Another demonstration of the dangers of recognition politics came in 1926 when Republicans tried to "liberalize" their state ticket. Representative Elijah Adlow, a Jew who did yeoman work for Governor Fuller in the 1924 campaign and on the floor of the legislature thereafter, entered the primary for the attorney general nomination against two old-stock contenders. In an attempt to implement the "Butler idea" a number of Republican leaders backed Adlow, and he was generally understood to be the organization candidate. The *Boston Transcript* and the *Boston Herald* endorsed him on the ground that his presence on the ticket would broaden the party's appeal to the newer elements of the population. Needless to say, Jewish spokesmen were strongly behind him.[10]

But the eyes of other New Immigrants were on this primary contest also. According to the *Italian News*:

> Adlow's candidacy should particularly appeal to the Italian voters since he is of foreign birth [sic]. . . As a former immigrant, with no claims that his ancestors came over on that prodigious ship, the Mayflower, he will be able to administer his office with great understanding and sympathy. . . For a cosmopolitan state like Massachusetts is needed an attorney general like Adlow. Italo-American citizens should be with him 100 per cent.[11]

As it turned out, one of the old-stock candidates beat Adlow in the primary. Various circumstances, especially the Prohibition issue, were involved in that result, but in some quarters one explanation blurred out all others: old-stock Republicans did not want a Newer American on their ticket. Democratic journals harped on that deduction. Senator Butler and other Republican leaders were alarmed, and the pro-Republican *Jewish Advocate* assured its readers that Adlow's Jewishness had nothing to do with the outcome of the contest. Adlow said the same thing, publicly, and campaigned for the party ticket.[12] But the results of the fiasco showed in election returns from Jewish wards in November.

The Democrats could only gain from Republican discomfiture over recognition, or "league of nations," politics.[13] Since the G.O.P. controlled the patronage purse on both the state and national levels, they were the ones besieged for rewards. When "just" recognition failed to come from that source, the unsatisfied nationality groups and their leaders had only the opposition party to turn to for consolation.

Moreover, the Democrats enjoyed another advantage over the Republicans, in the matter of the state ticket. Since Democratic candidates for the secondary executive offices on the ballot stood little chance of election in any case, competition for nomination to those jobs was not as strong as among Republicans. Democratic leaders therefore had a relatively easy time "clearing the field" for the man of their choice. In that way they were able to get the names of New Immigrants on the ballot under the Democratic label, usually for the position of secretary of state or state treasurer. In 1920 they ran a Jew; in 1922 a French-Canadian; in 1924 a Jew *and* a French-Canadian. All that was necessary was to make sure that an Irish name did not appear on the primary ballot in competition with the leaders' choice.

Events in 1926 demonstrated the working of this Democratic advantage, and its possible pitfalls. Party leaders, and especially ex-Senator Walsh, paid special attention to the construction of their ticket that year. Walsh desired as few Irish names as possible on the ballot with him in his quest to unseat Senator Butler. Only one received the leaders' blessing, for the position of secretary of state, and Yankee Democrats were given prominence. William A. Gaston, whose contributions to the party war chest were always welcome, gained a clear field for the gubernatorial nomination. Joseph Ely was to run for lieutenant governor. Another Yankee was endorsed for auditor and still a fourth, Harold Williams, was the organization's choice for attorney general. Daniel England, a Pittsfield Jew, was to have the nomination for state treasurer.

But there were two flies in the ointment in the persons of Irishmen. John Swift insisted on contesting Williams for the attorney general nomination, and a Boston Elevated Railway conductor named Harry Dooley wanted to run for lieutenant governor. Shortly before the election the leaders persuaded Dooley to withdraw, and he endorsed Ely. Nevertheless, his name remained on the ballot and on primary day, as had been feared, the two Irish names worked their magic at the polling places. Not only did Swift defeat Williams, but Harry Dooley of Boston beat the Yankee, Joseph Ely, from the western part of the state for the lieutenant governor nomination.[14]

This put the Democrats in a quandary. Dooley agreed to forfeit his nomination, but Ely refused to substitute for him under such embarrassing circumstances, despite Walsh's pleas. In the end, however, Democratic leaders struck upon a happy solution. French-Canadian Edmond Talbot, the Democratic mayor of Fall River (by virtue of "Republican" French-Canadian votes), accepted the nomination when it was offered to him.[15] Never before had a representative of a "newer race" appeared on the ballot for such an exalted position, and thus the chagrin caused by the "Dooleyizing" of the primary was turned to advantage. The Democratic ticket as finally presented to the voters consisted of three Irishmen, two Yankees, one Jew, and one French-Canadian. Its contrast with the pure old-stock Republican slate seemed to be a commentary on the question of which party practiced Senator Butler's open-door policy.

On the whole, the recognition movement hurt the Republicans and benefited the Democrats. Together with other, ideological factors it seemed to indicate that in Massachusetts the Democrats were the party of cultural liberalism. Republican spokesmen, fully recognizing the implications of the situation, were unable to remedy it. The composition of the two parties' tickets in 1926 forboded even more drastic defections from the G.O.P.

In the end, the Republicans' appeal for the votes of the newer groups was reduced to older tactics. One was the recitation of favors granted in the past to the ethnic group concerned — in the form of resolutions favoring the old country in the postwar reconstruction era, or in the form of patronage to Americans of foreign extraction. By the mid-1920's, however, the postwar troubles of the old country were largely dead issues, while the recognition already granted was never enough. More and more, then, Republicans were forced to rely on the time-honored appeal to their economic doctrines: that only the high protective tariff would safeguard the pocketbooks of New Immigrant workers — that only the Republican Party could guarantee "good times" for the modern industrial America in which the newer elements lived. But by 1926 that argument, too, sounded flat to many Massachusetts listeners.

"Business conditions in the country as a whole were extraordinarily stable and free from fluctuation in 1926," reported the Federal Reserve Bank of Boston at the end of that year, "but in New England there was a recession. . . The total value of business in the leading New England textile centers during 1926 was less than in 1925, and but little better than in 1924." [16] Such was the story of "Coolidge prosperity" in the President's home state. Until 1925 the ups and downs of the business picture in Massachusetts roughly paralleled national economic trends. Thereafter, the Bay State lagged far behind.[17]

The Commonwealth's two leading industries, shoes and textiles, were at the root of the trouble. Other types of activity like paper, jewelry, and confectionary manufacturing made advances. So did newer manufactures like silk and rayon goods, rubber goods, and electrical apparatus. But shoes and textiles were in the doldrums. Whereas 63,000 persons were employed in the shoe industry in the "recession" year 1924, only 59,700 were so employed in 1926. Between those two years the value of shoes produced in the state declined by approximately $3,000,000. The value of the state's cotton goods manufacture declined in the same period from almost $297,000,000 to about $292,000,000. The woolen and worsted goods industry showed only very small increases in employment and value of product.[18]

New England's shoe and textile industries were being outstripped by other parts of the country. While indexes of
employment and wages in New England shoe factories declined between 1924 and 1926, those for the north central
states increased. The same was true in the cotton goods industry, comparing New England with the South. In 1925
alone 530,000 new spindles were installed in southern cotton
mills, and in 1926 that section consumed more than twice as
much raw material as the industry's birthplace.[19]

The undermining of New England's former primacy by
other areas was ascribed to various causes. Some claimed that
nearness to the sources of raw materials favored her competitors. Others charged that discriminatory freight rates unduly
burdened the section's industries. More widely accepted in
Massachusetts was the idea that the Commonwealth's "progressive" labor laws, limiting the hours of work for women
and children and forbidding night work, gave her rivals an
advantage. Wage scales in New England were undeniably
higher than in other parts of the country. The average earn-
ings of shoe workers in Haverhill, for example, were 70 cents
an hour. In Philadelphia, Rochester, St. Louis, and Milwaukee
they ranged between 54 and 58 cents. Loom fixers in Massachusetts received 62 cents an hour; in North Carolina 42
cents.[20] That indicated another advantage often enjoyed by
New England's competitors — freedom from the influence of
labor unions. Southern mill workers (who were frequently
extolled as being one hundred per cent American) were more
"*amenable*," according to an advertisement by the Alabama
Power Company, "whether . . . operating twenty looms or
forty to the operative." And tax rates in the New England
states were higher, too. An advertisement sponsored by Alabama's state government proclaimed: "Move That Mill Down
South . . . Then Pay Your Dividends From Taxes Saved."

Alabama's average tax rate was $1.55 on one hundred dollars, according to the ad, while Massachusetts' was $2.54.[21]

Some pointed to still more profound reasons for New England's predicament. According to the *American Wool and Cotton Reporter*:

> It isn't southern competition . . . but superannuated equipment, poor management, poor merchandizing, poor styling . . . not knowing what is going on in the world . . . that is to blame for the failure or liquidation or abandonment of the Seaconnet Mills, the Hebronville, Dodgeville, Thorndike, Whitin, Shetucket and scores of other similar concerns. The tide just went out and left them on the beach.[22]

"Some of our industries," said another authority, "are still under the spell of the days when the shoe buyers of the United States came to Boston twice a year for their stocks." [23] The complaint was that earlier New England industrialists, meeting with success and prosperity, had grown stale — too intent on security and sure dividends. Lacking faith in their sons' ability to manage the industrial empires they amassed, the fathers bequeathed their properties in the form of trusts. Their sons became coupon clippers, and their properties passed under the control of absentee managers — conservative trustees with little industrial interest or know-how. Yankee ingenuity and the spirit of risk-taking vanished, and New England industry was allowed to lag behind modern developments.

The remedies proposed were as numerous as the alleged causes. A demand for higher tariff duties to shut out cheaply made foreign goods persisted throughout the decade. Pleas for a realignment of freight rates were carried to the federal agency concerned. Some proposed repeal or modification of the state's restrictive labor laws and changes in the tax structure to give corporations a "break." Management often seemed anxious to reduce wages as the easiest way of cutting production costs. And throughout the 1920's there were demands that New England's entrepreneurs re-invigorate themselves, catch up with the rest of the world, and begin applying "scientific methods to production and marketing." [24] In November 1925 a thousand delegates assembled in Worcester at the call of the six New England governors and established a permanent New England Conference, to find means for promoting the section's economic recovery. "Within the next ten years," the governor of Maine told the convention, "New England will experience a boom which will rival or exceed those of California or Florida." [25] Much talk resulted — but little improvement.

Meanwhile, the workers suffered. Of the total number of wage earners in Haverhill, 84 per cent were normally employed in shoe manufacturing. For Brockton the figure was 81 per cent. The situation was much the same in the great textile centers: in New Bedford 82 per cent of the wage earners normally worked in the textile mills; in Fall River 78 per cent; in Lawrence 76 per cent; in Lowell 62 per cent.[26] Similar conditions prevailed in numerous mill towns, where often one or two shoe or textile factories employed almost the total labor force. These were the places hardest hit by New England's depression. Comparison of the total number of wage earners employed in the cities mentioned in the last "good" year, 1923, with the number employed in 1926, bore out the prevalence of "hard times," as the accompanying tabulation shows.[27]

	1923	1926
Haverhill	12,673	11,917
Brockton	15,205	12,762
New Bedford	37,917	35,143
Fall River	37,018	31,353
Lawrence	35,292	26,777
Lowell	27,162	20,859

Many of those employed in 1926 were working only part time, and at reduced rates of pay.

Some workers in the depressed industries shifted to newer lines where employment and wage conditions were better, or to the growing ranks of "service" and commercial employees.[28] Thousands moved away altogether from the depressed cities and towns, as the next census figures revealed. But most, knowing only one occupation, held on, hoping that things would become better. In the meantime they scrimped along as best they could on reduced incomes or joined the growing number living off city relief rolls.

Laboring men were not alone in feeling the pinch in one-industry centers. "We live or die, sink or swim, survive or perish with the cotton cloth industry," said Monsignor Cassidy of Fall River.[29] By "we" he meant the entire community — workers, white-collar people, retailers, restaurateurs, theater owners, and even priests or ministers. When things were bad in shoes and textiles, everyone suffered in places like Haverhill and New Bedford — including middle-class Republican business and professional men. By 1926 even the latter were heard grumbling about the way Massachusetts — Cal Coolidge's own state — had been left out of the vaunted "Republican prosperity."

The political ramifications of the Bay State's economic situation were evident. "In the old days," said the *New Bedford Times* (which had supported Coolidge in 1924),

> the people here were led to associate the G.O.P. with the "full dinner pail" and to believe that the G.O.P. was their only safeguard against unemployment, wage reductions, and lower dividends. Five years of uninterrupted hard times under a Republican administration which has devoted most of its time to telling the people how prosperous they were has done little to confirm the city in those old ideas.[30]

When David I. Walsh made his first campaign appearance

in Fall River in 1926, the largest political audience in the city's history swept him off his feet and paraded him about the auditorium. From the ceiling dangled huge banners bearing but two words: "Prosperity — Hokum!" [31]

Another cause for Republican concern over 1926 became apparent when Mrs. Curtis Guild, widow of a former Republican governor of the Commonwealth, announced that she would vote Democratic. Her reason: to help induce the G.O.P. to break its connection with "the fanatical Anti-Saloon League." [32]

By 1926 the Republican Party was the dry party in Massachusetts, while the Democracy was the wet one. Earlier in the decade the distinction had not been so clear, at least as far as the Republicans were concerned. Indeed, in 1921 the personal wetness of many prominent Republicans was very amply demonstrated. In December of that year over three hundred party leaders, including the federal Prohibition enforcement director for Massachusetts, Elmer Potter, attended a testimonial dinner at Boston's Quincy House to launch Governor Cox's campaign for re-election in 1922. An improvised bar, featuring a tubfull of White Horse scotch, was set up on the second floor of the hotel for the guests' enjoyment. But during the festivities someone got in touch with one of Potter's assistants, who allegedly wanted the director's job, and shortly before midnight that zealous enforcer staged a full-scale raid on the Quincy House revelers, confiscating what remained of the refreshments. The story circulated that Governor Cox got away in the nick of time by a nearby fire escape, and left his hat behind in the rush. Actually he had left the scene earlier and supposedly knew nothing of the second-floor activities.[33]

But it was clear that the center of Republican voting

strength, the old-stock towns and suburban cities, was also the center of Prohibition sentiment. After the Quincy House episode the Republican leadership catered increasingly to that dry block of votes. When the legislature met in January 1922, Cox recommended that it enact the state Prohibition enforcement bill backed by the Anti-Saloon League. The legislature complied, with Republicans in the House voting 132 to 30 for the measure. (Democratic members voted 38 to 2 against it.) [34]

Cox's successor, Alvan T. Fuller, also sided with the drys, and in return enjoyed the Anti-Saloon League's support in his 1924 campaign. Moreover, in the senatorial race that year the Bay State Republican organization made a seemingly irrevocable commitment to the dry cause. Early in 1924 when Coolidge's confidant, William M. Butler, was expected to be the party's candidate against Walsh, the Prohibition forces were cool toward him because of his wet record. Through Charles Sumner Bird, a Progressive Party leader in the prewar years, the drys threatened to run their own candidate in the Republican primary. Butler issued a statement to ward off the danger:

> I favor the enforcement of the Volstead Act and would not amend it except if necessary after further fair and thorough trial, and then in no way which would tend to break down the principles involved in the Eighteenth Amendment. I frankly say I was not in favor of the Amendment when adopted, but I am convinced that it has brought about a great improvement in living and economic conditions in the country.[35]

When Speaker Gillett replaced Butler as the machine candidate, he too capitulated to the drys to win their support in the primary. Otherwise he might have lost to Representative Dallinger. Thereafter Butler's statement served as the credo of the regular Republican organization and cemented its ties with the Prohibitionists. The drys were satisfied and backed the G.O.P. completely.

But the Republican Party in Massachusetts embraced a wet
wing, too. The party's adherents among the New Immigrants
generally opposed the Eighteenth Amendment. And from the
beginning some old-stock business Republicans disliked Prohibition as an instance of "government meddling." [36] Those
elements were augmented by more recruits as disillusion with
the noble experiment grew during the 1920's. To some it
began to appear that certain results of Prohibition, among
them hypocrisy, lawlessness, and racketeering, were worse
than the evils that had brought passage of the Eighteenth
Amendment in the first place. Predominantly old-stock organizations like the Anti-Volstead League gained in membership. Demands for repeal, or some sort of modification, began
to come even from sources which earlier had advocated enforced temperance.

The wet Republicans of Massachusetts first made their
strength known in the 1924 senatorial primary. But their
man, Louis A. Coolidge, received only 94,000 votes compared
to a combined total of over 228,000 for Gillett, the newly
dried organization favorite, and Representative Dallinger, the
Anti-Saloon League candidate. Nevertheless, the wets continued their agitation, and the attorney general primary election of 1926 provided another test of strength. In that contest Alexander Lincoln, who wanted modification of Prohibition, ran against Arthur Reading, a favorite of the drys,
and Elijah Adlow, the organization candidate, who attempted
to straddle the issue. Again the Prohibition forces demonstrated their superior power as Reading topped the list in the
balloting.

Many wets, abiding by the *Boston Transcript*'s plea not to
make Prohibition the sole test of party loyalty, acquiesced in
their latest setback. But others, like Mrs. Guild, did not, and
they drifted toward the Democrats. The executive council of

predominantly Republican Massachusetts Constitutional
erty League urged voters to abandon party lines and sup-
t wet candidates in the election. Though Republican prog-
nosticators looking toward November could not foretell the
extent of defection from their party over the Prohibition
issue, they knew it was another factor unfavorable for the
prospects of G.O.P. victory.[37]

Threatened with desertions on many sides, Massachusetts
Republicans in 1926 confronted the task of re-electing Senator
William M. Butler, which in effect meant saving face for
President Coolidge. Butler was still chairman of the Republican national committee and the President's recognized spokesman in the Senate. Coolidge had been warned of Butler's draw-
backs in 1924, but paid no heed.[38] As a result, the G.O.P. was
represented by a particularly weak candidate in an election
which seemed to constitute a test of popularity for the Coolidge regime.

Many felt that Butler's connection with the prostrate textile industry made him a natural target for resentment against
prevailing economic conditions. "A rich man, let alone a rich
manufacturer of textiles, has no business having his name on
a ballot in this state," said the *Berkshire Evening Eagle*.[39]
Moreover, the precariousness of Butler's position had been increased in February when, during the annual legislative battle
over revision of the Commonwealth's "progressive" labor
laws, the head of the textile manufacturers' association testified that Senator Butler's cotton mills were among those favoring modification of the state's forty-eight-hour law for women
and children. Butler denied the allegation immediately, but the
damage was done. The idea that the Senator favored a return
to old-time exploitation of working women and children
hovered over his head throughout the campaign and conclu-

sively alienated labor leaders and advanced liberals from his cause.[40]

The Senator also was open to attack from the remaining partisans of the late Senator Lodge, who held him particularly responsible for the humiliation heaped on the elder statesman at the 1924 national convention. True, the old Senator's grandson, Henry Cabot Lodge, Jr., campaigned for Butler in his first appearance in the political limelight, and it was hoped that this fact would heal whatever hard feeling remained. But Mrs. Constance Lodge Williams, daughter of the Senator, endorsed David I. Walsh.[41] When the ballots were counted, Walsh carried not only Nahant, Lodge's home town, but Essex County as a whole. Neither place had ever voted Democratic in a state-wide election before. The Lodge faction had gained a measure of revenge on Calvin Coolidge's machine.

Finally, Butler was no match for Walsh as a campaigner. He read his speeches from typewritten sheets. (On one occasion, at an outdoor rally, the sheets blew away, leaving Butler literally speechless.) Accustomed to the staid businessman's club, he did not feel at home on the political stump. At a rally in Lynn four bagpipe players preceded him into the hall. "Mr. Butler's face," according to a reporter, "wore the kind of smile you might expect to see on the face of a boy detected stealing jam. He smiled, but he was not happy. It was plain that he felt ridiculous . . . Walsh, even Fuller, would have liked it." One newspaper referred to Butler as "the icy archpriest of the Coolidge doctrine of bloodless efficiency in office. . ." Even the *Boston Transcript* admitted that he lacked "the human element." [42]

Nevertheless, though Senator Butler disliked campaigning, he toured the state (in a caravan "headed by a Rolls Royce," people noticed), discussing some matters and evading others. The most important one to be evaded was Prohibition. The executive committee of one of the Commonwealth's leading Republican organizations, the Roosevelt Club, had voted that "liquor is the first political issue of the hour"; but Butler refused to recognize it in his campaign. His silence signified reiteration of his 1924 declaration on the subject, and the drys were happy. The Woman's Christian Temperance Union, the remnants of the state's old Prohibition Party, Methodist Bishop Edwin Hughes, and many Protestant ministers endorsed him. The only concession granted the wets was that the fiery and controversial head of the Anti-Saloon League, Wayne B. Wheeler, canceled his expected appearance in the Massachusetts campaign.[43]

Economic conditions could not be evaded, however. In his earliest campaign pronouncements Butler spoke in glowing terms of the nation-wide prosperity induced by the Republican Administration's economic policies, apparently oblivious to the true situation in Massachusetts. Even in mid-October Secretary of Commerce Hoover, in a speech beamed from New York on Senator Butler's behalf, boasted that "in America today the poorhouse has become nearly as extinct as the slave block." [44] But by that time Butler was aware of the statistics of employment published in the past two years by Governor Fuller's Department of Labor and Industries, and consequently Republican campaign tactics changed. "Most of our mills have been running part time," an advertisement in a North Adams paper conceded. But without a Republican Administration in power "the mills here could not have run even part time. They could not have run at all! . . . Because they have been able to run even part time . . . we have been able to get along." "This is not the time to be pessimistic," Butler added. Only patience was needed, and the prosperity enjoyed by the rest of the nation would sweep over New England "soon." [45]

The Republicans also tried hard to win back those among the newer nationality groups who had deserted the G.O.P. in recent years, or at least to hold on to what was left of their support. Representative Adlow was given a place of prominence at the state convention in September as chairman of the committee on permanent organization, and the personnel of the committees featured such names as Wasserman and Boruchoff; Zottoli, Campopiano, and Bizzozero; Gauthier and Legare; Speropoulos; and Vera. During the campaign all the nationality groups received "recognition," in the form of attendance at their rallies by old-stock Republican office seekers. New Immigrant officeholders like assistant United States attorneys Elihu Stone and Telesphore Le Beouf recited the party's record of past favors to the newer elements, contrasting it with the Democrats' niggardliness. Late in October Anthony Czarnecki, collector of the customs in Chicago and "the highest official of the Polish race in the Federal Government," was brought to Massachusetts on Senator Butler's behalf. Walter Cohen, the Negro collector of internal revenue at New Orleans, urged colored people of the Bay State to support Butler, who had advised Coolidge not to withdraw Cohen's nomination when it was under fire from southern Democrats in the Senate in 1924. Other Negro Republicans declared that although "there are Democrats of the 'Walsh' and 'Al Smith' type whose personal magnetism has endeared them to thousands of colored voters," still Walsh's victory would only enhance the power of the Democrats in the Senate and give control of that body to anti-Negro southerners.[46]

Again some old leaders of the newer ethnic groups — those already indebted to the G.O.P. for jobs or favors — pledged support to the Republican senatorial candidate. So did the State Federation of Polish-American Citizens Clubs, but a large number of the local clubs refused to ratify that endorsement.[47] In view of the facts that most of the New Immigrant people opposed Prohibition, that many of them were afflicted by the industrial depression, and that a growing number were coming to regard the Democrats as the party of cultural liberalism, there was doubt whether they would respond readily to their old leaders' endorsement of Butler's qualifications. So in the end Republican appeals to the newer elements, in editorials, advertisements, and speeches, boiled down to one thing: "Do You Believe in Calvin Coolidge Your President? If You Do You Have No Alternative but to Vote the Republican Ticket." [48]

That appeal, in fact, was the main basis of Senator Butler's campaign. Early in the spring of 1926 the Republican state chairman declared that "the issue in Massachusetts this year is Calvin Coolidge. . ." During the summer and fall a host of nationally prominent party leaders invaded the Bay State to emphasize that President Coolidge's legislative program, his prestige, and indeed his very re-election in 1928 depended on Butler's victory. According to the Senator, a shameful aggregation of "outside influences," the old La Follette crowd, and "the radical forces of discontent" were arrayed behind David I. Walsh, all seeking to embarrass the President by causing Butler's defeat.[49]

In May it was said that the President would come home to campaign personally for his friend and advisor. Early in October that possibility was discounted, since it was "not necessary." But by the end of the month Coolidge's personal intervention seemed essential. In a letter lavishly praising Butler and Governor Fuller, the President announced on October 25 that he and Mrs. Coolidge would come home on election day to vote. Bay State Republicans were elated, and assumed that the message would turn the tide conclusively in

Butler's favor. The voters of the Commonwealth would see clearly, now, that the issue was "Coolidge or Walsh," — or as the drys put it — "Coolidge or Rum." "There can be no doubt now that a vote for Butler is a vote for Coolidge, and conversely that a vote against Butler is a vote against the . . . head of the Republican party," said the *Boston Transcript*. Content with drawing that conclusion, the G.O.P. put its case in the hands of the people.[50]

David I. Walsh had no desire to run against President Coolidge in the senatorial election of 1926. Early in the year, when the Democratic national committee seemed to join the Republicans in an attempt to make Coolidge the issue in the Massachusetts contest, Walsh and his friends disavowed that interpretation. Throughout his campaign the former Senator insisted that a victory for him should not be considered a partisan one, and again he promised to support Coolidge when he thought the President right. "I am an independent. To be an independent in public office is not inconsistent with being a good Democrat . . . I never intend . . . to wear any party collar." [51] Again he emphasized his economic progressivism, winning endorsement from the Big Four railway brotherhoods, numerous other labor organizations, and the Progressive Action Committee, the remnant of the La Follette movement.[52] As in his race two years earlier against Gillett, he also touched on a variety of minor issues to attract support from diverse quarters. But his major efforts were devoted to cultivating the issues making for discontent in Massachusetts — ethnic, economic, and anti-Prohibition.

Though Walsh was always counted a wet and voted against both the Eighteenth Amendment and the Volstead Act in the Senate, in the early 1920's he felt that a majority of Americans favored the Prohibition experiment.[53] But by 1926 he was

convinced that the tide was running against Prohibition, especially in the Bay State, and so he condemned it in the
strongest terms available for Massachusetts audiences. "The
government which stands against the founder of Christianity
cannot survive," the ex-Senator told a Holyoke rally. "The
Volstead Law has put every Christian on the defensive, for
they are forbidden to do something which the founder of
their religion sanctioned." In another speech he declared that
if Christ came back to earth and performed the Cana miracle,
"He would be jailed and possibly crucified again." [54] The
Democratic campaign received financial backing from the
national Association against the Prohibition Amendment, and
the Massachusetts Constitutional Liberty League sponsored a
series of advertisements urging the mothers of the Commonwealth to remember that they themselves were once young-
sters, to whom the forbidden thing is always a temptation.
"Get rid of the 'pocket flask'. . . Vote For Colonel William
A. Gaston and David I. Walsh." [55]

The Bay State industrial depression was ready-made for
Walsh's oratory. "There is prosperity in this nation today,"
he declared in Fall River.

> The men and women with whom President Coolidge and Sena-
> tor Butler associate are indeed prosperous. The great corpora-
> tions outside those of Massachusetts are prosperous. The bankers
> and financiers are prosperous. But not until recently did Senator
> Butler admit that the workingmen of Massachusetts might not
> be prosperous.

Walsh provided little in the way of concrete recommendations for a solution. "The obvious remedy . . . is to stop the
reckless profiteering and the exploitation of the financial and
industrial tricksters," which Butler had done nothing about
in the past two years.[56] But in the atmosphere of resentment
against the "ins" created by hard times, the details of Walsh's

program for ending the depression didn't really matter. "God helping, I will go back to Washington and demand that the men who have been using every means to win a triumph for big business leave us alone." [57] That was enough for jobless or part-time workingmen, and for many "little fellows" in the business world.

Most significant of all were the Democrats' efforts to win the votes of the newer nationality groups. Much was heard of the "racial balance" featured by the party's state ticket. A widely circulated booklet listed its members and traced their backgrounds, concluding: "You will notice that the . . . ticket . . . embraces seven candidates of diversified racial and religious origins. . . Compare this truly 'open door' policy with the 'open door' policy of the Republican party, which puts the policy into its platform, but leaves it out of its ticket." Complaints against the Democrats' "groupiness" came from some quarters. The Democrats, according to the *Springfield Republican*,

> presented the picture of a political society in which nothing but "groups" . . . could live, and many will think it extreme, tending to reduce a simple, all-embracing Americanism to the vanishing point. This danger is the palpable consequence of the systematic construction of a state ticket according to the racial group principle of which the Democratic leaders of Massachusetts now openly boast.[58]

But an answer to such criticism was offered by Edmond Talbot, the party's nominee for lieutenant governor, who, speaking in French and English, told audiences:

> And why should it not be so? The American nation is a composite of racial elements with perhaps individual customs and ways of thinking, but nevertheless united in their allegiance to the government they helped to build. . . The time has come when all the racial elements that make up our nation should have a voice in the government. . . This is real Americanism.[59]

Politics, Talbot in effect was saying, must attune itself to the harmony of ethnic influences — to the principle of cultural liberalism.

David I. Walsh himself, like Al Smith of New York, was of Newer American stock, and people of the "newer races" familiar with his record and background recognized him as one of their own. Shortly after Walsh's first election to the Senate in 1918 he received a letter from a Boston Negro postal clerk, describing how race prejudice drove him from his home in Mississippi. "As I read the story of your life. . ." the Negro concluded, "I compared the struggles of your father with my own battle for a livelihood. . . Especially do colored people feel proud and hopeful at having such a staunch friend and so noble a character in the upper branch of Congress. . ." [60]

The drawback was that, in the early 1920's, thousands of Negroes and New Immigrants who traditionally voted Republican were unaware of the Irish Democrat's qualifications as a spokesman for cultural liberalism. By 1926 Julian D. Rainey and other campaigners, and Walsh himself, had largely erased that handicap. Colored audiences heard about Walsh's efforts to ban showing of *The Birth of a Nation* while he was governor, about his denunciation of the southern Democrats' filibuster against the Dyer federal anti-lynching bill in 1922, and about his deciding vote on the roll call which confirmed the appointment of Walter Cohen in 1924, 39 to 38.[61] Subsequently, one Negro Republican woman wrote the *Boston Transcript* during the 1926 campaign: "This year seems to be about the right time to give our party a stiff spanking." The Republican city committee of Springfield had to cancel a Butler rally at the Negro Congregational church, for fear that sparse attendance would embarrass their candidate. Reporting the incident, the *Springfield Republican* commented:

"It has been well known in this city for some time that many Negro voters were adherents of David I. Walsh because of the interest he evinced in that race. . ." [62]

In his 1924 contest with Gillett, and thereafter, Walsh had friends working for him among all the newer ethnic elements. A glimpse of the problems faced and of the tactics used by the Senator and his agents may be gleaned from reports which Walsh received during the 1924 campaign: "I had an article in the French newspaper, which covers Lawrence and Lowell. . . . The French people here are mostly Republicans, and I will try to wedge in for your interest." "I have talked with the French priest of Methuen, and he is willing to say a word for registration. . ." "I know of a meeting held this week of a church Sodality of about nine hundred young women . . . and the Spiritual Director urged these young women to be sure and register. This is the kind of work that is effective. . ." "I am attempting to get the most prominent men in Lowell of the different nationalities for your foreign language circular. Please let me know the last day I have to get these names in." "In regard to the New Bedford situation, I talked with Dr. Alphonse Normandin and he gave me the name of Peter Choquette. . . Mr. Choquette is the assistant superintendent of the Metropolitan Life Insurance Company and he has a good number of agents under him. I understand it is their practice to call on the French people to make weekly collections on policies. Dr. Normandin said Mr. Choquette could direct his men to make a canvass of the French people in your behalf. I understand he will have to be paid for this service. . ." "Monsignor Prevost, Pastor of the Notre Dame Church [Fall River] is a power among the French people. . . They have had a wonderful set of windows installed that were imported from France. If at any time you happened to be down this way it would be worth while to visit the Notre Dame Church to see those windows. The visit would be very effective with the French people." [63]

As a private citizen between 1924 and 1926 Walsh visited numerous foreign-born population centers throughout the state, both cities and mill towns, and no doubt admired many church windows.[64] He thus became better known to the New Immigrants, who saw in him an instrument for striking back at the cultural illiberalism of recent years. The *Italian News* of Boston spoke for many Bay State Newer Americans when it proclaimed in its pre-election issue:

> Senator Butler . . . belongs to that party which sponsored and supported the Johnson Immigration Bill, that damnable measure . . . As a result . . . it is recorded in Congress today that the Italian people and other races from Southern Europe have had their quota reduced because they do not belong to the Nordic strain and therefore they are inferior human beings. AND SO . . . OUR DAY IS AT HAND. IT WILL COME NEXT TUESDAY.[65]

In a sense, then, a victory for Walsh in itself would constitute recognition for the newer elements.

The forces promoting dissatisfaction in Massachusetts, and Walsh's strenuous campaign, indicated that the senatorial race would be close. Yet Republicans hoped their trump card, Calvin Coolidge, would save the day for Senator Butler. On election eve columnist David Lawrence summed up the situation: "Were it not for the Coolidge issue, [Walsh] would win easily. As it is Mr. Walsh is fighting the President of the United States, [the President's] campaign manager, the Klan influence, and a very well organized Republican party. Only a political miracle can win against such a combination. . ." [66]

In the gubernatorial contest Walsh's running mate, Colonel William A. Gaston, concentrated his fire almost exclusively on Prohibition. Ignoring or discounting unemployment and other potential issues, Gaston demanded modification of the

Volstead Act and inauguration of a state-controlled liquor dispensary system.[67] His campaign seemed to make headway at first, but before long dry Governor Fuller, seeking a second term, succeeded in convincing wets in both parties that Prohibition had no place in a gubernatorial election. In the end Gaston's tactics served only to reinforce his opponent's strength by rousing the drys to defense of the sacred Amendment. Aggregate registration in the towns — the center of Prohibition sentiment — actually showed a slight increase over the 1924 figure, while that for the cities decreased. On election day 74.1 per cent of the town registration went to the polls, in contrast to 69.0 per cent in the off-year election of 1922.

Governor Fuller also profited from his record of sustained "sound and economical" administration, his ability to link Gaston with various public utility "interests," and his friendship with certain Democratic leaders.[68] As a result he received 595,006 votes to Gaston's 407,389. The Colonel's 40.6 per cent of the two-party vote was the smallest received by any Democratic gubernatorial candidate since 1920. The G.O.P. retained its firm grip on all other elective executive offices, and actually increased slightly its margins of control in both houses of the legislature. On the state level Republican supremacy was unscathed.[69]

The story was different, however, in the senatorial contest. Walsh worked that "political miracle" and polled 52.8 per cent of the two-party vote, defeating Butler 525,303 to 469,989. The upset suffered by President Coolidge's personal favorite demonstrated that the political temper of the Bay State was changing. For one thing, though anti-Prohibition sentiment appeared to be of little aid to Colonel Gaston, it undoubtedly played a larger role in the senatorial election, since Prohibition was primarily a federal matter. Following

Butler's defeat an increasing number of Republican leaders joined Mrs. Guild in insisting that the G.O.P. "liberalize" its stand on the Eighteenth Amendment.

Moreover, the effects of the Bay State's economic plight showed in the returns from the most depressed of the industrial cities and towns. Comparison of the percentage of the senatorial vote won by Gaston in the off-year election of 1922 in the leading shoe and textile cities with the percentage won by Walsh in 1926, gave some indication of the political influence of sustained depression, as the accompanying tabulation shows.[70]

	1922	1926
Haverhill	32.4	47.4
Brockton	46.4	52.5
New Bedford	44.9	51.8
Fall River	46.5	51.1
Lawrence	68.0	72.5
Lowell	58.7	63.2

The figures for many industrial towns reflected similar increases in the drawing power of the Democratic senatorial candidate.

The returns also bore out Walsh's firm hold on the New Immigrant districts, which in many instances now supported him just as strongly as traditionally Democratic Irish wards. In cities where ward returns for 1922 and 1926 were comparable, the increases in the Democratic percentage of the senatorial vote were almost invariably largest in wards dominated by the newer ethnic elements. For example, while Walsh's percentage of the two-party senatorial vote in Chelsea was 11.0 points higher than Gaston's 1922 proportion of the three-party senatorial vote, in the city's two Jewish wards the figures were 18.6 and 16.8. For Haverhill as a whole the figure was 15.0, while in the city's two melting-pot wards it was 26.6 and 25.8. In New Bedford, Walsh bettered Gaston's mark by 6.9 points, but in the strongest French-Canadian ward the figure was 11.6.

Comparison of the proportion of the senatorial vote won by Walsh in 1926 with the proportion of the gubernatorial vote polled by Gaston in the same year likewise demonstrated the Senator's appeal to the New Immigrants. For while Walsh outdid Gaston's mark in all areas — old-stock, Irish, and New Immigrant — the discrepancy between the two Democratic candidates was especially marked in the latter strongholds. Though Walsh's percentage of the vote in Boston as a whole was 14.0 points higher than Gaston's, in the city's two Jewish wards it was 19.1 and 24.9 points higher. In Gardner, Walsh's percentage led Gaston's by 15.7 points, but in the city's two French-Canadian wards the figures were 23.8 and 22.9. In Lowell the discrepancy was 9.4 points, while in that city's strongest French-Canadian ward it was 17.9.

Finally, Walsh secured a majority of the aggregate vote of Boston's five Negro precincts, becoming the first Democrat in recent times to carry that traditionally Republican area in a state-wide election. He polled 53.8 per cent of the precincts' aggregate vote, while Gaston received only 37.9 per cent in the gubernatorial race. Walsh's feat here signified, as perhaps nothing else did, the evaporating of the G.O.P.'s appeal to the "newer races."

The number of people who went to the polls in Massachusetts in 1926 exceeded by 127,575 the number who voted in the last off-year election in 1922, indicating that apathy was not the outstanding characteristic of Bay State politics in the "Coolidge years." The result of the senatorial contest indicated also that complacency did not reign in the Commonwealth.

True, David I. Walsh's election had the aspects of a personal victory. His attractiveness as a candidate and his ability as a campaigner had much to do with the outcome. But only by skillfully mobilizing the forces making for political change in Massachusetts was he able to win against overwhelming odds. In the process, Walsh constructed a new and powerful coalition of voting elements. That alliance embraced both the Irish and Yankee Democrats. Advanced liberals and labor leaders adhered to it also. So did a considerable number of dissatisfied old-stock Republicans of a more independent stripe. And finally, it embraced the bulk of the New Immigrant voters. Walsh's coalition perhaps lacked the positive reform impulse of the old coalition that dominated Massachusetts politics in the Progressive era. Instead, its motivating force was a negative sort of discontent — with one hundred per cent Americanism, with economic depression, and with Prohibition. Nonetheless, it appeared equally capable of producing political upheaval in the Bay State.

As yet the Senator's coalition was a personal one and exercised wide discrimination among candidates. Its strength could not be shifted to a nominee like Gaston, even if Senator Walsh had desired to do so. He acknowledged as much in his post-election statement: "It is evident upon the returns that my victory is not a partisan one. It was brought about by the votes of thousands of men and women who arose above party affairs and turned from partisan appeals. . . I rejoice in that fact." [71] On the whole Walsh, who sometimes billed himself as "the People's candidate" rather than "the Democratic candidate," seemed willing to let it rest at that. Consequently some Democratic politicians — with considerable basis in fact — accused the Senator of interest only in "paddling his own canoe." [72]

Nevertheless, Walsh had laid the groundwork for party victory. Surveying the sources of his support after the election, the *Springfield Republican* concluded: "There is a potential

Democratic strength in the Commonwealth which needs only skillful Democratic leadership to become formidable." [73] The question remained of whether the Massachusetts Democracy and the national Democratic Party were capable of meeting that challenge and capitalizing on Senator Walsh's achievement.

Chapter Six

Al Smith's Revolution

THE Republican assertion of 1926 — that President Coolidge's re-election hinged on a victory for William M. Butler over David I. Walsh — was soon forgotten, and by the spring of 1927 most people expected that Coolidge would be a candidate in the next election. Then, in August, came the terse announcement: "I do not choose to run for President in 1928." Some discounted the President's sincerity and inferred that he merely sought the exhilaration of being drafted by the G.O.P., but there is no substantial proof that such was the case. At any rate, Coolidge discouraged talk of a draft in the months that followed, and eventually convinced most people that he meant what he said.[1]

By the beginning of the election year the search for an alternative candidate pointed most strongly in the direction of Secretary of Commerce Herbert Hoover, who in May 1928 had four hundred convention delegates lined up in his favor. Still uncertain of Coolidge's intentions, Hoover offered to swing his followers to the President should he desire to run. "If you have four hundred delegates you better keep them," was Coolidge's characteristically curt reply.[2] Hoover did so.

When the convention assembled in Kansas City the second week in June there was still talk of a Coolidge draft. But doubt of the outcome disappeared on the first day of the meeting when Secretary Mellon told the Pennsylvania caucus that Coolidge would not accept the nomination and then advised the delegates to vote for Hoover. The same morning ex-Senator Butler told the Massachusetts delegation that he intended to vote for Hoover and added that "in my opinion such a vote would be satisfactory not only to the people of Massachusetts but to the President." [3] Two days later the Secretary of Commerce became the party's candidate on the first roll call.

Hoover's nomination signified the continued supremacy of the conservative business wing in the G.O.P., and that pleased the homeward-bound Massachusetts delegates. Still, many of them would have breathed easier had Calvin Coolidge consented to head the ticket again, for by now Bay State party leaders knew they faced a tough fight in November. The reason was that all indications pointed to the nomination of Al Smith by the Democrats.

For a while after the disastrous 1924 convention in Madison Square Garden, the Democratic Party appeared headed straight for a repetition of that scene in 1928. The zeal of Smith and McAdoo partisans flagged not at all. Although John W. Davis lost New York State to Coolidge by a huge vote, Smith won his third gubernatorial term at the same election. Two years later he became the state's first four-term governor. In 1927 he was the country's outstanding Democrat.[4]

Meanwhile, William G. McAdoo launched his campaign on a platform of Prohibition enforcement. It gradually appeared, however, that McAdoo's drive lacked the spark of earlier years. Labor leaders and economic liberals no longer rallied to his support. Even professional politicians of the South and West, who had supported McAdoo in 1924, realized that his nomination bore little promise of slaking their thirst for federal patronage, for he would have no chance of carrying the great industrial states of the Northeast which now seemed essential for victory. Better perhaps to try the alternative strategy of letting Smith run, hoping that he might win by uniting the East and the South. Even if Smith lost, at least the Newer American wing of the party would have gotten the left-over resentment of 1924 out of its system, and then the Democrats might make a new start on a united basis in 1932. Facing up to the fact that his star had descended while Smith's had risen, McAdoo in September 1927 announced his retirement from the field.[5]

When the Democrats convened in Houston late in June, Smith counted the support of 705 delegates, just a few short of the required two-thirds majority. After the first roll call enough states switched votes to give him the nomination. But Smith got no votes at all from South Carolina, Georgia, Florida, and Texas, and no attempt was made to make the nomination unanimous. At the very end the Governor upset the equilibrium which his campaign managers had nurtured by sending a message to the convention reaffirming his belief that the Volstead Act should be changed fundamentally. His words jarred the dry delegates, but it was too late.[6] Smith was the candidate and the convention adjourned, having witnessed a remarkable change. The days of southern and western supremacy in the party — the times of Bryan, Wilson, and McAdoo — were over, and the Newer American wing of the party was in control. For better or worse, the Democratic Party was under new management.

If political apathy really was characteristic of many Americans during the 1920's, the election of 1928 ended it. Al Smith's presence on the Democratic ticket revived the nation's

interest in politics. Though concentrating on carrying his
native East, he also attempted to hold the support of his an-
tipodal Democratic brethren in the South and invaded the
West to bid for the votes of disgruntled agrarians. In straight-
forward manner he discussed the topics that might interest
voters — economic conditions, prosperity, and the tariff;
agricultural relief, public utilities, and water power; corruption, government reorganization, and foreign affairs; Prohibition, the Ku Klux Klan, and religion. Hoover, on the
other hand, preferred the tactic of "standing on the record"
through most of the summer and fall. Only toward the end
did he assume the role of an active candidate.[7]

To post-New Deal Americans, Smith's position on national
economic issues in the 1928 campaign perhaps seems only
mildly advanced, and there has been a tendency rather to
emphasize his ideological agreement with Hoover in some
matters. But to the action-starved progressives of the 1920's
the Governor, with a long list of state reform measures to his
credit, came as a refreshing breeze amidst the stifling atmosphere of normalcy. Professor Felix Frankfurter of the Harvard Law School voiced their tribute: "Alfred E. Smith has
proved himself the greatest master of adult education in
America. He has vitalized politics and lifted them to their
rightful place of discussion, debate, controversy, exchange of
opinion, full and frank, about the pressing problems of society." [8] Politics were no longer passé in America, and even
for this alone, progressives could be thankful. On election
day nearly 36,800,000 people cast ballots in the presidential
contest, an increase of more than 7,700,000 — or 26 per cent
— over the number who voted in 1924.[9]

Most of the matters discussed in party platforms and campaign speeches, however, exerted little effect on the outcome
of the election. Specific issues paled in significance beside the

one overbearing fact that Al Smith's nomination projected the conflict of old-stock and Newer American cultures that had disrupted the Democrats in 1924 onto the national, inter-party stage. The fears and resentments inherent in one hundred per cent Americanism and Ku Kluxism culminated in the 1928 election, and perceptive observers noted the significance of the encounter. "For the first time," said the *New Republic*, "a representative of the unpedigreed, foreign-born, city-bred, many-tongued recent arrivals on the American scene has knocked on the door and aspired seriously to the presiding seat in the national Council Chamber." "Here is no trivial conflict," wrote Walter Lippmann. "Here are the new people, clamoring . . . and the older people defending their household gods. The rise of Al Smith has made the conflict plain, and his career has come to involve a major aspect of the destiny of American civilization." [10]

In the midst of this clash of value systems, then, what the candidates thought about the water-power issue or the tariff issue was relatively unimportant. Two contemporary students of the election summed up the situation: "The basis of . . . faith was not what Smith *said* or what the platform of his party suggested. . . The issue . . . was not one which intelligent men could solve by abstract logic or by mathematical analysis. You *felt* with Smith, or you *felt* with Hoover." [11] In the end, on the face of the returns, most Americans felt with Hoover.

In Massachusetts, however, enough people felt with Smith to give the Democrats a majority of the Commonwealth's presidential vote for the first time in history. The Bay State campaign centered on the same issues that had dominated the senatorial contest of 1926 — Prohibition, the economic situation, and ethnic politics. The Democrats sought to reinforce the Walsh coalition, while the Republicans tried to overwhelm it; and neither side left a stone unturned. The result was an intensive campaign — and a degree of popular political interest — unequaled in the modern history of the state.

Though the national Democratic Party remained as divided as ever over the merits of the Eighteenth Amendment, Smith's nomination gave <u>Prohibition</u> the semblance of being a partisan issue. In August the New York governor outlined his position: amendment of the Volstead Act to "liberalize" the definition of intoxicating liquors, and revision of the Eighteenth Amendment to allow individual states, by referendum, to legalize such alcoholic beverages, provided they be sold by the states themselves. Federal enforcement would thus be retained for states choosing to remain dry, and the return of the "saloon" inhibited. Bay State Democrats were in full accord with Smith's program, but they had no desire to repeat Colonel Gaston's mistake of 1926 by turning the campaign into a wet crusade. The Democratic state convention therefore neglected to mention the issue at all in its platform, and party campaigners carefully refrained from giving the matter undue emphasis in their appeals. But everyone knew that Herbert Hoover was friendly toward the Eighteenth Amendment and that Al Smith was not.[12]

Especially aware of the discrepancy between the candidates' views on liquor were those old-stock Protestant inhabitants of the towns and suburban cities who regarded the Volstead Act as sacred. Al Smith's name was anathema to these people for many reasons, but his stand on Prohibition was the one most frequently cited in their indictment. Methodist Bishop William F. Anderson of Boston, calling Prohibition "the greatest economic and social reform of the ages," denounced the Democratic candidate as a man "who appeals to a group who have back of them only physical appetite and no regard for law or reform." Mrs. Henry W. Peabody of Beverly, chairman of the Women's National Committee for Law Enforcement, told delegates at the Northfield Foreign Missionary Conference that the election was "a crusade. We must go before God, and then go out and work for God. We want a great victory." [13] Across the state the call to arms was sounded from Protestant pulpits, especially those of the Methodists. "The greatest moral menace on the present political horizon," the Reverend A. A. Schoolcraft of Lunenburg told his flock, "is the dripping-wet figure of Governor Smith," while the Reverend Edson Leach of the First Methodist Church of Lynn deemed Smith "the greatest menace that has faced America since the Civil War." Inspired by the Massachusetts W.C.T.U., which endorsed Hoover, thousands of Prohibitionists met in local churches the day before the election to pray for a continued national drought. [14]

The dry elements still claimed to be the backbone of the Republican Party in Massachusetts, and in deference to them the G.O.P. state convention adopted a platform pledging "vigorous enforcement" of Prohibition. Nevertheless, party leaders were distressingly aware of the growing wet sentiment among some traditionally Republican voters. In the September primary, a wet challenger made a strong showing in the race for the senatorial nomination (to oppose David I. Walsh for a full term) against the machine's candidate, who supported the party's dry platform. [15] The returns demonstrated that the wet vote in the G.O.P. primary had increased considerably in comparison with earlier years. Clearly this anti-Prohibition sentiment must be appeased, somehow, to forestall desertion.

The danger of defection was especially great among New Immigrant Republicans, and so campaigners tried to explain that Smith's election would not automatically bring a return of legalized "vino" and other favorite forms of refreshment. Only Congress, they stressed, could institute the necessary steps for a change in the Constitution, and the matter of repeal or revision therefore had no place in the presidential contest.[16] Thus, while Protestant divines called for a crusade to save Prohibition from "the dripping-wet figure of Governor Smith," Republican orators told wet audiences that the Eighteenth Amendment was not a real issue at all.

Party directors hit upon another device for consoling the anti-Prohibitionists. Wet elements in each state senatorial district were seeking during 1928 to have a question put on the ballot, whether the state senator should vote for a legislative resolution requesting Massachusetts' congressional delegation to favor repeal of the Eightenth Amendment. Republican leaders got behind the movement, and by election time enough signatures had been secured to have the matter placed on the ballot in thirty-six of the forty senatorial districts. This round-about referendum, it was hoped, might siphon off the resentment of the party's wets by enabling them to register a protest against national dryness without bolting the party's national ticket.[17]

If dissatisfaction with Prohibition caused headaches for those running the Hoover campaign in Massachusetts, the Commonwealth's economic condition caused even more. Again figures published by the state's Department of Labor and Industries described the unfavorable situation. In 1926 (a year that was bad enough itself), Massachusetts' manufacturing industries employed 602,343 operatives, and produced goods valued at nearly $3,420,000,000. For the presidential year 1928 the corresponding figures were 540,927 operatives and approximately $3,224,000,000.[18] The Republican campaign across the nation was predicated on the existence of

"Republican prosperity," but in the Bay State prosperity of any brand was hard to find.

Again the textile industry accounted in largest part for Massachusetts' plight. Liquidations and shut-downs continued apace. What the depression meant in concrete terms is suggested by the employment and production figures for the Commonwealth's leading textile cities shown in the accompanying table.[19]

	Employment		Value of Products	
	1926	1928	1926	1928
New Bedford	35,143	21,249	$121,034,981	$82,640,906
Fall River	31,353	25,547	127,637,287	105,224,884
Lawrence	26,777	21,047	175,251,666	120,296,210
Lowell	20,859	17,234	77,546,542	70,287,441

The disintegration of the textile industry was abetted by the New Bedford cotton operatives' strike of 1928, which lasted from April to October. In the former month mill owners announced a 10 per cent reduction in wages, alleging inability to compete with the South under existing wage structures. Shortly thereafter, in this city of 120,000 inhabitants, 27,000 workers were on strike and the municipality's economic life was at a standstill. Public opinion tended to side with the workers in the belief that improvement of management techniques, rather than further reduction of already low wages, constituted the only cure for the industry's ailments. But in the end, on October 6, the workers agreed to a 5 per cent reduction of wages and went back to the mills.[20] The textile depression continued, however, and the effects of one of the industry's bitterest strikes hung like a pall over what had once been the queen city of the New England textile trade. "The conditions that the strikers have undergone . . ." said a correspondent for the *Springfield Republican*, "will be the governing factor in the marking of their ballots." [21]

The general absence of "boom times" in Massachusetts, and the genuinely desperate conditions in certain of her strategic industrial centers, provided the Democrats a fertile issue. They found no difficulty compiling lists of firms that had sold out or suspended operations during the recent years of Republican rule — in Lowell, in Pittsfield, in North Adams, and elsewhere. Invariably the newspaper advertisements ended with some form of the same punch line: "Locally, do you think the Republican Party can take credit for prosperity during the past eight years?" [22]

Democratic campaigners were not specific in proposing remedies, but they did emphasize the "new look" in their party's tariff doctrine. With the ascendancy of the eastern wing of the party, which came with Smith's nomination, the Democrats abandoned what remained of their traditional "low tariff" ideology and adopted instead the tariff philosophy advocated by Senator Walsh in his earlier campaigns. The 1928 platform, which Walsh had a large hand in writing, espoused duties that would permit "effective competition" and safeguard the interests of American workers and "legitimate business," while promising to reduce "monopolistic" and "extortionate" rates. Governor Smith, determined to erase the "anti-business" label which had attached to the party in the days of Bryan, reiterated the platform's principles and pledged that no drastic changes would be made in the tariff structure following his election. The *Boston Transcript* complained that the Democrats had stolen the G.O.P.'s "protectionist" position.[23]

In the end, cultivation of existing discontent was enough for Democratic purposes. The tactics pursued by Republicans in other parts of the country, where they touted votes on the basis of "Coolidge prosperity," increased the difficulty of their task in Massachusetts. Elsewhere, the Republican national committee sponsored full-page advertisements claiming that G.O.P. economic policies had put a chicken in every pot and a car in every back yard, and placed the whole nation in "the silk-stocking class." But when Al Smith spoke in Boston on October 24, he cited the average weekly pay of Massachusetts mill workers as computed by the federal Bureau of Labor Statistics — $17.30. "Now just draw on your imagination for a moment," the Governor continued, "and see if you can in your mind's eye, picture a man at $17.30 a week going out to a chicken dinner, in his own automobile, with silk socks on." [24] His Boston audience got the point, and laughter shook the Arena. The New Bedford radio audience got the point, too, though there the laughter was likely more subdued.

The famous "Chicken in Every Pot" advertisement did not appear in Massachusetts newspapers. Instead, those in charge of the Hoover campaign concentrated on rationalizing the absence of good times in President Coolidge's own state. "The mill workers are glad to be working as much as three and one-half days a week," one speaker told his audience, "for they feel that without the protective tariff they would not be working at all. The textile workers in England are working no days a week. I am sure the Republicans will be victorious this year and that business conditions will improve." [25] Again, as in 1924 and 1926, Republican candidates promised to increase protective duties on the staples of the Bay State's manufacturing economy.

Republican spokesmen also claimed that Smith's election would endanger two other policies essential to economic well-being and recovery: economy in government and immigration restriction. Without restriction, it was said, thousands more immigrants would have flooded the country to compete for jobs with Massachusetts inhabitants. With Smith in the White House the bars would come down, and even greater depression would follow.[26] As for the question of "economy and sound administration," Republicans saw no comparison between Hoover and Smith. President Coolidge had reduced taxes and the national debt, releasing capital for business investment and expansion. Smith, on the other hand, had a record as a "spender" in New York State. He was "too free with bond issues and too liberal with expenditures." But Hoover would carry on Coolidge's policies, for he was "the enemy of bureaucracy . . . and a fine managing director for the greatest corporation in the world, in which we are all stockholders." [27]

Finally, Republicans alleged, Smith's election would weaken the fibre of American business in another way. The Governor, according to Congressman Fort of New Jersey in a Boston address, stood committed "to the broadest policy of Government in business ever proposed to the people of any nation except Russia." He referred to Smith's proposals for government intervention in agriculture, public utilities, and the liquor business, and levied the charge of "state socialism." A few days later candidate Hoover repeated the charge in a major speech and put the issue as one between rugged individualism and despotic socialism.[28] Toward the end of the campaign the electorate heard from Roger Babson, the famed Boston financial advisor and forecaster, that "an era of business depression and unemployment" would follow a victory for the Democratic candidate.[29] Republican leaders in Massachusetts hoped that such words would make an impression, somehow, on unemployed mill hands.

During October a correspondent for the *Springfield Republican* surveyed the political situation in cities and towns across the state. "You talk of politics," he reported in one dispatch, and sooner or later race and religion come in unbidden. The minute you ask for "facts" you get them in terms of French, Irish, Pole and Yankee, or Catholic and non-Catholic. Votes will undoubtedly be cast on other issues, particularly prohibition and prosperity, but when you get down to the ground there's "dirt." [30]

For old-stock Republicans who subscribed to the cult of one hundred per cent Americanism, the vision of Al Smith ensconced in the White House was a nightmare. The reaction to Smith's candidacy among the Newer Americans was just as violent, but in the opposite direction.

The one hundred per cent Americans' opposition to Al Smith was a blend of various elements, whose proportions differed in individual cases. For one thing there was the matter of religion. The exchange of letters between C. C. Marshall and Smith in the *Atlantic Monthly* during 1927 convinced some readers that the Governor's Catholicism was compatible with patriotism, but not all.[31] Throughout the campaign the issue was debated frankly in the letters-to-the-editor columns of the Commonwealth's press. On the anti-Smith side the arguments boiled down to the precept voiced by a Bay State Unitarian minister, the Reverend Dr. Dieffenbach, in a speech delivered in Virginia: that no Catholic should ever be President.[32] In addition Smith, a product of New York City and Tammany Hall, represented as much as any man could the urban, industrialized, polyglot Newer America. His surroundings, in the eyes of people who still cherished Old American values, unfit him for the task of leading the country, and they rebelled at the idea of making the mores of New York the standard of the nation. "The stability and continuation of our democratic form of government," according to Mrs. Elizabeth Tilton of Cambridge, a prominent Republican prohibitionist, depends on keeping in the political saddle what we used to call the frontier and what today we call Main Street; the virile, clean-minded, middle class mentality. . . America stands at the crossroads. Can her democracy survive if she puts in the White House what Bryce calls "her failures in government" — the big cities? Here is the question of the hour! [33]

In still other ways some old-stock people found Smith offensive to their conception of proper presidential fitness. The meagerness of his formal education was the basis for one complaint. The Governor's East Side accent grated on some ears, and his use of "ain't" and "between you and I" in campaign speeches touched off a nation-wide grammatical debate. Nor did Mrs. Smith, a housewifely person tending toward plumpness, escape invidious comparison with the more pert Lou Hoover. [34]

On the other hand, the Republican nominee represented to the one hundred per cent Americans everything that Smith did not. Protestant and of old-stock lineage, Hoover was born on an Iowa farm. Largely through his own efforts, he acquired an adequate education and, in business, amassed a sizable fortune at an early age. Only then had he entered public life, and at the top. By heredity, environment, and record, Hoover measured up to the ideal standards which, in 1928 at least, seemed for many to describe the "typical" real American. He was an almost perfect protagonist to withstand the assault being made by Newer America on the highest office in the land. Though some old-stock people sympathized with Smith as the victim of snobbishness and as the exponent of cultural liberalism, most of them responded to Hoover's cause, which was the cause of an Older America.

To the Irish Democrats of Massachusetts, however, Al Smith was a <u>folk hero</u>, and there was no doubt where their sympathies lay in the campaign. So many of them wanted to go all the way to Houston to see their idol nominated that four delegates were sent from each district instead of the usual two. The Democratic state chairman explained that "money doesn't enter into the situation with them, for they look upon this as an event of a lifetime." [35]

The task among Irish-Americans was primarily one of registration, and Democratic politicians in the Irish wards of Boston and other centers virtually fell over one another adding names to the voting lists, particularly the names of women who had never bothered to exercise the suffrage. Moreover, Irishmen who had joined the Republicans for one reason or another, a small number to begin with, were forced back to their "natural habitat" by the stress of pro-Smith sentiment. Republican Mayor John E. Walsh of Revere, who owed his election to the votes of Irish Democrats, publicly announced that he was deserting the head of his party's ticket. In Worcester, Republican Mayor Michael J. O'Hara found it convenient to take a vacation trip during the campaign, and local papers reported that O'Hara's machine would swing its support to Smith. Obviously the directors of the Hoover campaign could hope to garner few votes among Massachusetts' Sons of Erin, and they made little effort to do so.[36]

With old-stock Republicans and Irish Democrats mobilized behind their representative candidates, both parties campaigned as never before for the votes of the New Immigrant groups, who now controlled the balance of power. From the very beginning the Democrats faced the easier task, for the considerations that endeared Smith to the basically Irish Democracy of Massachusetts were also the most effective arguments that could be used in any appeal to New Immigrant voters.

The vital issue of Catholicism raised against Smith by old-stock Protestants produced a strong reaction among the French-Canadians, the Italians, the Poles, the Portuguese, and the Lithuanians, most of whom shared the Governor's religious convictions. Though the Catholic clergy abstained from public participation in the fray,[37] Democratic politicians felt no compunction in emphasizing the religious issue before Catholic audiences. In Boston, James Michael Curley plastered the exterior of the building used for his daily Smith rallies with quotations from Abraham Lincoln condemning religious bigotry. Inside, frequent attacks on Protestant intolerance received wild applause.[38] The Catholic New Immigrants' response to the religious appeal stemmed from two emotions: pride that one of their co-religionists should finally attain the status of a contender for the presidency, and resentment that his faith should bar him from that office.

> Say, Daddy, won't you tell me, the terrible news I heard?
> I scarcely can believe it, each cold and cruel word.
> They say because I worship Christ, and Catholic doctrines share,
> I never can be President, or hope to fill that Chair.
>
> You fought beneath Old Glory, in the late and terrible war,
> And the shot and shell that rose and fell, some Catholic hearts
> it tore.
> Both pain and desolation, the Catholic home did share,
> And if I serve my country, Dad, why can't I fill that Chair?
>
> And far away in Europe, in many a silent grave,
> There rests the form of a Catholic boy, so noble, true and brave.
> And they didn't tell him, Daddy, as he started "over there,"
> He was only fit to fight and die, and not to fill the Chair.
>
> O, Glorious Flag of Freedom, O, Flag of our native land,
> Uphold the Constitution, and by its doctrine stand.
> Protect your native children, let despots not ensnare,
> And give to them their birthright — the right to FILL THAT CHAIR.[39]

Moreover, the raising of the religious issue attracted to Smith's cause thousands of New Immigrants outside the Catholic Church. The Ku Klux years had taught the ethnic minority groups that an attack on one was an attack on all and in-

✓ culcated a trend toward unity among them. The response to Smith's candidacy on the part of <u>Jews</u> and, to a lesser extent, of <u>Negroes</u>, reflected an intensification of that trend, and Democratic spokesmen encouraged it. Prominently displayed at Curley's headquarters were posters depicting the Tomb of the Unknown Soldier with the legend: "What a tragedy if we should learn that he was a Jew, Catholic or Negro." [40] The most eloquent appeal for unity was spoken by Rabbi Stephen S. Wise at a Symphony Hall rally late in October. Answering those who wondered why he should defend a Catholic in view of the Church's persecution of Jewry in other times and places, Rabbi Wise declared that American ideals were at stake, not just the presidency — "whether minority religious groups shall be declared permanently and incurably inferior through substantive and actual violation of the Constitution." He concluded with a now-familiar call for cultural liberalism as the American ideal. "This is a Protestant country," Wise conceded. "A majority of the citizens of the United States are perhaps members of the Protestant churches. But what does America mean if not the most scrupulous safeguarding of the rights of minorities and, above all, of religious minorities?" [41]

✓ In addition to the religious issue, <u>immigration restriction</u> played a part in the campaign as another aspect of cultural liberalism. In his acceptance speech Governor Smith denounced use of the 1890 census for the base date in establishing quotas as a device purposely discriminating against "certain nationalities." It soon became evident, however, that use of a later census, which seemed to be the gist of Smith's solution, would mean a reduction in the quotas for Ireland and Germany. Confronted with a dilemma, Smith said nothing more during the campaign about changing the base date. Instead he joined Hoover in denouncing the still-pending National Origins Clause as an unworkable scheme which should be discarded — a move that would leave the existing law, based on the 1890 figures, in effect. Shortly before the election the Democratic candidate also challenged the wisdom of the literacy test.[42]

Though the exigencies of ethnic politics caused confusion in Smith's attitude on the tricky restriction issue, Democratic spokesmen in Massachusetts encouraged the belief that support of their candidate was the surest way of obtaining "justice and equality in legislation" for the New Immigrant groups, "because he understands them." [43] Moreover, the Republicans' tactics on the immigration issue inured to the Governor's benefit among Newer Americans. Despite Smith's insistence that, in compliance with the party platform, he favored continuation of nondiscriminatory restriction, G.O.P. campaigners persited in telling old-stock and organized labor groups that with his election the bars would come down completely and a host of foreigners would flood the country. In a Maryland speech urging Hoover's election the famous dry crusader, Methodist Bishop James Cannon, was quoted as saying:

> Governor Smith wants the Italians, the Sicilians, the Poles and the Russian Jews. That kind has given us a stomach ache. We have been unable to assimilate such people in our national life, so we shut the door to them until we could digest those we have here. But Smith says "Give me that kind of people." He wants the kind of people that you find today on the sidewalks of New York.[44]

That message might aid Hoover's cause in the South, but in the North it helped his opponent. Bishop Cannon's sentiments provided material for Democratic campaign advertisements in centers where the Italians, the Sicilians, the Poles, and the Russian Jews were not a negligible element.

In soliciting the votes of Newer Americans, the Democrats

X

also stressed <u>Smith</u>'s record of "progressive legislation" for the advancement of working men and women, for the protection of child welfare, and for the promotion of public health and housing, implying that his performance as President would match his performance as governor. The New Immigrant groups responded favorably. A columnist in the *Jewish Advocate* saw Smith "as the expression of . . . the strongly humanitarian spirit. The war and the machine age have tended to repress this spirit," the writer continued, "yet deep within, it surges, and through 'Al' it obtains an outlet." [45]

The reason for the Newer Americans' <u>revived interest in</u> "<u>reform</u>," as embodied in Smith's candidacy, was expressed by the *New Republic*. "While he has been a peculiarly successful reformer himself, he has <u>none</u> of the dogmatism, the self-righteousness, the legalistic bias and the psychological fundamentalism of the clerical politicians who are chiefly responsible for imposing prohibition on the war-bewildered American people." This quality of Smith's liberalism, the *New Republic* believed, owed much to his association with Tammany Hall which, in its solicitude for the "underdog," represented "the true inheritor, in the conditions of modern city life, of the Jacksonian Democratic tradition." [46]

Through Tammany, Smith had learned early in life the needs of the urban masses. In a speech during the 1928 campaign, he recalled how "as an assemblyman . . . I went down to that Oliver Street clubhouse six nights a week . . . just the same as a doctor who has his office hours, and I had a line of patients there night after night. And I had interpreters there, too, because a great many of them could not speak English." As legislator and governor, Smith also learned how the government might be made to serve the welfare of his kind of people, but <u>without</u> injecting into its "reforms" those condescending interferences with their personal and group preferences which had tended to make them suspicious of "government meddling" toward the end of the Progressive era. Thus New York, under his administration, was one of the very few states in which the urban tradition of social and humanitarian reform remained strong during the 1920's. When Smith became a presidential candidate in 1928, that tradition reasserted itself among Newer Americans elsewhere in the country. Their distrust of government action declined, and economic liberalism gained a new lease on life in their ranks.

Finally, serving as the capstone of the Democratic ethnic campaign, was the "recognition" of the Newer Americans implicit in Al Smith's candidacy. Writing in the *Baltimore Sun*, correspondent John Owens reported:

> If we would understand the real heart of the movement behind Governor Smith we must go back . . . to the massive circumstance that millions of people in the great cities, and to some extent on the farms, people who are in the second or third or fourth generation after the immigrants, find in Governor Smith evidence that they have achieved equality.[47]

In Massachusetts the composition of the state tickets again enhanced the Democratic Party's status as the party of "recognition."[48] But Smith's presence at the head of the roster was the main talking point. So what if the Bay State listees in *Who's Who* did favor Hoover eight to one?[49] And no matter that Smith occasionally said "ain't," or that Mrs. Smith was stouter than Mrs. Hoover and did her own housework. (After all, Smith's wife probably conformed more closely to the mother image of most Newer Americans than did Hoover's.) "What a glorious thing to know a boy who lived a life of labor and poverty can become President of the United States," Senator Walsh proclaimed. "There will be a silent throb in the heart of every mother . . . to learn next Wednesday morning that a poor boy from the East Side of New York is elected President." The *Springfield Republican*, supporting Hoover, conceded that "there is inherent in the Smith candidacy a call to the deeps of democratic sentiment and aspiration that is heard all along 'the new frontier' of American life. It is heard most clearly and distinctly, however, here in our own Commonwealth." [50]

Republican efforts to retain support among the various nationality groups were handicapped from the start, for the considerations that rallied the old-stock backbone of the party behind Hoover were also the ones most responsible for defection among the party's newer wing. What Republican campaigners told New Immigrant audiences on certain issues, then, necessarily differed from what their fellow workers were telling old-stock audiences at the same time. In spite of its dilemma, the G.O.P. in 1928 realized how essential the votes of the Commonwealth's newer citizens were and waged a desperate campaign to win them.

While Protestant zealots told one another that no Catholic must ever be President, managers of the Bay State Republican machine made every effort to dissociate themselves from such sentiments. Congressman A. Piatt Andrew of the Sixth District urged the Republican national committee to "muzzle" Mrs. Mabel Walker Willebrandt, an assistant attorney general of the United States who made a specialty of denouncing Smith before audiences of evangelical Protestant ministers. Robert Washburn, president of the Roosevelt Club, felt that Mrs. Willebrandt should be "camphored and carried into seclusion." [51] When copies of a viciously anti-Catholic publication, *The Fellowship Forum*, were distributed on the streets of North Adams, local party officials denounced the action and denied any connection with it. Instead, Republican campaign literature which circulated among New Immi-

grants quoted the praise heaped on Hoover for his war reconstruction work by the Pope, Cardinal Gibbons, and the
King of Italy.[52] Joseph Scott, a prominent Los Angeles attorney who was a Knight of St. Gregory and an official of the
Knights of Columbus, toured Massachusetts pointing out that
Hoover, like Smith, had denounced those who sought votes on
religious grounds.[53] Consequently, Republican spokesmen
told their Newer American audiences, religion — like Prohibition — was not an issue at all in the election.

While some Hooverites warned old-stock audiences that a
Smith victory would bring a lowering of immigration bars
and a flood of unwanted aliens, others told New Immigrant
gatherings that after Hoover's election the restrictions would
be liberalized. As a member of the committee charged with
working out the provisions of the National Origins Clause,
Secretary Hoover had concluded that the scheme was im-
practicable, and he urged that it be abandoned. He promised
as well a revision of the immigration laws to eliminate provisions that caused separation of families and other special
hardships. Though little was heard of such matters in Republican appeals to old-stock audiences, much was made of
them before New Immigrant crowds.[54]

To offset Smith's appeal to the Newer Americans' instincts
toward humanitarian reform, Republican spokesmen lauded
Hoover's war-relief work in European countries and hailed
him as the world's "Good Samaritan." [55] But Hoover monopo-
lized the support of those one hundred per cent Americans
who continued to view "reform" as primarily a job of uplifting "inferior" immigrant standards, and this caused Newer
Americans to distrust his brand of liberalism.

In the end, the Republican bid for the votes of the "newer
races" rested on appeals to tradition, gratitude, and long-
standing Irish–New Immigrant hostility. The G.O.P.'s record

of legislative enactments favorable to the newer elements and their homelands paraded in review. Party spokesmen recited the list of patronage already extended to Newer Americans, and promised even more in the future. One hard-working campaigner asked a standard question of the New Immigrant voters whom he addressed: "What have the Irish ever done for you?" [56] That was the question asked, implicitly, whenever Republican orators cited the party's record of boons to the newer ethnic groups. Though the traditional enmity between Irishmen and the later arrivals had obviously declined in recent years, directors of the Hoover campaign in Massachusetts relied on the hope that enough of the old feeling still persisted to prevent a mass movement of New Immigrants to the side of the Democratic presidential candidate.

Republican efforts to cultivate Irish–New Immigrant enmity were particularly marked among the French-Canadians. A large element in the population of Massachusetts, that group traditionally voted Republican in national elections, and the G.O.P. in 1928 counted heavily on retaining its allegiance.[57] Not only political differences but also sporadic arguments over religious affairs had served to keep the Frenchmen at odds with their Irish co-religionists. The most recent dispute occurred in the neighboring state of Rhode Island, where, throughout the 1920's, French-Canadian spokesmen wrangled with the dominantly Irish Catholic hierarchy over the disposition of parochial school funds. The upshot of the affair was the excommunication of a number of the insurgents, led by Elphege Daignault, for instituting suit in civil courts against Bishop Hickey of Providence. In 1928 Daignault headed the Republican campaign among his countrymen in Rhode Island, stirring up resentment against the Irish. "We can't expect anything from the Democratic party," Daignault told his audiences, "which is controlled by men of the same race as those

with whom we are having trouble. . ." [58] The French of
Massachusetts had followed the Daignault-Hickey affair, and
Republican leaders in the Bay State trusted that it would keep
them in the G.O.P. presidential column. Late in the campaign
they brought Daignault across the border to speak for Hoover.

Straws in the wind indicated, however, that the Republicans were failing in their efforts to prevent a union of the
"newer races" with the Irish Democrats behind the popular
figure of Al Smith. A few nights before the election Daignault was forced to interrupt a pro-Hoover speech in Man-
ville, Rhode Island, and beat a hasty retreat under police protection when the audience "abandoned the opera house . . .
and, armed with eggs, waited for the speakers to leave the
building." [59] The Republicans had to cancel rallies for Polish
and French citizens in a number of Massachusetts communities
because of sparse attendance. Only forty-two persons attended
an Italian-American meeting for Hoover in Springfield, but
when the city's Italian-American League for Smith sponsored
a rally a few nights later, four thousand men, women, and
children turned out. "To the uninitiated," a reporter commented, "it seemed as if even the coming back to earth of
Columbus would not have attracted such a motley gathering." [60] Another reporter found the Portuguese-Americans
of Provincetown on Cape Cod unusually well organized,
politically, all on Governor Smith's behalf. A columnist in
the *Jewish Advocate* felt it worth recording that "despite reports to the contrary, all Jews are not going to vote for
Smith!" Other observers noted that "Negro voters have been
divided in this campaign as never before." The *Chicago De-
fender*, the most widely read Negro paper in the nation, bolted
its traditional Republican allegiance to endorse the Democratic nominee, as did the *Boston Guardian*. Viewing the
storm clouds, a prominent Republican worker among the

ethnic groups told correspondent Carter Field that he was "more hopeful than confident." [61]

Meanwhile, other components of the Walsh coalition responded favorably to the Democrats' campaign efforts in 1928. Prohibition and economic depression could be counted upon to win the votes of some disaffected old-stock Republicans. And the Bay State labor leaders who had supported Senator Walsh in his earlier contests now worked for Governor Smith. Though the national A.F. of L. refrained from endorsing either candidate, President William Green praised Smith's acceptance speech and added: "I am certain that when the working men and women of America go to the polls, they will stand by those who stood by them in their hours of need." The political committee of the Massachusetts Federation endorsed Smith officially, as did central labor unions in various cities.[62]

Advanced liberals were somewhat more divided among Smith, Norman Thomas, and Hoover. Nevertheless, Smith's record won him the bulk of the votes of the professional reformers, at least in the East and in Massachusetts. "Among all the prominent candidates for President in both parties," the *New Republic* declared in 1927, "there is only one thorough-going progressive — Governor Alfred Smith of New York." That journal endorsed him in 1928, and admonished those liberals who shied away from him because of his Tammany affiliation that "if he is not elected, progressives, in so far as they are responsible for his failure, will have proved blind and false to the one man who at this moment is capable of putting an end to the postwar stagnation of political opinion and to issue new marching orders to American government." [63]

Moreover, the matter of cultural liberalism earned votes for Smith among independents. "Everywhere one goes . . ." wrote the editors of the *Nation*, "it is prejudice that seems to be electing Herbert Hoover — prejudice against the Pope; against Tammany Hall; against the man who waxes ungrammatical as he waxes eloquent; against his wife . . . ; prejudice because Al Smith represents the immigrant part of our population." Though the *Nation*, torn between the Democratic nominee and Norman Thomas, refrained from endorsing either candidate, it conceded that "the present emergency is so great that many will overlook everything else save the height to which the tides of prejudice have gone in order to rebuke this treason to Americanism at the polls by voting for Smith." [64]

A survey of *Nation* subscribers revealed an overwhelming preference for the Democratic nominee. Dr. John Dewey and H. L. Mencken, the idol of America's "lost generation," backed him. [65] In Massachusetts, many who had been prominent in the 1924 La Follette Progressive movement transferred their allegiance to Smith. A number of "intellectual" Democrats, who had abstained from active participation in Bay State politics since their disappointment in 1920 over the League of Nations campaign, now worked for Democratic success. [66] Forty distinguished Harvard professors issued an endorsement of Smith, "notwithstanding his Bowery dialect," as one columnist observed. A group of Harvard students formed the "Brown Derby Brigade" and toured the Commonwealth practicing their oratorical talents for the Democratic candidate. At the climactic Democratic rally in Boston a delegation of them, all "the typical college-boy type," made a flamboyant entry into the hall waving Harvard banners. The chairman called them to the stage where they stood "grinning and blushing" at the ovation, and "for perhaps the first time in any political rally in this city, three cheers were given for Harvard." Sons of Erin acclaiming Sons of Harvard — the Smith campaign made strange bed-fellows! [67]

The decisiveness of the election, for both parties, produced in Massachusetts a volume of organizational activity beyond anything witnessed in a previous campaign. The phenomenon was particularly marked among the Democrats, if only because of the dilapidated condition of the party's machinery since at least the end of the war. Al Smith's appearance on the scene ended that. For one thing the Democratic national committee, far from "writing off" the Bay State as had been the case earlier, in this instance regarded it as one of the crucial fighting grounds. Another unusual circumstance from the Democratic point of view was the availability of money — that vital lubricant for registration and campaign work — which now flowed abundantly from both local and out-of-state sources.[68]

Even the Democratic state committee came to life following Smith's nomination at Houston. For the first time in his career Senator Walsh showed a desire to assume a larger control of internal party affairs. At his behest the incumbent state chairman was ousted and replaced by Frank Donahue, formerly secretary of state during Walsh's gubernatorial terms. "Intellectual" Democrats, including Mrs. Jessie Woodrow Sayre, daughter of Woodrow Wilson, were added to the committee's roster and lent it an unaccustomed air of "refinement." The revivified committee then fostered establishment of "Smith for President" clubs in cities and towns where a regular Democratic organization was nonexistent or weak. More than two hundred of them dotted the Commonwealth by election day, bringing organization to communities where the idea of establishing a Democratic city or town committee had seemed useless before.[69]

In Boston, however, the incomparable James Michael Curley stole the show. Ruffled by what he regarded as Senator Walsh's usurpation of party control, Curley was piqued by the thought that he was being left out of things. The ex-Mayor rented an abandoned hotel in the heart of the Hub, dubbed it "the bull-pen," and daily conducted the liveliest rallies in town which attracted anywhere from two to five thousand people at each session. "Nothing approaching the cleverness of Mr. Curley's stroke . . . has been noted in Boston politics for a generation," the pro-Hoover *Boston Transcript* declared.[70]

The rift between Curley and Walsh bore seeds of a dispute which later gave the party trouble, but that was not noticeable yet. For in 1928 their competition, together with that of all the actual or would-be party chieftains, had one end in view: to outdo one another in assuring a victory for Al Smith. The Democrats could only benefit from such rivalry.

Supplementing the work of the regular Democratic politicians and their machines were groups like the Smith-Robinson Veterans' Organization and the Smith First-Voters League.[71] Most important of all were the ethnic organizations. French-Canadians, Italian-Americans, Poles, Greeks, Lithuanians, Jews, Negroes — each had a Smith for President club. Generally, Smith headquarters in New York City designated a man to lead the drive among his countrymen in Massachusetts, doled out funds, and maintained a loose supervision over his work.[72] The leader then began the task of organizing the state, setting up a local club wherever a large enough number of "his people" lived, and leaving it in the hands of local directors. In every case the job of registration, especially among the women, enjoyed priority. After that, the rest was easy — rallies, editorials and advertisements in local newspapers, campaign speeches and distribution of literature, often in foreign tongues, parades — and the response was encouraging. In some cases these ethnic leaders were men who had already associated themselves with the Democrats, and particularly with David I. Walsh, in earlier campaigns. In other instances they were younger professional men — lawyers, doctors, dentists, journalists — anxious to make a name in their communities. All saw Smith's candidacy as a vehicle for recognition for their ethnic group and — who could tell — perhaps for themselves, personally.

Never before had so many aspiring politicians worked so hard for a Democratic presidential victory in Massachusetts. The reason was evident when Governor Smith himself came to the state on October 24. At Pittsfield, the first city his train reached after crossing the border from New York, a crowd of ten thousand was gathered, though no stop was scheduled. It was the same all along the route to Boston, and the reception accorded the Governor in the Hub outdid anything ever seen there. The Boston Arena — built to accommodate nine thousand people — opened its doors at noon, and by three o'clock all seats were taken. At 9:00 P.M., when the rally began, fifteen thousand persons had somehow squeezed into the hall.[73]

Democratic politicians took heed, closed ranks — at least temporarily — and gave their all. It was essential to one's future, and the plainer one made his devotion to the idol's cause, the better. James Michael Curley, for example, managed to secure a coveted seat in the car that carried the Governor through Boston's streets and, together with Senator Walsh, responded to the plaudits aimed at Smith. That no onlooker might miss him, "Mr. Curley," the newspapers reported, "was conspicuously attired in a silk hat and raccoon coat." [74]

On the other side of the political fence, the long-perfected Bay State Republican organization functioned more effectively than ever. Coolidge's retirement and the Hoover movement brought to the fore a new and younger element of Republicans, led by Boston lawyer John Richardson and journalist

Christian Herter, but the old-timers retained control of party reins. When William M. Butler surrendered his post as national committeeman at the Kansas City convention, his successor was Louis K. Liggett, the drugstore magnate who previously held a prominent place in the Coolidge machine as chief fundraiser. Liggett promised due representation in party councils to the younger men, and throughout the campaign the two elements co-operated wholeheartedly.[75]

Under the new national committeeman's direction, the Republican city and town committees spearheaded the Hoover drive. Assisting their operations were the independent Volunteers for Hoover, headed by Richardson and Herter, which enrolled 26,000 active members during the course of the campaign.[76] Moreover, the Republicans too had their ethnic organizations, led in most cases by the old-time "prominenti" of each nationality — office holders, businessmen, and others who had benefited from Republican rule. The efforts of the ethnic groups, however, seemed the least productive of encouraging results. Hoover campaign headquarters in the Italian-dominated North End of Boston were attacked by a mob, the pictures of the Secretary adorning the building torn down, and much of the campaign literature destroyed.[77]

Again, as in the case of the Democrats, registration work was essential. Liggett and his co-workers knew they faced defection among groups that had supported the party in previous years, and to offset it they relied on enlisting every possible new recruit among those elements that constituted the backbone of the party. Consequently, Republican volunteers combed the towns, the suburban cities, and the industrial city enclaves in search of new voters wherever Prohibition fervor, economic conservatism, and old-stock American sentiment seemed to prevail. As registration figures mounted in Republican strongholds, party leaders felt they had done everything possible to hold the Bay State to her traditional allegiance, and observers concurred that they had. Liggett told reporters of his hopes: to hold Smith to a 100,000 vote lead in Boston, to limit him to 25,000 more in the other cities of the Commonwealth, and to roll up a margin of 150,000 votes for Hoover in the towns. The Republican candidate, he concluded, would carry Massachusetts by 25,000.[78]

Between them the two parties added almost 330,000 names to the registration lists compared with 1924 — an increase of 23.7 per cent.[79] On election day voters went to the polls early and strong. By noon 50 per cent of Boston's registered vote had been cast, and in Holyoke and Pittsfield the figure was 70 per cent.[80] When the polls closed, 93.5 per cent of the registered voters in Massachusetts had exercised the franchise, breaking all records (in 1924 the figure was 87.1). While 1,129,902 persons had voted for President in the Commonwealth in 1924, in 1928 1,577,813 did so, an increase of nearly 40 per cent over the former total (the national increase was 26 per cent).

Al Smith polled 792,758 votes to 775,566 for Hoover, giving him a lead of 17,192. In Boston the Democratic candidate's margin was 98,835, and thus Louis Liggett achieved his objective of keeping Smith's majority in the city below 100,000. But in the thirty-eight cities outside Boston, where Liggett's plans required Smith to be limited to a 25,000 vote advantage, the Democrats actually rolled up a 47,150 vote majority for their candidate. And in the towns, where Liggett hoped for a 150,000 vote margin in Hoover's favor, the Republican candidate's lead was only 128,793. Despite the outpouring of voters in Republican centers, the G.O.P. had failed to accomplish its ends outside the Commonwealth's capital city.

Smith's state-wide vote was 50.5 per cent of the two-party

presidential total, representing an increase of 13.0 points over Davis and La Follette's combined 37.5 per cent of the total three-party vote in 1924. In Boston the increase was 14.3 points, while in the thirty-eight other cities it was even higher, 14.8; and in the towns it was 9.8.

In so close an election every vote counted, and each element making up the victorious Democratic coalition might claim, with some justification, that without its backing Smith would not have carried the state. Labor leaders and advanced liberals undoubtedly rendered valuable support (the Socialist candidate, Norman Thomas, received only 6,256 votes in Massachusetts, while the Communist nominee polled a mere 2,461). The votes of disaffected old-stock Republicans were also needed. Anti-Prohibition sentiment in G.O.P. ranks, and the response of some old-stock people to Smith's appeal as a cultural liberal, accounted in part for the increased Democratic percentage of the vote in certain Republican strongholds. Moreover in New Bedford, where the depression was severe, traditionally Republican precincts heavily populated with old-stock English textile workers were listed in the Democratic column. Discontent with the economic situation affected old-stock Republicans in other depressed centers too, as in the town of Methuen, where English workers were numerous and where the Democratic presidential vote showed a large increase.

But while support from each of these elements was essential to Smith's success, most of the swollen Democratic vote came from two sources: the Irish and the New Immigrants. In the three wards embracing the Irish areas of Charlestown and South Boston in the Hub, Smith's percentages of the vote were 90.0, 89.2, and 86.8. The one dominantly Irish ward in the city of Malden turned in 2,257 votes for Smith, 135 for Hoover. Elsewhere it was the same. Across the state the tra-

X

ditionally Democratic Irish Catholics turned out at the polls en masse. There, for the first time in a presidential election, they were joined by the bulk of the Commonwealth's newer citizens.

The New Immigrants left the Republican Party in droves. Overlooking previous antagonisms, they joined the Massachusetts Irish to an extent that shocked Republican leaders and broke their hopes of carrying the state. "The defection of the so-called foreign groups . . ." an Associated Press dispatch reported, "is regarded by the Republican managers as having turned the tide for Smith. . ." [81] Election statistics confirmed the Republican appraisal of the seriousness of the New Immigrant switch. While the increase in Smith's percentage of the two-party vote compared with the combined Davis–La Follette percentage of the three-party vote in 1924 was 13.0 points for the state as a whole, the figure was 18.5 for the aggregate vote of the ten other Newer American cities over 25,000 outside Boston (each having 70 per cent or more foreign-stock population). By contrast, the figure for the thirteen old-stock cities of that class (each having more than 30 per cent "native white of native parentage" population), was only 12.3. And in the latter places the Democratic increases in melting-pot wards far outdistanced those in wards which were old-stock strongholds. Comparing the figures for towns between 2,500 and 10,000 inhabitants, the increase in the Democratic percentage of the aggregate vote of the sixteen Newer American towns of that class (each having 70 per cent or more foreign-stock population) was found to be 14.8 points, while for the twenty-nine old-stock towns of that class (each having 50 per cent or more "native white of native parentage" population), the figure was only 6.1. Clearly, the foreign-stock cities and towns and the foreign-stock wards of the "native" cities accounted in largest part for the disruption of Liggett's plans.

With the exception of Worcester, Smith carried all of the ten Newer American cities referred to above, none of which had gone Democratic in a presidential election since at least 1916. In addition, he carried a large number of industrial towns such as Adams, Easthampton, Southbridge, Webster, Montague, and Ludlow — all heavily populated with New Immigrant factory workers — most of which had never gone to a Democratic presidential nominee before. The little agricultural towns of Hadley and Hatfield in the Connecticut River Valley, where Poles and other New Immigrants had taken over the farms abandoned by Yankees,[82] also fell into the Democratic column.

The increases in the Democratic percentage of the presidential vote were most marked in those New Immigrant centers which were also hardest hit by industrial depression. In New Bedford the increase was 22.3 points, in Fall River it was 22.2, and in Lawrence 21.9 points. Nevertheless, it is notable that among all the cities of Massachusetts the increase was largest in Chicopee (23.6 points) where, contrary to the trend in the places just mentioned, employment and payroll figures indicated an actual improvement in the economic situation compared with 1926 and 1927.[83] The Democratic gain in Chicopee was due to increased registration and the switching of votes away from the Republican Party among the city's large French-Canadian and Polish populations. Apparently the matter of "recognition" involved in Smith's candidacy, with all the resentments and aspirations implied in that term, sufficed in itself to cause a political revolution among those elements, even though unabetted by acute economic distress.

Analysis of ward returns demonstrated the effectiveness of the work done among the newer nationality groups by Democratic politicians and the ethnic "Smith for President" clubs. In Boston, for example, dominantly Irish-Italian Ward One gave Smith 82.2 per cent of its vote; while in Martin Lomasney's Italian-Jewish stronghold, Ward Three, the Democratic candidate received 81.7 per cent. The North End precincts of Lomasney's ward, an almost solidly Italian neighborhood, recorded 2,325 votes for Smith, 134 for Hoover. Jewish areas in the outlying parts of the city had always been Republican strongholds in presidential elections, but now they too went to Smith, one ward giving him 55.5 per cent of its two-party vote and the other, 64.2 per cent. Smith also received 40 per cent of the aggregate vote in the city's Negro precincts, a proportion higher than that of any previous Democratic presidential nominee.

In New Bedford's Ward Five, where Portuguese-Americans and Negroes counted heavily in the population, Smith received 51.1 per cent of the vote, a phenomenal increase over the 18.9 per cent garnered by Davis and La Follette in 1924. In Chelsea's strongest Jewish ward Smith got 81.0 per cent, just 2.0 points less than his mark in the city's strongest Irish ward, and representing an increase of 18.0 points over the combined Davis–La Follette percentage in 1924. In Malden the predominantly Jewish Ward Seven gave Smith 64.0 per cent of the vote, an increase of 17.0 points over the Davis–La Follette mark. The Democratic percentage in Haverhill showed an increase of 14.7 points for the city as a whole, but in Ward Three, with a heavy Greek population, the figure was 20.3. It was even greater, 24.4, in Haverhill's melting-pot Ward Five, which had received a large influx of French-Canadians, Italians, Poles, and Jews (by contrast, the increase in the city's strongest old-stock Republican ward was only 5.2).

The massive defection among voters of French-Canadian extraction was particularly disappointing to the Republicans.

In New Bedford, Fall River, Lowell, and other centers, that element led the way in the New Immigrant trend toward Smith. In Lowell the two wards dominated by Frenchmen gave him 65.6 per cent and 66.3 per cent of the vote, and in Holyoke the French ward gave him 84.1 per cent. Chicopee's Ward Seven came through with 71.5 per cent. While Smith's percentage of the vote in Gardner compared with the Davis–La Follette percentage in 1924 showed an increase of 19.0 points for the city as a whole, the figures for the two French-Canadian wards were 27.9 and 37.9 (by contrast, the increase in the city's strongest old-stock Republican ward was a mere 5.9). In Fitchburg the Democratic percentage increased by only 4.6 points in the city's strongest old-stock Republican ward, but by 20.1 points in the French ward.

A few days after the election an Associated Press dispatch from Boston reported that "there is talk of a reorganization of the Republican party machinery which would give greater recognition to the various elements of State population." [84]

The election that gave Massachusetts' electoral vote to Al Smith also returned David I. Walsh to a full term as senator. The Republican candidate, B. Loring Young, was more adept at electioneering than Walsh's previous opponents, but no match for the popular incumbent. The expanded Democratic coalition, which the Senator had been the first to muster in 1926, now brought him one of the most overwhelming victories of his career. Walsh actually polled 25,000 votes more than Smith, while Young received 82,000 fewer than Hoover. Walsh defeated his opponent by nearly 125,000 votes.

But the presidency and the senatorship marked the end of the Democratic victory drive in Massachusetts, as far as statewide contests were concerned. In the gubernatorial election Lieutenant Governor Frank Allen, a classic product of the

Republican "escalator," managed to defeat General Charles H. Cole, the "original Smith man" who had crashed the Democratic convention slate in 1924, by a narrow margin of 19,235 votes. Although the strategy of the gubernatorial campaign followed the lines marked out in the presidential race, it possessed a significance of its own. Reflecting the reinvigoration of the urban tradition of reform which came with Al Smith's nomination for the presidency, the Democratic state convention had written a platform endorsing a state old-age pension system, broadening of the workmen's compensation law, stricter regulation of public utility corporations, restrictions on the labor injunction and the "yellow dog" contract, and a variety of similar economic and social reform measures. Launching a vigorous campaign, General Cole and other Democratic spokesmen espoused those proposals with a fervor reminiscent of the Progressive era. Recounting and denouncing Allen's record of opposition to liberal measures while a member of the legislature in that period, Cole called for a new regime which would concern itself with "legislation that will improve working conditions and make for more happiness . . . in the home and social life." "A state is more than a mere business machine," the General declared. "It must have a human side, a sympathetic side . . . it should perform the service of formulating into laws in an orderly and practical manner the aspirations, hopes, and desires of its people." Obviously, Democratic campaign tactics were different now from those of 1922, when John F. Fitzgerald bemoaned the rise of state "paternalism." The temper of the times — and of the Democrats' Newer American constituents in Massachusetts — had changed, for while 1922 was a year of one hundred per cent Americanism and of fear, 1928 seemed to be the year of Al Smith and of confidence. Smith himself set the pattern for the new departure in his Boston campaign speech, which he devoted largely to defending his record of welfare legislation against the Republicans' hackneyed charge of "socialism." Subsequently Cole and other Massachusetts progressives, enjoying the Governor's blessing, felt safe once again in talking of "reform" to their Irish and New Immigrant audiences.[85] Bay State Democrats no longer lacked issues, and thus the spell of normalcy over state politicking was broken. Its spell over the actual administration of state government might have been broken too, and Cole would have been governor, had not thousands of Newer American first-voters, in their anxiousness to vote for Al Smith, neglected to put their marks in the gubernatorial column on the ballot.

The Republicans also retained control of the other state executive offices, but in every case the margin of victory was far reduced below that of former, "normal" years. The balance in Massachusetts' congressional delegation remained heavily weighted in the Republicans' favor, thirteen to three, but several incumbents saw their percentages of the vote decline to an alarming extent.

Democratic representation in the legislature, on the other hand, registered a considerable gain. Democrats in the state Senate increased from five to nine, and in the lower house, from sixty-two to eighty. Particularly significant among the names of the new members of the House were those of New Immigrant extraction. In 1926 only three of the sixty-two Democrats elected had names of other than Irish or Yankee connotation, but in 1928 eleven of the eighty victors were of New Immigrant stock. Many of these Newer American Democrats came from constituencies formerly represented by Republicans of either old-stock or New Immigrant lineage. Their election signified again that infusion of new blood into the party which accompanied the Al Smith upheaval.

Finally, in the voting on referenda, the people of the Commonwealth recorded an overwhelming opposition to Prohibition and approved a measure authorizing admission charges at Sunday sports events. In the thirty-six state senatorial districts (out of forty) in which the Prohibition question appeared on the ballot, the aggregate majority in favor of repeal totaled nearly 285,000.[86] Only two districts, in rural parts of the state, favored the dry side of the issue. The Sunday sports measure, denounced by evangelical Protestant ministers and many old-stock "reformers" as an infringement on their "American" moral code,[87] received a state-wide majority of over 335,000 votes. Only three rural counties returned majorities against the proposal. The outcome on these matters, too, fittingly accompanied the rise of a new political order in Massachusetts.

Nationally, the Democrats' strategy of catering to the party's Newer American wing in 1928 was no more productive of success than the foredoomed candidacy of John W. Davis had been in 1924. Al Smith carried only six states in what remained of the formerly solid South, plus Rhode Island and Massachusetts. Nevertheless, throughout the country Smith attracted to the Democratic standard hundreds of thousands of Newer American voters who had not been found there before. This was the "Al Smith revolution" which, in the aggregate vote of the nation's twelve largest cities, turned a 1924 Republican plurality of 1,252,000 votes into a 38,000-vote Democratic plurality in 1928.[88]

At the same time, hundreds of thousands of old-stock Americans also came to the polls for the first time and voted for Herbert Hoover, while others who had voted Democratic all their lives deserted the party in favor of the G.O.P. This was the old-stock "counterrevolution" which put Virginia, North Carolina, Florida, and Texas in the Republican column.

Hoover overwhelmed his opponent in both popular and electoral votes, signifying that the older people had successfully defended their household gods against the assault of the newcomers. "America is not yet dominated by its great cities," a Minnesota newspaper exulted. "Control of its destinies still remains in the smaller communities and rural regions, with their traditional conservatism and solid virtues. . . Main Street is still the principal thoroughfare of the nation." [89]

Smith's defeat indicated that a candidate whose appeal was directed primarily to Newer Americans had little prospect of victory, just as La Follette's experience four years earlier revealed the futility of an appeal limited almost entirely to agrarian radicals. There were too many old-stock Americans left in the country, and Republican economic doctrines were still too attractive to many Newer Americans in prosperous parts of the nation. Nonetheless, Smith's candidacy gave the new-stock citizens an adequate voice for the first time in the nation's history, and it was not likely that this voice would be quiet thereafter. Politicians would have to heed the aspirations of the Newer Americans in future elections.

While the Al Smith revolution raised the Democratic percentage of the vote in a number of states where Newer Americans were strong, it was most effective in Massachusetts and Rhode Island, where economic depression left Republican New Immigrants freer than they were elsewhere to express their preference for the Democratic nominee. In Massachusetts the unity achieved by the Irish Democrats and the "newer races" surpassed all expectations. The union of those two elements constituted the backbone of the new Democratic coalition which, with the aid of its labor, liberal, and disaffected old-stock Republican components, was on the verge of reshaping the Commonwealth's politics.

Though some Massachusetts Republicans saw nothing but

the darkness of their immediate situation, most took a more optimistic view of the future. Attributing the Democrats' gains to the ethnic aspects of Smith's campaign, Republican leaders trusted that they were merely temporary. "Strike out all the non-political factors, the prejudices and passions which have marked the campaign in this state," declared the *Boston Herald*, "and the net result is a state as fundamentally Republican as it ever has been." [90]

The *Herald's* notion, that ethnic politics and cultural liberalism were somehow "nonpolitical factors," was wrong; for indeed those were the most significant issues of American politics in the 1920's. [91] Similarly mistaken was the belief that such issues could be stricken out entirely in future political contests. Nonetheless, Republican optimists had some reason for their hopefulness, especially as far as presidential elections were concerned. For it was unlikely that the Democratic Party would again nominate Al Smith, or any other man so completely identified with the Newer America, for a long time to come. The "nonpolitical factors" which had embarrassed the Bay State Republicans in the Smith campaign might thus subside, and then the G.O.P., on the basis of more "traditional" issues, could hope to win back the allegiance of some of its former and essential allies among the newer groups. "It is inevitable that, with the influences of 1928 at work, a great many persons who have been Republican, and who will be Republican, should have gone for a little outing behind the Democratic donkey," the *Herald* contended. "But the holiday will be short, the picknickers will return for their regular home fare, and Massachusetts will stand where she has stood always." [92]

The editors could not be expected to foresee that a new political era had begun in the Bay State, and that the picknickers would not begin to return until twenty-four years had passed.

Chapter Seven

Bread, Beer, and Beacon Hill

T HE political turmoil of 1928 gave way, in the following year, to a final fling of prosperity across the nation. The stock market climbed to new heights, and even New England tagged along in the wake of "good times." Massachusetts' enjoyment of the boom was limited, however; for while centers of diversified industry like Boston, Cambridge, Springfield, Worcester, and Pittsfield saw notable increases in employment and production, signs of improvement in shoe and textile cities were scanty or nonexistent.[1] Nevertheless, the upsurge of economic activity throughout the country encouraged optimists in even the least blessed of the state's textile centers. In August of 1929 the *Fall River Herald News* felt certain that the "fortunate wave" of prosperity engulfing the nation must soon sweep over that city. "The industrial tide has actually turned and is coming in with a rush."[2] Such sentiments heartened those who hoped to see the Commonwealth return to its Republican allegiance at the state and senatorial elections in 1930.

Then, in October, came the stock market crash. From Washington President Hoover assured the country that its basic economic condition was sound and announced plans for a tax reduction as a token of confidence. The deflation of stock values, according to most Republican observers, re-sulted merely from overspeculation. The plungers would be hurt, but the flurry would soon pass leaving the rest of the nation unharmed. "The wind that blew through Wall Street," according to the *Boston Transcript*, would actually prove beneficial to the American economy in the long run.[3]

Despite the optimism of the country's leaders and the pledges of its industrialists, workers soon felt the effects of recession. Between October and November 1929 the number of industrial wage earners employed in Massachusetts dropped 4.4 per cent and aggregate weekly pay rolls decreased 8.0 per cent.[4] The startling decline in industrial employment be-tween the month of the crash and the first month of the new year was traced by statistics of the state's Department of Labor and Industries: October 1929, 573,445; November, 552,402; December, 531,077; January 1930, 502,813.[5] On February 3 Boston's first unemployment demonstration took place when a motley crowd of about a hundred people marched on the State House carrying banners: "We Want Work!"[6]

Following Hoover's lead, Governor Frank Allen in De-cember urged Bay State employers to maintain employment and wage standards. Conforming with the President's appeal for acceleration of public works construction as a means of taking up the slack in employment, Allen instigated a survey of the projects contemplated by the cities and towns of Massa-chusetts for the coming year. In addition, the Governor's budget message of January 1930 included provision for an expanded program of state building and highway construc-tion, to be carried out on a pay-as-you-go basis.[7]

The turn of economic events in the latter part of 1929 posed a dismal contrast to the expectations of Bay State Re-publican leaders, yet — trusting that the measures inaugurated by Hoover and Allen would soon end the recession — they were not deeply perturbed. On February 3 of the election year the *Boston Transcript's* Washington correspondent reported that the stock market trouble of a few months ago was "no longer of concern," and that President Hoover felt sure 1930 would be as good a year, economically, as 1929. The "Hoover panic" had "died a-borning," the reporter concluded, and Democrats would have to look elsewhere for ammunition to use in the fall elections.[8]

More disconcerting to Massachusetts Republicans than the economic situation was a matter which seemed to affect more directly the structure and strength of the party — the Prohibition issue. The overwhelming wet majority in the 1928 Prohibition referendum precipitated a crucial battle between Republican wets and drys for party control. Throughout 1929 Republican anti-Prohibitionists helped collect signatures for an iniative-referendum measure repealing the state's Prohibition enforcement act, to be introduced at the 1930 meeting of the legislature. Then in December, when Senator Gillett announced that he would not stand for re-election in 1930, Eben Draper declared himself a candidate to be Gillett's successor. Draper had opposed B. Loring Young, the machine's candidate for senator in the 1928 primary, on a platform featuring modification of the Volstead Law. The wets rallied to his support again and promised to make the 1930 senatorial primary another test of anti-Prohibition strength in the ranks of the G.O.P.[9]

The party's dry wing, on the other hand, was equally active. Assailing the initiative measure for repeal of the state's Prohibition law as an act of disloyalty to President Hoover, dry spokesmen demanded that the Republican state committee back up the enforcement planks of the state and national platforms by denouncing the repeal movement. In July

1929 delegates from twelve counties attending the Northfield Foreign Missionary Conference threatened to bolt the party, should it fail to uphold the President's position on Prohibition. And in January 1930, after announcement of Draper's moist candidacy, a group of dry Republican women urged Mrs. Elizabeth Tilton of Cambridge to run as an independent candidate for senator if neither party nominated a real enforcer in the primaries.[10]

In the middle of the controversy stood National Committeeman Louis Liggett, State Chairman Amos Taylor, and the other directors of the once-powerful Republican organization of Coolidge days. That organization had been dry, at least officially, through the greatest part of the 1920's, but now it faced a dilemma. In the summer of 1929 State Chairman Taylor sought to solve the matter by suggesting that, after all, Prohibition was not really a party issue and should not be counted as such by Bay State Republicans, be they for or against liquor. Prohibition, like religion, he declared, must be eliminated from politics if the Republicans were to carry the state again. A short while later National Committeeman Liggett said the same thing and then added: "These are individual matters. We have a right to go to church where we want to and when we want to or not at all, and to take a drink if we want to." [11] But to Prohibitionists such utterances were heretical. Prohibition *was* a party matter, they insisted to the state chairman: the Democrats were the wet party and the G.O.P. must remain the dry party. The uproar against Liggett's pronouncement was even more violent, and calls for his resignation as national committeeman came thick and fast from dry sources.[12]

Wet and dry Republicans alike, then, seemed resolved that the party choose between them. Governor Allen decided early to abide by the dry cause, and denounced the proposed repeal of the state enforcement act in his message opening the 1930 legislative session.[13] But when the election year began, the problem regarding the party's senatorial nomination was far from settled. The search for a solution engrossed the attention of Republican leaders through the first weeks of 1930 — even while employment in the state's manufacturing industries descended to the lowest level of the decade.

The perplexities facing the Republicans were accentuated by the outcome of a special election held February 11, 1930, in the Second Congressional District to fill a vacancy caused by the death of Representative William K. Kaynor. By a vote of 31,170 to 24,748 the district — which had never been represented by a Democrat in the forty years of its existence — chose William Granfield over Frederick Griggs, the Republican candidate. Prohibition played a large part in the campaign. Griggs, formerly counted a dry, bowed to the fact that the district had returned a wet majority of 25,000 in the 1928 referendum and promised to vote for repeal or modification if the matter came up in Congress. Nevertheless, he had the support of the W.C.T.U., which preferred him to his dripping-wet Democratic opponent. And he lost the election. Consequently, the *Boston Transcript* concluded, "it is time to utter the plain truth, that the voters of Massachusetts are out of sympathy with the President in his efforts to make the country dry by compulsion, although heartily supporting him on virtually every other issue." [14]

Other observers emphasized a different aspect of the contest, however. The Second District embraced the industrial cities of Springfield, Chicopee, and Northampton, and manufacturing towns like West Springfield, Easthampton, and Ludlow in the Connecticut River Valley. During the campaign Granfield made much of "hard times," and Senator Walsh toured the district urging votes for the Democratic candidate "as a protest against the refusal of the Republican Administration to at least admit there is something wrong with the country economically." Subsequently Granfield carried each of the industrial cities and towns in the district. Post-election statements by Walsh and Democratic Chairman Donahue declared that economic conditions, rather than Prohibition, had turned the trick for their man.[15]

Although interpreters of the upset disagreed over the relative importance of the two factors that brought it about, the net result made it clear that unemployment and Prohibition together presented serious obstacles to the Republicans' plans for returning Massachusetts to her G.O.P. moorings. Recognition of the importance of the depression issue came a few days after Granfield's victory when ex-Senator and former National Chairman William M. Butler, the organization's choice for the 1930 senatorial nomination, in announcing his candidacy declared that economic conditions would be the most important consideration in the fall campaign. And as "an immediate sequel" to the Second District balloting, Governor Allen conferred with his department heads on the unemployment situation, directed that the state's public works program be pushed ahead of schedule, and again urged municipal governing bodies to co-operate in advancing necessary public improvements as a means of relieving the jobless.[16]

The heads of the Republican machine also prepared to "liberalize" the party's stand on Prohibition for the forthcoming senatorial contest. Butler, State Chairman Taylor, and other leaders worked out a declaration favoring modification of the Volstead Act, which the organization's candidate was to unveil at a press conference on March 14. But at the last minute Butler, yielding to pressure from the drys, changed his mind, and Taylor was amazed to read in the newspapers that the ex-Senator had come out with a bone-dry statement

— against repeal of the Eighteenth Amendment, against modification of the Volstead Law, and against repeal of the Massachusetts enforcement act. Soon after Butler's pronouncement, Eben Draper changed his position from one of modification of the Volstead Law to outright repeal of the Eighteenth Amendment, which he now condemned as a failure.[17]

Contrary to the wishes of some organization leaders, then, the senatorial primary was turned into a wet-and-dry fight that could only detract from the party's strength regardless of the outcome. While Butler's position as a charter member of the Coolidge coterie held for him the support of the machine managers, his staunchest backers were the old-stock women's groups and other drys who loudly proclaimed their determination to desert the G.O.P. should Butler be defeated. Draper, on the other hand, enjoyed the support of the proliferating anti-Prohibition organizations in the state. Spearheading his campaign were a group of wets from the younger aspiring party leaders — men like Christian Herter, Henry Cabot Lodge, Jr., and Mayor Sinclair Weeks of Newton — who were growing restive under continued domination of the party by the "Old Guard" of Calvin Coolidge's day. Throughout the summer Draper insisted that Prohibition was the matter uppermost in people's minds, while Butler told his audiences that the state of business was the paramount issue of the day. When the debate ended and Republican voters went to the polls on September 16, the organization candidate defeated Draper by a narrow margin — 163,336 to 156,745. A third contender, the erratic Mayor Andrew J. "Bossy" Gillis of Newburyport, who had announced himself as "moist," received nearly 23,000 votes.[18]

The outcome of the voting had two important results. It destroyed the idea that the drys still exercised an overwhelming control of the Republican primary. Even more significantly, it sent the G.O.P. into the 1930 campaign labeled as the dry party. That such a label constituted a handicap, in a state that voted so strongly against Prohibition in 1928, seemed clear.

The Republicans' troubles heartened Massachusetts Democrats, whose own morale remained high during the year following the Smith campaign. The subsequent evaporation of "Republican prosperity" across the nation provided new grist for the Democratic mill. So did ex-Senator Butler's decision to remain dry, and the Republican legislature's rejection of the initiative bill repealing the state Prohibition law at the 1930 session.[19] Moreover, the "unprogressive" record of the legislature elected in 1928 invited attack. The coalition of Democratic lawmakers and working-class Republican representatives from the mill districts, who supported labor and welfare reform measures, was stronger now than at any previous time in the 1920's. But they were still outvoted by the bulk of the Republican membership coming from the towns and suburban cities, who continued to think in terms of normalcy. During 1929 and 1930 the votes of the latter group accounted for the legislature's rejection of bills providing for a noncontributory old-age pension system, increased workmen's compensation benefits, restrictions on the use of injunctions in labor disputes, the outlawing of "yellow dog" contracts, and stricter regulation of public utility corporations.[20] The Democrats prepared to hammer away at those issues, confident that their Newer American constituents' support for economic liberalism, which Al Smith and General Cole had reawakened in 1928, would be even stronger in the depression-ridden year 1930.

If the abundance of issues encouraged the Democrats, so did the apparent persistence of the unity and organization achieved on Smith's behalf in 1928. State Chairman Frank Donahue won unanimous re-election when the state committee met in 1929, and thereafter, contrary to the practice of his predecessors, the chairman made the rounds of the Commonwealth bolstering attempts to perfect local party machinery.[21]

Co-operating with Donahue in his effort to hold the new Democratic organization intact was the Jeffersonian Society, established in May 1929 by the advanced liberals and "intellectual" Democrats summoned to active political service the previous fall. Dedicated to economic and cultural liberalism — "the principles of Alfred E. Smith" — the society aimed at aligning the independent voters of Massachusetts with the Democratic Party. LaRue Brown headed the organization, and prominent among its charter members were Joseph Ely, Mrs. Jessie Woodrow Sayre, Ray Stannard Baker, and a number of Harvard University professors including Zechariah Chaffee, William Yandell Elliott, and Benjamin F. Wright.[22] In 1929 and 1930 the Jeffersonians held frequent meetings and heard leading Democrats of national reputation discuss the issues facing the country's liberals. Though some Boston Irish Democrats looked askance at the new "high-brow" organization, and although James Michael Curley was absent from its meetings, Chairman Donahue and other old-timers like John F. Fitzgerald took part in its affairs. After all, the votes of the high-brows had helped carry the state, and it was encouraging to know they were still with the party.

Finally, the outcome of elections in 1929 and 1930 also cheered the Democrats. In November 1929 Curley defeated the candidate of the Good Government Association to become, for the third time, mayor of Boston. That Curley's candidacy this time enjoyed the acquiescence of all the party leaders seemed to augur well for Democratic unity in the future and helped make his plurality the largest he had yet received. In other mayoral elections the following month, the outpouring of voters recruited originally for the Smith campaign gave the city of Springfield its first Democratic mayor in seventeen years, while in Somerville the Democrats took control of city hall for the first time in history.[23] Granfield's victory in the Second Congressional District in February 1930 gave a finishing touch to the party's off-year success.

But in the end, the scent of victory pervading the Democratic camp threatened to undo the party's favorable prospects. The likelihood of election whetted the office-holding ambitions of politicians and increased their competition for places on the ballot. By the middle of 1930 so many candidacies had been launched for the state primary that Chairman Donahue was rumored ready to resign in disgust. With this situation came a recurrence of the factionalism that had plagued the party earlier in the 1920's and which now menaced the unity achieved in 1928.

Five men were anxious to contend for the seat about to be vacated by Senator Gillett, but the lead went early to Marcus A. Coolidge. A wealthy manufacturer who had served a term as mayor of Fitchburg, Coolidge had been the nominee of the Wilson Democrats for lieutenant governor in 1920. By 1928 he was reconciled to Senator Walsh and the regular organization, however, and was appointed treasurer of the state committee for the Smith election. His service in that capacity, and his ability to finance a campaign and lend "racial balance" to the ticket, won him the backing of the Walsh-Donahue organization for the senatorial nomination in 1930, giving him a head start in the race.[24]

The real battle centered about the gubernatorial nomination. Leading the field in that contest were the old war-horse, John F. Fitzgerald, and Joseph Ely, the Yankee Democrat from the western part of the state who had been "Dooley-ized" out of the nomination for lieutenant governor in 1926. Chairman Donahue, among others, felt that Fitzgerald's appearance on the ballot would not enhance the party's chances of victory in November. But Honey Fitz's hold on the Boston Irish, and the support accorded him by Martin Lomasney and Mayor Curley, seemed to assure his nomination.[25]

Curley's motives in supporting Fitzgerald, with whom he had feuded long and bitterly, were not unmixed and gave Fitzgerald's candidacy a special significance. The Mayor, according to common reports, was not particularly interested in seeing Governor Allen unseated in 1930. Curley expected to run for governor himself in 1932, when the Republican escalator was scheduled to bring forth as the G.O.P. candidate Lieutenant Governor William A. Youngman — an interloper who was out of favor with the party organization and was expected to be a weak candidate. Interference with the completion of Governor Allen's traditional two-term stint might upset the Republican promotional system and thus undo Curley's own scheme of advancement. Moreover, Curley and Honey Fitz supposedly had an understanding whereby Fitzgerald, if elected, would make way voluntarily for the Mayor's candidacy in 1932. For Curley, then, Fitzgerald's nomination seemed the best method of paving his own way to the State House.[26]

Donahue's efforts to induce Fitzgerald to withdraw from the race were ineffective, and in August and September the battle raged. Ely attacked Fitzgerald and Curley as men "who believe the party a chattel to be controlled by a private arrangement, or a thing to be delivered to the opposition for a price." They responded in kind. A third contender, Boston Irishman John Cummings, enlivened things further by recalling Ely's support of Woodrow Wilson and the League of

Nations at the 1919 state convention — proof that Ely was a foe of the Irish.[27]

Then, on September 9, Fitzgerald announced from a hospital bed his retirement from the contest. This seemed to open the way for Ely's nomination, but James Michael Curley had other ideas. Claiming that neither Ely nor Cummings measured up to gubernatorial stature, Curley urged that Democratic voters nominate Fitzgerald anyway and then let the state committee pick a substitute candidate after the primary. The Mayor's suggestion was a desperate attempt to salvage his plans for 1932 and was denounced as such by Martin Lomasney and other party leaders, who now rallied to Ely's side. Nevertheless, in the remaining week before the balloting Curley and his followers waged a strong campaign on Fitzgerald's behalf, pleading that a victory might make him well enough to run himself, and repeating the charges first leveled against Ely by Cummings. According to Curley: "No Irishman worthy of the name can cast a vote for Ely after the facts of his black record of opposition to their race are publicly known." [28]

The climax came the day before the election when Chairman Donahue, abandoning all pretense of neutrality, denounced Curley's "nefarious plan." That evening Donahue took to the airwaves and leveled a series of blasts at the Mayor, condemning his use of the "Irish issue" and charging, among other things, that Curley was trying to re-elect Governor Allen, that in 1928 Curley refused to help the state committee raise money for the Al Smith campaign, and that Curley's presence on the ballot in 1924 was the sole reason for Senator Walsh's defeat that year. Thus far Walsh had kept his name from figuring prominently in the primary contest, and even prolonged a vacation in Cuba to avoid involvement. But now

Donahue asked that every friend of the Senator join in defeating Curley's scheme on election day.

As the state chairman concluded his broadcast, Curley and his cohorts swarmed into the studio. Foul names were exchanged, and before Donahue managed to escape, blows were struck. A member of Donahue's party was "kneed in the groin" and threatened to have the Mayor arrested for assault. At midnight the state chairman was back on the radio relating what had happened. "The Democrats of Massachusetts should know what kind of a man this Curley is," Donahue concluded. "Tonight he reverted to type. . . Tonight he gave the finishing touch by showing himself as Curley, the thug." At eleven o'clock the next morning — election day — the Mayor was on the air answering Donahue's charges and denying that he had assaulted the state chairman: "Nobody assaults little children like Mr. Donahue, he is too small to notice. . ." [29]

When the votes were counted Ely defeated Fitzgerald 117,548 to 84,744. Marcus A. Coolidge won the senatorial nomination and still a third Yankee Democrat, Strabo V. Claggett, was nominated for lieutenant governor, the bulk of the vote being split among three Irish contenders. Also significant was the defeat of Joseph Santosuosso by an Irishman, Chester O'Brien, in the race for the secretary of state position on the ballot.[30]

The bitterness generated in the Democratic primary gratified the Republicans, who talked much about the emasculation Ely would receive at the hands of Curley partisans in November. But the Mayor, as usual, proved magnanimous in defeat. At the Democratic state convention two weeks later, Curley delivered one of his more grandiloquent orations lavishing praise on the members of the state ticket, including the gubernatorial candidate. Having finished, he presented Ely a check for a thousand dollars to aid his campaign, amid cheers from the delegates. (The check, it was soon discovered, was made out to the Democratic city committee of Boston, which Curley controlled, rather than the Walsh-Donahue-Ely-dominated state committee.) [31]

The flare-up of factionalism simmered down, then. Temporarily, at least, a semblance of party unity was preserved.

The Democratic ticket for 1930 was unique in that those leading it — Coolidge for senator, Ely for governor, and Claggett for lieutenant governor — were as thoroughly "Anglo-Saxon" as their Republican counterparts, Butler, Allen, and Youngman. Even the Boston Irish were unrepresented at the ticket's head, and the one New Immigrant who competed for a minor place had been defeated in the primary. Encouraged by these circumstances, Republicans made a strenuous effort to recapture their lost allies among the "newer races." According to a reputable Springfield newspaper the G.O.P. spent "barrels of money" in the industrial centers, and foreign-language broadcasts in French, Polish, Lithuanian, and other tongues were beamed out over the state's leading radio network. In 1929 and 1930 Governor Allen gave seats on the Superior Court to Abraham Pinanski and Raoul Beaudreau, and a number of other Newer Americans — including Frank Vera, a Portuguese-American attorney of New Bedford — were commissioned to municipal and district courts. Consequently, Allen's record of judicial appointments received particular attention from Republican spokesmen during the campaign.[32]

Moreover, after the Second Congressional District's special election, in which Granfield won the bulk of the Polish-American voters who counted heavily in the area, Governor Allen appointed Frank Lewandowski a justice of the Holyoke

Municipal Court, and federal authorities made Harry J. Meleski of Worcester an assistant United States attorney.[33] Lewandowski was the first judge of Polish extraction in the Commonwealth's history, as Frank Vera was the first Portuguese-American one. In November the Republicans made a concerted attempt to unseat Granfield, importing former Representative John Sosnowski of Detroit to campaign in the Connecticut River Valley. Another attraction at G.O.P. rallies in the Second District was Al Simmons (Aloysius Harry Szymanski), the popular outfielder of the Philadelphia Athletics who had just won the American League batting title.[34]

Though Stanley Wisnioski, Julian Rainey, Edmond Talbot, and other Democratic leaders of the "newer races" again took to the field, the Democratic ticket in 1930 lacked the special appeals it bore to Newer Americans in years when David I. Walsh or Alfred E. Smith headed it. If Yankees Ely and Coolidge were to retain the votes of the Irish and the New Immigrants, they could not rely on ethnic considerations for doing so. To a large extent the so-called "nonpolitical factors," about which the Republicans complained in the Smith election, had been eliminated. The 1930 campaign would be conducted more strictly on the basis of traditional, "political" issues.

In the senatorial race Coolidge and Butler, both manufacturers, traded blows over the merits of their respective labor records, with the Democratic nominee coming out on top by winning endorsement from the Massachusetts A.F. of L.[35] Former Senator Butler, meanwhile, contrasted his experience in office-holding with his opponent's lack of it, and promised to carry on the Massachusetts tradition of "ability in the Senate" embodied in "Webster, Hoar, Lodge, Crane and

Walsh." [36] In the contest for the governorship, Ely and Allen both spoke of the need for increased state regulation of public utility corporations. The Democratic platform also promised enactment of the welfare and labor reform measures rejected by the legislature in the past two years. Governor Allen, on the Republican's behalf, acclaimed the improvements in the Commonwealth's institutional facilities made during his first administration.[37]

While such matters provided material for campaign speeches and advertisements, Prohibition and the depression were the things people talked about most in the fall of 1930. On the Prohibition issue, the Democratic candidates too did a lot of talking. Late in September Ely promised to take the lead, if elected, in convoking a national constitutional convention to repeal the Eighteenth Amendment should Congress refuse to act.[38] In the senatorial contest, where the brunt of the liquor issue was expected to be felt, Marcus Coolidge pledged to work for immediate modification of the Volstead Act until repeal could be effected. In return Coolidge won endorsement from the Constitutional Liberty League and other wet organizations, whose membership included many thirsty old-stock Republicans.[39]

Butler and Allen, on the other hand, maintained complete silence on the issue. Wet Republicans would have a chance to vent their sentiments in the referendum on repeal of the state Prohibition act, and perhaps — if the Republican candidates muffled their dryness during the campaign — they would remain loyal to the party when it came to voting for offices. However, the G.O.P. organization did make a more direct bid for the allegiance of its wet wing in the Prohibition plank adopted at the state convention. Pledging strict enforcement of all laws, including the Eighteenth Amendment, the platform then went on to affirm the right of citizens to work for a change in the Constitution. "All present waited breath-lessly for the prohibition plank," said the *Springfield Republi-can*, "and, as the wets cheered it immediately after the drys cheered it, the plank was felt to be a masterpiece. . ." [40] Sub-sequently, Mayor Weeks of Newton and others who backed Eben Draper in the primary made their peace with the or-ganization and worked for Butler. But Draper himself de-nounced the plank as a "meaningless straddle," making it ob-vious that he did not intend to vote for the Republican senatorial candidate in November.[41] A substantial number of Draper's supporters perhaps felt the same way, and largely for that reason betting odds in Boston ran consistently in Coolidge's favor throughout the campaign.

While the Republican nominees were silent on Prohibition, those who retained faith in the Eighteenth Amendment were not. As far as Massachusetts was concerned, the drys were making their last desperate stand behind Allen, Butler, and the state enforcement law, and they viewed the impending election as the most serious since 1860. "The dangerous Reds are in our midst," declared one dry pronouncement, "men and women who defy and break down the law passed by the great majority of the people. To yield to the forces of lawlessness means crime in our great un-American cities." The National Women's Committee for Law Enforcement, headed by Mrs. Henry W. Peabody of Beverly, designated the Sunday before election a day of prayer throughout the country, so that the people of the Bay State might come "to the help of the Lord on November 4." [42]

Nevertheless, though Mrs. Peabody was apt to disagree, most observers concurred in the final weeks of the campaign that economic conditions had outstripped Prohibition as the main issue of the election. Early in March President Hoover had declared that the worst effects of the stock market crash would be a thing of the past in sixty days. At the end of two months, however, the United States Bureau of Labor Statistics' index of employment in the nation's manufacturing industries, which stood at 90.5 the month the President spoke, had declined two more points. By October it was down to 79.9.[43]

Acceleration of the federal government's public works program provided some jobs. But the President turned a deaf ear to those who demanded that the government's construction schedule be expanded beyond the limits of the budget. That would involve either a rise in taxes or deficit financing, the Administration reasoned, both of which must be avoided. By mid-October it was evident that a hard winter lay ahead, and the President appointed two new committees: one to supervise existing federal work-giving projects and another to mobilize local and voluntary relief efforts across the nation. Creation of neither agency involved any new outlay of federal funds to provide employment or relief.[44]

By the time the 1930 campaign got underway, then, the stock market crash had turned into a full-scale depression. Since Butler and Marcus Coolidge both acknowledged this to be the leading concern of the country, debate over its origins and the assigning of responsibility for it dominated the senatorial contest. According to Coolidge, the Administration's failure to control the orgy of speculation in 1928 and 1929 played a large part in bringing about the economic slump, as did the Hawley-Smoot Tariff, which produced retaliation abroad and a subsequent decline in American exports. Butler and other Republican spokesmen, finding their earlier "overspeculation" theory of the crisis untenable in the face of Democratic attack, now resorted to other arguments. The depression was a world-wide phenomenon, they said, with its roots going back to the World War. It was an *economic*

Alvan T. Fuller leaving the State House after the inauguration of his successor, Governor Frank G. Allen, January 1929.

Commissioner of Conservation W. A. L. Bazeley, Governor Frank G. Allen, and Speaker of the Massachusetts House of Representatives Leverett Saltonstall in conference, March 1930.

Al Smith amid throng during his visit to Boston before the 1930 election. Wearing glasses in the front seat is Democratic State Chairman Frank J. Donahue; seated in front of Smith and wearing a derby is Joseph Ely, the Democratic gubernatorial candidate.

Mr. and Mrs. Al Smith, with a group of welcomers, on their 1930 visit to Boston.

depression, not a political, "Republican" depression. Democrats pointed out that the G.O.P. had not been so hesitant
to dub the vaunted "prosperity" that preceded the crash "Republican." [45]

Such debate had little constructive value. As for remedying
the situation, ex-Senator Butler revived the idea of a national
forty-eight-hour law as a means of bolstering Massachusetts'
economy, if not the rest of the nation's.[46] His Democratic
opponents had little more to offer. Charging that President
Hoover was not fighting the depression hard enough, they
insisted that he do more without specifying what should be
done. Mayor Curley asked votes for Coolidge as a protest
against a President who "does nothing to relieve unemployment save to give the people proclamations and commissions."
Senator Walsh stressed that the country was waiting for
leadership and was anxious to follow it when it should come.
"Just as we look to our Commander-in-Chief to lead and direct
us and to say what is to be done in time of war," he told the
national A.F. of L. convention assembled in Boston, "so we
ask for the same effort in a domestic crisis that is just as bad
as war." Hoover's failure to provide that leadership, according
to the Democrats, called for a rebuke at the polls.[47]

The depression's effect on Massachusetts' economy was
reflected in the downward trend of the index of New England
business activity compiled by the Federal Reserve Bank of
Boston. Various components of the index showed marked declines for the year 1930 from their 1929 levels. Cotton consumption in the six New England states was down 32 per
cent; wool consumption 23 per cent; shoe production 14 per
cent; consumption of electrical power for manufacturing purposes 19 per cent. The value of construction contracts awarded
was 11 per cent less than in 1929, department store sales declined 6 per cent, and the sale of automobiles was down 23

per cent. The number of wage earners employed in the Bay State's manufacturing industries continued to decline in the spring and early summer of 1930, with only a slight increase in the fall. While 510,878 persons were employed in March 1930, the figure for October was 469,218 (one year earlier, in October 1929, it had been 573,445).[48] Even as the number of totally unemployed persons steadily mounted, many of those who kept their jobs were taking home smaller pay envelopes. A Department of Labor and Industries survey covering a large portion of the state's labor force in October revealed that only 59 per cent of those included in the study were working full time.[49]

Governor Allen's determination to speed up the state's public works program following the Democratic upset in the Second Congressional District has already been mentioned. The appropriations bill pursuant to the Governor's budget message was rushed through the legislature in record time, and when the 1930 campaign got under way, the state had awarded contracts for new building and highway construction totaling fifteen million dollars. In addition, Allen approved measures authorizing Boston and other cities to borrow money beyond their legal debt limits in order to foster their own public improvement projects. He also urged other places to follow the example of the municipalities that had established free local employment agencies where persons out of work might register. Finally, on October 27 the Governor announced appointment of a committee consisting of thirty-seven representatives of industry, labor, civic groups, and the churches, to co-operate with President Hoover's new national relief commission.[50]

Pointing to Mayor Curley's praise of his public works program earlier in the year, Allen contended in his campaign speeches that the state's expenditure on building projects in

1930 far exceeded the record of any recent administration. He stressed that the expansion had taken place entirely on a pay-as-you-go basis, without resort to borrowing. The Commonwealth's balanced budget had been maintained despite the emergency, and her financial integrity was unquestioned. Allen promised to continue efforts to provide jobs through public works in his next term of office.[51]

In his campaign to unseat Governor Allen, Joseph Ely felt his way warily, but finally became an advocate of deficit financing. Talk of unbalancing the budget was still regarded as heresy by many people, and it took a while for Ely to state definitely what was on his mind. At first he was content to say that his opponent had not done enough to fight the depression. Becoming more specific, Ely next accused the Governor of having spent for public works only the routine amounts appropriated at the beginning of the year, despite the deepening of the crisis since January. Finally, just a few days before the election, he charged that Allen had merely "passed the buck" to the mayors and selectmen, just as the President had passed it to the governors. If the Commonwealth's financial rating was as high as the Governor claimed it to be, Ely demanded, "I'd like to know why the credit of the State wasn't resorted to some months ago and roads and buildings in addition — in addition, I repeat, to the routine program weren't built as a means of helping the present critical unemployment situation." In the end, the Democratic nominee had launched a direct attack against the golden calf of the 1920's — the balanced budget, the hallmark of "economy and sound administration." [52]

As the economic issue came to dominate the campaign and as Ely's aggressiveness increased, observers acknowledged that he had made good progress in overcoming Allen's early advantage. But they found it hard to forecast the outcome, for by common report people seemed unusually indifferent to the noise and hullabaloo that accompanied the ending of the contest. The voters, according to most commentators, had made up their minds early in the campaign, and the speeches and rallies thereafter meant little.

Only Al Smith's appearance in Boston on October 29, repaying the debt he owed the Bay State Democrats from 1928, brought a show of enthusiasm — and that was a remarkable one. The Happy Warrior seemed only to have gained in popularity with the people of the Hub after his defeat, and "he rode through the streets like a conquering hero. . . . Even his dearest enemies admitted that he achieved a triumph such as no other living American could hope to achieve," in the state of Calvin Coolidge.[53]

Attempting to offset the effects of Smith's visit, Republican leaders persuaded the former President to make a radio broadcast for the party's ticket the evening of October 30 — his first political speech since leaving office. In retirement at Northampton, Calvin Coolidge had pondered the evils that befell the country after he left the White House in those happier days. But the message he gave the people that night was not an uplifting one: "I do not know of anything which the Federal or State governments have failed to do which either would have prevented the depression or now would cause a healthy revival of business." Of only one thing was he certain as he delivered his endorsement of Butler and Allen: "This is no time for rash experiments in men or measures." [54]

Five days later the voters of Massachusetts indicated their lack of sympathy with the ex-President's sentiments by sending both Republican candidates down to defeat.

Marcus Coolidge outdistanced former Senator Butler

651,939 to 539,226, winning 54.7 per cent of the two-party vote, a slight increase over the 54.1 per cent attained by Senator Walsh against B. Loring Young two years earlier. Joseph Ely's margin over Governor Allen was much smaller — 606,920 to 590,238. His vote represented a bare 50.7 per cent of the two-party total, but was enough to win Democratic control of the executive suite on Beacon Hill for the first time in fifteen years. The election also put two Irish Democrats named Hurley, Charles F. and Francis X., in office as state treasurer and state auditor. The only survivors on the Republican ticket were the candidates for lieutenant governor, secretary of state, and attorney general.[55]

In the legislature the Democrats increased their membership in the Senate from nine to ten, and in the House from eighty to ninety-seven. Congressman Granfield retained his seat in the Second District. All the incumbent Republican congressmen won re-election, but in most cases their margins were even slimmer than in 1928. Effects of the Democrats' newfound strength began to be felt on the level of county government, too, where for decades — with the exception of Suffolk County (Boston) — Republican "county rings" had been solidly entrenched in power. But now in Hampden County (Springfield, Holyoke, Chicopee, and environs) the Democrats unseated the incumbent Republican county treasurer who had held office for twenty-four years, and won control of all other county offices for the first time in history.[56]

Finally, by referendum, the people of Massachusetts repealed their Prohibition enforcement act. The anti-Prohibition vote was overwhelming: 649,592 to 368,544. Rural Franklin County, alone among the state's fourteen counties, returned a majority in favor of keeping the enforcement law on the statute books.

Analysis of election returns revealed none of that extensive "cutting" of Ely and Coolidge which the Republicans hoped would result from the Democratic primary fireworks. In Boston's Ward Eight, the home of Mayor Curley's old Tammany Club, Ely got 83.6 per cent of the two-party vote, actually one point higher than Al Smith's mark in 1928. In Irish Wards Two (Charlestown) and Six and Seven (South Boston), the Democratic gubernatorial candidate's percentage of the vote was 89.0, 87.3, and 85.2, which in each case was a mere two points below Smith's achievement two years earlier. In each of the wards cited, Marcus Coolidge's proportion of the two-party vote in the senatorial race was even higher than Smith's record. In Boston, and in other centers across the state, the two Yankee Democrats won unflinching support from the backbone of the party, the Irish Catholics.

The Democratic percentage of the vote in 1930, compared with 1928, declined in areas dominated by the New Immigrants, indicating that the hold of Ely and Coolidge on the votes of these people was not so firm as had been the case with Smith and Walsh. While Ely's proportion of the two-party vote in the state as a whole showed an increase of 0.2 over Smith's 1928 mark, in the aggregate vote of the ten other Newer American cities over 25,000 outside Boston (each having 70 per cent or more foreign-stock population), there was a decrease of 3.4 points. In those same places Marcus Coolidge's percentage of the aggregate senatorial vote was 1.5 points less than Walsh's 1928 record, although in the state as a whole Coolidge exceeded Walsh's mark by 0.6.

In Boston's two Jewish wards, for example, Ely got 53.3 and 57.2 per cent of the vote, whereas in 1928 Smith received 55.5 and 64.2 per cent respectively. In Chelsea's Jewish Ward Two the difference between Smith and Ely was a minus 5.7 percentage points. In Lowell's two French-Canadian wards Smith polled 65.6 and 66.3 per cent of the vote, and Ely but

61.3 and 60.6 per cent respectively. In Gardner's two French wards Ely's percentage fell below Smith's by approximately 5 points in each case. The French-dominated ward in Leominster gave Ely 77.7 per cent of the vote, which was 4.2 points less than Smith's mark. In Worcester Ely's percentage was less than Smith's in each of the city's three great melting-pot wards.

In view of their ethnic lineage, however, it was not surprising that Ely and Coolidge should fail to equal the achievements of Smith and Walsh in winning the support of the New Immigrants. Nevertheless, the two Yankee Democrats carried the areas which these citizens dominated, and by very substantial margins. Obviously the great bulk of the New Immigrant vote had stayed with the Democratic Party, to an extent that sorely disappointed the Republicans. In fact, according to one reporter who spent election night at G.O.P. headquarters, it was the announcement of returns from the Jewish precincts of Boston that convinced the directors of the Republican organization it was time to go home.[57]

Compensating for whatever losses the Democrats suffered among the Newer Americans in 1930 was the increased percentage of the vote they won in areas counted as old-stock Republican strongholds. Among the cities carried by Ely were Springfield, Everett, and Lynn, all of which had remained in the Republican column in the 1928 presidential election. Compared with Ely's increase of 0.2 over Smith's mark in the state as a whole, in the aggregate vote of the thirteen old-stock cities over 25,000 (each having more than 30 per cent "native white of native parentage" population), the increase was 1.1 points. In those same places Coolidge's bettering of Senator's Walsh's 1928 record was 1.4 points, compared with a 0.6 increase for the state as a whole. In many cities across the Commonwealth, then, the Democratic per-

centage of the vote increased in old-stock Republican wards
even as it decreased in Newer American wards.

Moreover, in the twenty-nine old-stock towns of 2,500 to
10,000 (each having 50 per cent or more "native white of
native parentage" population), Ely got 32.2 per cent of the
aggregate two-party vote compared to Smith's 29.3 per cent
in 1928, an increase of 2.9 points. The Democratic percentage
of the aggregate senatorial vote in those places rose from 34.4
to 36.4, or 2 points. In the case of both candidates the increase in the percentage of the vote won in these old-stock Republican towns exceeded the increase in the state as a whole.

The election of 1930 tested the cohesiveness of the Democratic coalition assembled by David I. Walsh and Al Smith,
and found it sufficient. On the whole, the coalition's Irish and
New Immigrant components responded well to a predominantly Yankee Democrat ticket. Labor leaders and advanced
liberals also continued their support of the party. In addition, the Democratic camp was reinforced by even more new
recruits from among the Commonwealth's old-stock Republicans. All this had been accomplished on the basis of "political" issues, unabetted by the ethnic, "nonpolitical factors"
of 1928.

"The American people have served notice upon the Republican machine at Washington that bread and beer are more
potent than proclamations and promises," declared James
Michael Curley after the election, and there was no denying
that the Prohibition and depression issues won the day for the
Democrats.[58] The outcome of the voting put an end to liquor
as a debatable matter in Bay State politics even though Arthur
Davis, director of the Constitutional Defense Committee, asserted that drys "do not take this as a defeat, but rather as a
challenge to greater effort." The chairman of the National

Women's Committee for Law Enforcement faced up to reality more squarely. Denouncing Massachusetts as an "outlaw State," Mrs. Henry W. Peabody announced that she was packing up her grandson and moving to Florida, promising not to return "until Massachusetts has found herself. . . If I must live in a Democratic state," she proclaimed in a parting shot, "it will have to be a dry Democratic state." Meanwhile, Eben Draper issued his statement: "I am thoroughly satisfied that the people of Massachusetts are against Federal Prohibition and the hypocrisy of candidates for high office." Some foresaw a reorganization of Republican machinery in which the younger elements of party leadership would "clean house" and "start things on a new and wetter basis." [59]

Nevertheless, most post-election statements cited economic conditions as the main cause of the Democrats' triumph. Here was a purely "traditional" issue that had turned out disastrously for the Republicans, and they acknowledged that only an alleviation of depression and unemployment could restore people's faith in the G.O.P. as "the party of prosperity." Butler, Allen, and Amos Taylor felt certain President Hoover's measures would soon bring about that result, and then the Bay State would return to the Republican fold. [60]

The victors, on the other hand, saw Massachusetts fast approaching the status of a Democratic paradise. For the first time in history the party held both United States senatorships. Half the state's elective constitutional offices, including above all the governorship, had passed under its control. On the state level the people of the Commonwealth had expressed their desire for an end to the ideals of "normalcy" in government, and for the inauguration of a time of "experiments in men and measures." Even in congressional, legislative, and county elections — where local popularity, local issues, and gerrymandering favored entrenched Republican incumbents — the Democrats had made considerable gains.

But the flare-up of personal rivalries that attended the Democratic primary in 1930 already indicated that actual or prospective success might be too much for the party to endure. The ascendancy of the Walsh-Donahue-Ely organization, which came with the election victory, turned James Michael Curley further out into the cold, and promised to intensify factional pretensions. Their comminglement with rivalries within the national Democratic organization, and the reinjection of ethnic considerations into the conduct of party affairs, would provide another test of the substantialness of the new Massachusetts Democratic coalition in 1932.

Chapter Eight

Action To Make Things Better

Aᴛᴛᴇᴍᴘᴛs to ward off depression in 1931 led both the Republican Administration in Washington and the Democratic administration in Massachusetts far beyond the concepts of proper government activity prevalent in the preceding decade of normalcy. Chief among the new policies was the idea that expensive public works programs, by relieving unemployment and sustaining purchasing power, might help end recession. But by the end of 1931 the economic barometer had dropped even further, and government spending seemingly produced only deficits and doubts. Consequently, some urged a return to "safe and sane" standards of government behavior. Others, however, asserted that the experiments with economic and social engineering had been too timid rather than too rash. In any case, confusion reigned by 1932, when the political problems of a presidential election year augmented the already baffling economic problems of the Great Depression.[1]

When Congress assembled in December 1930 after the midterm election, President Hoover reported that federal construction work already approved for the coming year stood at a record high, but he recommended nonetheless that Congress make additional appropriations for public works at its present sitting. The House and Senate complied quickly with the President's request, and within three weeks he signed a bill allotting $116,000,000 for new public improvements. Consequently, the White House announced, job-producing federal construction projects would total about $724,000,000 in 1931.[2]

Some Democrats and insurgent Republicans were unwilling to stop the spending at limits set by the President, however. Even as Hoover delivered his State of the Union message, returning congressmen and senators filed a flood of bills providing further expansion of the public works program for the jobless or direct outlays of federal money for relief payments to the destitute. Assailing the President's program as a "drop in the bucket," Senator David I. Walsh introduced a measure appropriating one hundred million dollars to reimburse states and municipalities for one-half their relief payments. According to the Administration's calculations, the various schemes expounded in Congress would increase federal expenditures by nearly four and a half billion dollars over the next two fiscal years, and the President was determined to resist them. On December 9 Hoover attacked such proposals as "raids on the public treasury" which would necessitate increased taxes or deficit financing, either of which would inevitably impede recovery. Members of Congress who sponsored fantastic unemployment legislation, he asserted, were playing politics at the expense of human misery.[3]

Though the presidential veto successfully blocked some spending proposals approved by the Congress which ended March 4, 1931, declining tax revenues thwarted Hoover's attempt to keep the budget balanced, and at the end of the fiscal year there was a deficit of $903,000,000.[4] By fall, moreover, the depression was deeper than ever. Between March — the best month of the year — and November 1931 the index of employment in the nation's manufacturing industries dropped from 75.9 to 67.1. In the same period the index of pay roll totals declined from 69.6 to 52.5, following a general breakdown of the wage-maintenance pledges made to the President in 1929.[5]

The persistence of hard times, coupled with the debut of deficit financing, prompted a reappraisal of government depression policy. Governor Franklin D. Roosevelt, seeking a tax increase from the New York legislature to finance a state relief fund, insisted that

> it would be very foolish to follow the precedent established by the Federal Government. . . We cannot and must not borrow against the future, because depression is today's problem. The government should pay expenses as they arise instead of creating a debt through long bond issues to be paid off in future years.[6]

Those who earlier questioned the usefulness of public works as a cure for depression now saw their doubts confirmed by the seemingly little effect produced thus far. Even some among the most vociferous early spenders were affected. One was Senator Walsh who, arriving in Washington for the opening session of the new Congress in December 1931, was more docile than a year earlier. "I found no sympathy in Massachusetts for extreme measures, nor is there any sentiment for radical action. The feeling seems to be that this is the time for caution and prudence." [7]

President Hoover's message to Congress on December 8 reflected the changed approach to the depression produced by the previous year's efforts to combat it. As a start toward bringing the budget in balance the President recommended an increase in taxes. Again he called for the practice of rigid economy, reiterating his opposition to any form of government "dole," since the matter of direct relief was being cared for by charitable and local government agencies in "true

American fashion." While expenditures on public works in 1932 would be continued at a level slightly higher than in 1931, Hoover recommended no sweeping intensification in that phase of government activity. Instead, federal efforts to solve the problem of unemployment directly, through public works construction, were to be subordinated to the tactic of revivifying the private sector of the economy, through creation of an Emergency Reconstruction Corporation and other credit-loosening measures.[8]

The course of anti-depression efforts on the national level in 1931 had its parallel in Massachusetts. Assuming office in January, Governor Joseph Ely soon made clear his status as a spender and an advocate of the public works cure. In his inaugural address Ely asked the legislature for an immediate appropriation of $300,000 to put men to work cleaning up the state's forests, roads, and buildings, and for a one-million-dollar emergency fund to be doled out as relief payments at the Governor's discretion either directly to individuals or to municipal welfare agencies. In addition, he urged that it be made easier for cities and towns to borrow outside their legal debt limits for public improvement projects. The capstone of the Governor's message was a proposal for a vast program of state road and building construction totaling twenty million dollars. Opposing a tax increase to finance the undertaking, Ely recommended instead an issue of long-term bonds to mature over the next fifteen years.[9]

The legislature soon complied with Ely's request for the $300,000 emergency work fund, and additional amounts were appropriated for such "boondoggling" projects several times during the session. The lawmakers also authorized various cities and towns to borrow a total of fourteen million dollars above their debt limits for public works projects, with Mayor Curley's Boston alone accounting for half that amount. Other parts of the Governor's program received less favor, however. The proposed million-dollar relief fund was quickly shelved and never materialized, the burden of direct relief payments remaining with the municipalities.[10]

But the proposal for abandonment of the pay-as-you-go principle aroused the greatest antagonism. Alvan T. Fuller and other Republican spokesmen attacked the Governor and his supporters as "lavish spenders," and urged that rigid economy in government — not bond issues — would cure the depression.[11] Nevertheless, a number of Republicans in the legislature saw need for some loosening of the state's financial policy in the crisis. With their aid — and a great deal of legislative back-scratching — the Democrats managed to push through a fragmentary version of Ely's public works program against the opposition of die-hard Republican conservatives. The legislation finally approved, however, reduced considerably the total volume of expenditures involved. Even more distasteful to the Governor was a provision that the improvements be financed by a tax increase and issuance of short-term notes maturing in four years, rather than the fifteen-year bonds he favored.[12]

The new administration's policies gave employment to thousands of men during 1931 — on a temporary basis clearing away underbrush in the forests and along the highways, or on more substantial public building projects. The cities and towns gave similar jobs to thousands of others. Nevertheless, after the second quarter of the year the depression in Massachusetts — as in the rest of the nation — became worse. The 454,987 persons employed in the Commonwealth's manufacturing industries in April, the best month of the year, declined to 423,395 by October, and in that month only 44.7 per cent of the workers covered in a Department of Labor and Industries survey were employed full time. By

December the number of wage earners was down to 387,551.[13]

Faced with discouraging conditions and a rising clamor against mounting debt, Governor Ely abandoned his earlier enthusiasm for spending, and announced late in October that he would return to the pay-as-you-go basis. When the legislature convened in January 1932, Ely presented a balanced budget featuring a tax increase, a 10 per cent cut in the salaries of state employees, and expenditures totaling three million dollars less than the budget recommended by his Republican predecessor in 1930. Though he felt that his 1931 program had been "temporarily helpful," the Governor acknowledged that it was based on a belief that conditions would be better in a year's time, and now a different tack must be pursued. The essential thing this year was to protect the credit of the state and its municipalities. To accomplish these ends the Governor recommended that cities be allowed to exceed their debt limits only in rare instances, and that the legislature exercise strict economy so as to safeguard the balanced budget. "It may seem to you that the recommendations of this message are a departure from the elaborate plans of unemployment relief advocated in 1931. They are. . ."[14]

Republican spokesmen had their chance to chortle at Ely's about-face. Addressing the lower house of the legislature, Speaker Leverett Saltonstall admonished: "Our Commonwealth does not want, nor does it expect us to give it legislative palliatives for its economic difficulties. Such methods of relief have proved of doubtful value. . . Our people, this year, desire certainty, not change."[15]

Election year, 1932, brought even greater distress. By July the national index of industrial employment was down to 55.2 from a mark of 82.7 in July 1930, while the pay roll index had slumped from 77.0 to 36.2 in the same period.[16] The de-

Al Smith speaking for Roosevelt at the Boston Arena, October 1932.

Democratic Senator Marcus A. Coolidge, Senator David I. Walsh, and Mayor Curley at a Boston Arena Roosevelt rally, October 31, 1932.

Mayor Curley stands beside Franklin D. Roosevelt in his campaign appearance at the Boston Arena, October 31, 1932. Governor Ely, his hair full of confetti, is at Roosevelt's left. Wide World Photo.

mand for direct relief presented by the swollen ranks of unemployed now clearly overtaxed the resources of those charitable and local government agencies which, according to uni-
versal opinion, bore primary responsibility in the matter. Late
in December 1931 the directors of the national Association of
Community Chests and the American Association of Public
Welfare Officials told a United States Senate committee that
private and local funds could no longer handle the job of relief, and federal aid must come. In June 1932 a conference of
mayors summoned by Mayor Frank Murphy of Detroit also
turned to the national government for help. Selecting James
Michael Curley head of a committee to present a petition to
President Hoover and congressional leaders, the mayors re-
quested an appropriation of five billion dollars for direct federal relief payments to distressed individuals during the coming
winter.[17]

Moreover, although public works spending had lost favor
with some leaders during 1931, others, like Mayor Curley,
retained faith in it. The trouble lay not in the expenditures
made for such purposes, the believers contended, but in the
fact that they were not of sufficient magnitude. As conditions
grew worse during 1932, the spenders again gained recruits.
It was evident now, however, that cities and states — their
treasuries depleted — could not finance programs large enough
to put the public works theory into full effect. Only the immense credit resources of the national government appeared
sufficient for the task. Consequently, the mayors' committee
headed by Curley also petitioned the nation's lawmakers for a
new five-billion-dollar federal public works program to be
paid for by a bond issue.

As election year wore on, then, Americans looked more and
more toward Washington in search of relief dollars, jobs, and
a solution to the country's economic dilemma. Agitators like

Father Coughlin joined in the chorus of demands for expanded federal activities and expenditures. In the summer months the Bonus Expeditionary Force assembled in the capital to petition for full payment of the veterans' bonus certificates. Even the Red Cross reversed its former position and now accepted donations of surplus wheat voted by Congress for distribution to the needy.[18]

Meanwhile, President Hoover in January 1932 secured passage of the Reconstruction Finance Corporation bill and his other measures for thawing out the nation's private credit resources.[19] Thereafter, until the adjournment of Congress in July, the President devoted much of his energy to warding off proposals for more drastic government action. Hoover remained unmoved in his opposition to full payment of the veterans' bonus, to proposals for a bond issue to finance any vast increase in public works, and to appropriations for direct federal relief payments.

In May, however, the White House unveiled a new plan involving an expansion of the R.F.C.'s resources, in order that it might *lend* money to states for relief purposes and for self-liquidating public works. Through the next two months the President parried the counterproposals of Democrats and insurgent Republicans, and in July — after the Republican national convention had nominated him for a second term — Hoover signed his measure.[20] With employment in the nation tumbling to new lows, the President took his record to the people.

While economic conditions occupied the attention of Republican leaders in Washington during 1931, Republican leaders in Massachusetts were busy in other ways preparing for the 1932 election. By the middle of the election year the issue regarding control of the G.O.P. organization had been decided in favor of the future, rather than the past. An attempt by the younger, anti-Prohibition element to remove State Chairman Amos Taylor from office following the defeat of Butler and Allen in 1930 proved abortive.[21] But when Louis Liggett decided to relinquish his post as national committeeman, the younger element made good their opportunity. The delegates at the 1932 national convention chose between two aspirants for Liggett's place: William M. Butler, the Old Guard candidate, and John Richardson, who headed the Volunteers for Hoover in 1928. Richardson won, and clearly the coterie of managers who had controlled Massachusetts Republicanism since Calvin Coolidge's rise to fame was on the way out.[22]

Meanwhile, the Bay State Republican Party buried the corpse of its dryness. After the disastrous election of 1930, wet Republicans insisted more strongly than ever that the state organization take a stand favoring revision of the Volstead Act, resubmission of the Eighteenth Amendment to the people for another vote, or outright repeal. The head of the Massachusetts W.C.T.U. demanded to know: "Where do you expect the drys to go?" Fewer Republican leaders seemed to care, however, and by the time the national convention met in June even former Governor Fuller and ex-Senator Butler had come out in favor of resubmitting the Eighteenth Amendment to the people. The drys' hold on the Bay State G.O.P., tenacious during the Coolidge years, was broken.[23]

President Hoover's continued allegiance to Prohibition during 1931 worried the leaders of the Massachusetts organization, and constituted the one qualification in their loyalty to him. The President himself relieved that situation, however, by deciding during the winter of 1932 that unfortunately the evil of drink could not be suppressed by federal law "in the present stage of human progress." Subsequently the national convention endorsed a plank, approved by the White House, favoring submission of a new constitutional amendment that would allow states desiring to do so to recover control of the liquor traffic within their borders, while guaranteeing federal protection for those that chose to honor the Eighteenth Amendment.[24]

With the troublesome Prohibition issue out of the way, the new leaders of Massachusetts Republicanism congratulated themselves on the strides made since the party's undoing in 1930. True, the depression remained. Governor Ely's 1931 program had temporarily disjointed Republican thinking on economic matters, as some party leaders went along with him, hesitantly, while others defended conservative fiscal doctrines to the bitter end. But Ely's countermarch in January 1932 restored the unity of Republican allegiance to the fetish of "economy and sound administration." Soon G.O.P. spokesmen were attacking the heresies of Ely's first year in office and the alleged damage done to the Commonwealth. As for national economic policy, a convention of six hundred party leaders in May 1932 condemned the anti-depression proposals introduced in Congress by Democrats and insurgent Republicans as productive of taxes, deficits, centralization, bureaucracy, paternalism, and other evils.[25] Confident in Senator Walsh's earlier declaration that he found no sympathy in Massachusetts for either "extreme measures" or "radical action," they felt certain the Bay State would sustain President Hoover's course at the polls in November.

And finally, the political antics of their Democratic opponents encouraged the Massachusetts Republicans most of all.

Al Smith's defeat in 1928 opened a new round in the struggle for control of the national Democratic Party. The southern and western wing, feeling that eastern Democrats had

had their chance and lost, was determined to regain the upper hand. But National Chairman John J. Raskob, the former chairman of the board of General Motors whom Smith appointed to run the 1928 campaign, had other ideas. Raskob and his followers were intent on having the party continue the strategy of attempting to win over the populous East, and that meant keeping the southern and western wing — the devotees of Bryan and McAdoo — out of control.[26] Their strategy had several aspects. One was an effort to make Prohibition the dominant issue on which the Democrats would campaign in the next election, and even as late as the spring of 1931 the national chairman named liquor the leading issue of the day, ahead of the depression.[27] Another aspect of their plan was to continue Smith's work of erasing the "anti-business" label which had attached to the party in earlier times. Raskob hoped that Democratic representatives in Congress would refrain from joining Republican insurgents to enact radical legislation that might frighten wet but economically conservative businessmen — converts of 1928 — away from the Democratic standard. As a token of the party's "soundness," he issued, after the 1930 mid-term election, a manifesto bearing the names of Smith, John W. Davis, and James M. Cox pledging co-operation with President Hoover.[28] Finally, Raskob and his faction hoped to capture the presidential nomination in 1932 for someone favorable to their views.

The deepening of the economic crisis in 1931 and 1932 did much to undermine Raskob's plans. As unemployment grew, the depression clearly overshadowed Prohibition as the uppermost concern of the public. "What is the mission of the Democratic Party?" demanded David I. Walsh on the floor of the Senate. "Is it to exploit religion, rum, or race? Or is it to heed the call of the millions?"[29] Before long some Democratic congressmen were introducing proposals for government handouts to the needy, for federal public works bond issues, and other measures which surely savored of radicalism to the business community. Chairman Raskob's efforts to give the Democratic Party a conservative tinge had only limited success, at least as far as its record in Congress was concerned.

Moreover, Raskob and his friends soon found their program as it pertained to the 1932 presidential nomination menaced by the ambitions of Franklin D. Roosevelt. Following his re-election as governor of New York in 1930, Roosevelt was acknowledged to hold first place among Democratic aspirants to the White House. Although a New Yorker and a staunch supporter of Al Smith in earlier days, Roosevelt shunned the pro-East strategy of the Smith-Raskob group in his own drive for nomination. Soliciting the good-will of sulking southern and western Democrats, he refused to recognize the divisive Prohibition issue as the primary question facing the party and emphasized economic issues instead. With time, Roosevelt's candidacy acquired strong backing in the South and the West — much of it coming from the same elements that had fought Al Smith tooth and nail in 1924 and 1928 and now desired the unseating of Raskob. On the other hand, it was evident that Roosevelt was not another William G. McAdoo of Klan-tainted fame, and his popularity with the old-stock wing of the party did not prevent him from garnering substantial support among its Newer American ranks in places like New York and Massachusetts. But Roosevelt's tactics offended Raskob and the group that had come to power through Smith. By 1931 they knew the New York governor was the man to beat if they were to retain their supremacy in party councils.[30]

A number of possible nominees figured as favorites of the anti-Roosevelt combine. There was Owen D. Young, chair-

man of the board of General Electric, who could be counted
on to open up the pocketbooks of wet conservatives better
than anyone else. There was Governor Albert Ritchie of
Maryland, an ardent opponent of Prohibition and federal centralization who, in his 1931 inaugural address, scored those
who ran to Washington "for increasing access to the Federal
Treasury." Others, like Newton D. Baker and Chicago banker
Melvin Traylor were spoken of, too. And there was Alfred
E. Smith himself.[31]

While Raskob was the self-appointed spokesman for the
eastern wing of the party after 1928, Al Smith remained its
idol and its leader in a more than figurative sense. His continued popularity with the Newer American masses was amply
demonstrated when he appeared in Boston and other places
during the 1930 campaign, while his hold on Democratic
leaders in the great industrial states, who were indebted to
him for invigorating their organizations in 1928, assured him
a voice in the matter of selecting delegates to the national
convention. Significantly, though Roosevelt's candidacy found
increasing favor across the nation, Smith refrained from using
his power on behalf of the man who succeeded him as governor.

The cooling of friendship between Smith and Roosevelt
began soon after 1928, when Roosevelt made clear his determination to be independent in matters of patronage and
policy at Albany. Moreover, the tactics of Roosevelt's pre-
convention campaign were bound to offend the older party
leader. After Smith's encounters with the Democrats of the
South and West in 1924 and 1928, he might well be suspicious
of one who seemed anxious to abandon the course he had set
for the party — the aggrandizement of its eastern, Newer
American wing. Like Raskob, Smith also remained adamant
in his demand that the Democrats be outspokenly anti-Pro-

hibitionist in 1932, and Roosevelt's evasive strategy on that issue disturbed him. Then, too, Smith became a businessman following his retirement from politics. After 1928 he associated more than ever with men high in the ranks of the business world, such as Raskob and John W. Davis, and possibly he began to share their fear that Roosevelt seemed too friendly with the agrarian radical wing of the party. Finally, as the prospects for Democratic victory in 1932 brightened, Smith probably came to feel, as his admirers did, that he deserved another chance at the presidency himself.[32]

Whatever the reasons, anticipation of an outright break between Smith and Roosevelt grew during 1931, and the titular head of the party was sometimes identified with the stop-Roosevelt combine.[33] If Smith actually joined the movement he would have a lot to say about its strategy — particularly if he decided to become a candidate himself. Meanwhile, organization leaders in Rhode Island, Connecticut, New Jersey, and other Newer American states waited for Al to make up his mind, before charting their courses for the 1932 convention.

Factional strife in the national organization soon meshed with a struggle for control of the party in Massachusetts, threatening a complete disruption of the Democratic coalition in the Bay State. The dominant Walsh-Ely organization retained its affection for Al Smith in 1931, and in May of that year Senator Walsh told reporters that he would support Smith if he chose to throw his hat in the ring. But at the same time Walsh, Ely, and State Chairman Donahue maintained friendly relations with Governor Roosevelt, and regarded him a likely prospect for nomination if Smith interposed no objection. In fact, Senators Walsh and Coolidge met with Roosevelt on June 13, 1931, at the summer home of Colonel Edward

M. House, and when the session ended Walsh declared himself for Smith first and Roosevelt second.[34]

As it happened, however, the train that carried Roosevelt from New York City toward Massachusetts for the House rendezvous also had among its passengers Mayor James Michael Curley, returning to Boston after a European tour. The two men did much talking en route, and probably there was mention of a political plum that might come Curley's way in return for supporting Roosevelt. At any rate, even before the train arrived in Boston, the Mayor announced to reporters on board that he was "with Roosevelt." A week later in a statement to the press Curley asserted that Smith could not be elected President, and that he too should end his silence and endorse Roosevelt for nomination.[35]

The Roosevelt-Curley meeting, and the Mayor's announcement, put a new face on Democratic presidential politics in Massachusetts. Curley's action seemed to be aimed less at improving Roosevelt's fortunes than at bolstering the Mayor's own political stock. Many regarded his seizing the leadership of the Roosevelt forces in the state as a challenge to the regular Walsh-Ely organization, and perhaps a prelude to a contest with Ely for the gubernatorial nomination in 1932. The leaders of the organization believed it to be so, and moved to head off the Mayor.[36] In the fall it was rumored that Curley would be kept off the unpledged (but pro-Smith) slate of delegates that State Chairman Donahue was drawing up for the national convention. Curley countered with a threat to run a "pledged to Roosevelt" slate headed by himself in the primary against the Walsh-Ely delegation, and in January of 1932 the Mayor went to Albany to confer with Roosevelt on the Massachusetts situation. Back home, he announced he was going ahead with plans to contest the regular slate in the primary. Roosevelt, interviewed later, declared that he had not yet decided what to do in the Bay State.[37]

It was a ticklish problem that the leading contender for the nomination faced. According to all reports — except Curley's — Massachusetts was still a "Smith state." Roosevelt's less pugnacious friends there, headed by LaRue Brown of the Jeffersonian Society, urged him to keep out.[38] Better to desist from antagonizing the dominant Walsh-Ely organization, let it send an unpledged delegation to the convention, and hope to pick up Massachusetts votes on the later ballots as the Roosevelt bandwagon gained momentum. There was no reason why he should become involved in James Michael Curley's siege of the Walsh-Ely machine.

The arguments of the moderates gained force when, on February 8, 1932, Al Smith finally broke silence and announced his willingness to accept the nomination if the convention decided it wanted him, although he would make no active campaign for delegates. The statement elated the leaders of the Massachusetts organization, who felt confident now that Roosevelt would not dare authorize a campaign against their slate. But a week later Roosevelt's son James, who had teamed up with Curley, called on Governor Ely and informed him a contest would be made. Shortly thereafter, "Roosevelt for President" headquarters opened in Curley's . . . downtown Boston.[39]

Goaded by Curley's activities, the Walsh-Ely faction pressured Smith during the remainder of February for the required legal permission to run a slate of delegates pledged to Smith in the primary, instead of the unpledged delegation hitherto contemplated. Heads of regular party organizations in other states dominated by Newer American Democrats, finding their supremacy challenged by new aspirants for leadership attached to Roosevelt's cause, similarly beseeched Smith to lend them the full prestige of his name. Largely out of loyalty to those who had been loyal to him, Smith consented at the beginning of March to enter primaries in a number of states. On March 1 State Chairman Donahue received power-of-attorney to select a delegation pledged to Smith for the Massachusetts election on April 26.[40]

That took some wind from the sails of the Roosevelt faction, and compromise negotiations got under way. Even Mayor Curley indicated he would be satisfied if the organization delegates would promise to vote for Roosevelt as their second choice after Smith dropped out, but his offer was rejected. The more moderate group of Roosevelt admirers, less exacting in their demands, were willing to settle for the concession of having at least a few Roosevelt sympathizers included on the organization slate. A meeting which LaRue Brown had with Walsh, Ely, and Donahue on March 9 seemed to be making progress in that direction. But right in the midst of their conversations Mayor Curley, a few blocks away at City Hall, issued a statement that in effect termed Al Smith a liar. When word of Curley's outburst came to the conferees, Senator Walsh, enraged, terminated the discussion. The next day Chairman Donahue announced the personnel of the slate pledged to Smith — with no "break" for the Roosevelt people.[41]

Believing enough damage was done already, Brown again advised Roosevelt to avoid a direct clash with the Walsh-Ely organization. But Curley's counsels, with the aid of James Roosevelt and Louis McHenry Howe, prevailed at Albany. In the end Governor Roosevelt left the decision up to the Mayor, which meant, in the words of a *Boston Transcript* correspondent, that "a battle royal is assured." On March 16 the Mayor unveiled the slate which he hoped would win convention votes for Franklin Roosevelt, and at the same time

gain control of the Bay State party organization for James
Michael Curley.[42]

The campaign was a bitter one. In a move that surprised
many, Curley announced that "under no conditions will I be
a candidate for Governor — this year." Nevertheless he
opened a strong attack against Ely's record in the State House,
Walsh's record in the Senate, and Donahue's performance as
state chairman. Al Smith's dog-in-the-manger attitude might
mean Democratic defeat in November, the Mayor asserted,
in which case he would be responsible "for the injury that
may result to the millions in America" suffering from the depression. Smith's opposition to the leading contender, Curley
inferred, was attributable to either "emotions that border on
unexplainable jealousy" or "the bankers of Wall Street, the
power combinations, and the other trusts who fear, with justi-
fiable reason, the election of Roosevelt." [43]

Active in Roosevelt's behalf besides the Curley organization
were others who held grudges against the Walsh-Ely machine
— former officeholders of Woodrow Wilson's day, deposed
state chairmen, and the man who led McAdoo's ill-fated campaign in Massachusetts in 1924. But the more moderate
Roosevelt supporters of LaRue Brown's type took little part
in the contest, fearing perhaps — as the *Springfield Republican*
did — that "the destruction of the Walsh-Ely-Donahue organization under Curley's blows might be a major disaster for
the Democratic Party in Massachusetts." [44]

Smith retained the support of practically all the prominent
party leaders, including John F. Fitzgerald, Martin Lomasney,
and the spokesmen for the "newer races" who had come to
the fore since 1928. At first the regular organization concentrated its fire on Mayor Curley. It also spent much time com-
bating Curley's claim that Smith was not really an active
candidate. Speculation on that matter ended April 13, how-

ever, when Smith, speaking at a Jefferson Day dinner in Washington, promised to "fight to the bitter end any candidate who persists in any demagogic appeal to the masses of the working people of this country to destroy themselves by setting class against class and rich against poor." [45] The speech was a direct thrust at Roosevelt, who had recently denounced the Hoover Administration's alleged neglect of the "little fellows" and the "forgotten man," and it ended all doubt that Smith was joining in earnest the stop-Roosevelt movement. Thereafter the Walsh-Ely machine stepped up its frontal attack on the New York governor.

In the end, all the talking influenced few votes. The contest boiled down to a choice between Al Smith and James Michael Curley, and there was little doubt where the bulk of Bay State Democratic sympathy lay in that case. While most observers believed that Curley himself might displace the low man on the organization's delegate-at-large slate, and that Roosevelt might win a few district seats, it was a foregone conclusion that Smith would control a large majority of the Massachusetts delegation. Primary day demonstrated just how strong a hold the 1928 candidate retained. Curley received 56,500 votes, but the low man on the Walsh-Ely ticket got over 134,000. The Roosevelt slate carried not one of the thirty-nine cities in the Commonwealth. Nor did Roosevelt win any of the district contests. [46]

Massachusetts truly remained a "Smith state." Moreover, the worst forebodings of Roosevelt's moderate advisors had also materialized, for Curley's tactics had greatly antagonized Walsh, Ely, and Donahue. More clearly than ever their continued supremacy in the state would be endangered if Roosevelt succeeded in carrying off the nomination after all. The Mayor's primary fight had converted the regular organization into die-hard Smithites, or die-hard anti-Roosevelt men, which now meant the same thing.[47]

To some extent the Democratic national convention that met in Chicago on June 27 resembled the convention of 1924 all over again, especially as far as Massachusetts was concerned. Roosevelt, his strength centering in the southern and western states, was by far the leading contender. But Smith had the support of Massachusetts, Rhode Island, Connecticut, the Tammany element in New York, and a large part of the Pennsylvania delegation. Those votes, together with the ninety controlled by John N. Garner (Texas and California), and the ones tied up by favorite sons, totaled more than the one-third necessary to deny the nomination to Roosevelt. On the first three roll calls his total rose only from 666 to 683 — considerably short of the 770 needed to win — and the Massachusetts delegation was delighted.[48]

The gratification of the Smith delegates ended there, however, for during the recess that followed the third ballot Garner released his delegates. When the convention reassembled, none other than William G. McAdoo took the rostrum to announce that California was shifting her votes to Franklin Roosevelt, and that turned the trick. On the fourth roll call — the one that gave Roosevelt 945 votes and the nomination — Massachusetts defiantly cast her thirty-six votes for Al Smith again. Few of her delegates were present the next afternoon when the nominee, after a dramatic flight from the East, appeared in person to deliver his acceptance speech. Most Bay Staters had already started home, in a mood no less bitter than that in which they left Madison Square Garden in the summer of 1924.[49]

Several circumstances made Roosevelt's victory more galling to the Walsh-Ely organization than it might have been. For one thing, it was accomplished through the retirement of

Garner, the hero of one of the Democratic states that deserted Smith in 1928. Moreover, the announcement of the
coup by McAdoo, an arch-villain in the Massachusetts scheme
of things, added insult to injury. Also Garner, as reward for
his capitulation, received second place on the Roosevelt ticket.
Finally, there was the fact that the Roosevelt-dominated cre-
dentials committee had permitted James Michael Curley to
sit as an alternate delegate from Puerto Rico. On the last
ballot the chairman of the island delegation allowed "Don
Jaime" of Boston to announce its vote — all for Roosevelt —
which he proceeded to do in his most eloquent tones.[50]

Back in Boston delegate Daniel Gallagher declared that
"the Anti-Saloon League and the Ku Klux Klan have won.
. . . I do not intend to vote for either Roosevelt or Garner."
Said the *Italian News*, which supported the Democratic ticket
in 1928: "Al Smith has nothing in common with those who
now control the Democratic Party. . . Today Roosevelt is
a symbol of all that is antagonistic to the immigrant groups
whereas in 1928 Al Smith was quite the contrary. . . In the
background hovers the gaunt figure of McAdoo. . ." And
Governor Ely, whose fight for Smith made him the new idol
of Bay State Democrats, had vowed that he would not run
for re-election if Roosevelt was victorious.[51]

With the convention over, however, candidate Roosevelt
and his high command reconsidered the situation they had
created in Massachusetts, and concluded that it was time to
conciliate the regular organization if the state were to be carried in November. The wounds of Senators Walsh and Coolidge, John F. Fitzgerald, and some other key men healed
quickly, and they issued endorsements of the party's ticket
a short time after the convention's adjournment. But Governor Ely proved a tougher customer. He was a crucial cog in
Roosevelt's plans, for his speech nominating Smith at Chicago

endeared Ely to devotees of the 1928 candidate everywhere, and to Smith himself. Perhaps he alone could convince the Happy Warrior to come forth and actually work for party success in November.[52]

But as the days passed Ely said nothing, and the Roosevelt managers redoubled their efforts to gain his favor. Even Mayor Curley concurred in the judgment that Ely's support was necessary for a Roosevelt victory in Massachusetts, and contributed to the peace overtures by declaring that "it is clearly the duty of Governor Ely to be a candidate for re-election." [53] On July 18 Roosevelt himself, ending a vacation cruise of the Massachusetts coast at Swampscott, conferred with some friends of the Governor and enlisted their aid. On the twenty-second James Farley called on Ely in Springfield. A few days later Ely visited Roosevelt in Albany, and they talked for two hours. Finally, on July 31, Ely endorsed the party's candidates and announced that he would stand for re-election, although his statement hardly flattered Roosevelt. He had hoped, Ely declared, that the convention would pick "a man of expressed convictions. . ." Nevertheless, he was now convinced the party's platform was the important thing, and that Roosevelt would carry out its promises — reduction of government expenses, repeal of Prohibition, and liberal social measures — with "earnest and energetic action." With that understanding, he urged Massachusetts voters to support the Democratic ticket.[54]

One of Ely's prices for surrender was that James Michael Curley be relegated to a back seat in the Massachusetts campaign, and that its direction be left in the hands of the regular organization's state committee. The Roosevelt managers agreed. Curley acquiesced — "I am still a self-effacing Roosevelt man." There would be no "bull pen" this time, and the Mayor arranged to be out of the state during the entire month of September on a country-wide speaking tour for the national ticket, paying the expenses himself. When he returned, he promised, his services would be at the disposal of the state committee.[55]

At the beginning, then, the Democratic campaign in Massachusetts centered around Governor Ely. By all reports his first administration was popular — "not radical and not conservative" — and the man scheduled to oppose him, Lieutenant Governor William Youngman, was disliked even in Republican circles. On the other hand, the outlook for the Democrats in the presidential race was dark, and seemed to hinge on the size of Ely's majority. Roosevelt, many observers believed, could ride to victory in Massachusetts only on the Governor's coat-tails.[56]

Nevertheless, party spokesmen did what they could to offset the impression that the Chicago convention had delivered the Democratic Party back to its southern and western elements, to the followers of Bryan and McAdoo whose cultural views and economic interests were inimical to those of the Newer American wing in the East. The party's nominee, they insisted, was not a bigot. Nor was he the tool of agrarian radicals, whose inflationist and low-tariff doctrines would further reduce the purchasing power and job opportunities of urban industrial workers. In various campaign speeches Roosevelt himself promised to maintain a sound currency, denounced the Republicans' alleged inflationary policies, and pledged that tariff rates would be kept high enough to safeguard the standards of American workingmen. His lieutenants in Massachusetts tended to emphasize these aspects of the candidate's program in the early stages of the campaign, along with his opposition to Prohibition.[57] Moreover, attempts were made to dispel the antagonism aroused by "Cactus Jack" Garner's presence on the ticket. In mid-August the Texas congressman

paid a personal call on Al Smith in New York City. Later
Garner addressed a meeting of state chairmen from the New
England states and, "with tears in his eyes," denounced religious prejudice, apologized for Texas' defection in 1928,
and assured them he was not a Prohibitionist.[58]

But the Democrats' tactics appeared to bear little fruit. As
August gave way to September, Smith still refused to amplify
his bare post-convention statement that he remained a Democrat and would support the ticket. Early in September *The
Catholic Mirror*, official organ of the Diocese of Springfield,
attacked the Chicago convention as one dominated by bigotry
and denounced attempts to "white-wash" that "fact." The
delegates denied Smith the nomination solely because of his
religion, the *Mirror* asserted, and then proceeded to select as
their vice-presidential nominee "a representative of . . .
bigotry's banner state four years ago." [59]

Under the circumstances, the Democratic camp in Massachusetts showed little activity, and what there was seemed
half-hearted. With Mayor Curley out of the state the whole
of September, things were especially quiet. Governor Ely,
it was understood, did not intend to start a real drive until
two weeks before the election.

Because the Democratic campaign got off to a slow start
and a bad one in Massachusetts, the spirit of the Commonwealth's Republican organization was necessarily high. One
reflection of Republican confidence during the summer of
1932 was the revived talk of displacing Youngman with someone more amenable to the regular organization, since it now
appeared that the size of the Hoover vote might even sweep
Governor Ely out of office. The movement never materialized,
however, and Youngman's only opponent in the September

gubernatorial primary was another interloper like himself, whom he managed to defeat.[60]

Youngman's campaign tactics were summed up by a press correspondent who remarked that the Lieutenant Governor had "shaken every hand in the state at least twice." [61] An ubiquitous attender at party rallies and meetings of veterans' and women's organizations, Youngman also boldly sought the votes of ethnic groups in his attempt to unseat Ely. In appeals to Italian-Americans he harped on the Democratic administration's alleged failure to grant them recognition. To people of German extraction he sent letters promising to "appoint public officials on merit solely, with fair representation for German-Americans. . ." Speaking in French to audiences in the Connecticut River Valley, Youngman promised bilingual transaction of business at the State House after his election. Over the door to the executive suite, he vowed, would be a sign similar to those seen in the store windows of Holyoke and Chicopee — "Ici on parle francais." [62]

Among many regular Republicans, however, there was little more than a mere willingness to let Youngman have his fling and go down to defeat, so that the party "escalator" might resume its normal operations in time for the 1934 contest, when Ely would be retiring. Therefore, the only chance for a Youngman victory seemed to lie in the expected overwhelming vote for President Hoover.[63]

In his August acceptance speech, Hoover conceded that Prohibition was a failure — a statement which went even further than the party's platform. Thereafter, Republican campaigners in Massachusetts told their audiences that the G.O.P. was just as wet as the Democratic Party. Indeed, they asserted, the Republicans could bring repeal more quickly than their opponents, for the promise of federal protection for dry states put forth in the G.O.P. plan would hasten acquiescence in the ending of nation-wide Prohibition.[64]

But with both parties wet, the Eighteenth Amendment was dead, and clearly the depression was the overshadowing issue of the election. During August and September indexes of employment and economic activity showed some improvement compared with the depths reached in the early part of the summer.[65] Acclaiming the signs of recovery as a product of the President's reconstruction measures, Republicans called for endorsement of the Administration's program at the polls. This was a time for men with "known" views, not for those who dealt only in "fine-spun theories." While charging that the Democratic candidate's views were vague, Bay State Republicans insisted, nonetheless, that they were contrary to the interests of the industrial East, for his chief supporters at the Chicago convention had been the agrarian radicals. And had not Roosevelt asserted in his acceptance speech: "We must lay hold of the fact that economic laws are not made by nature. They are made by human beings"? "Two more glaring misstatements of the truth," the *Boston Transcript* declared, "could hardly have been packed into so little space." "It was not without some justification," the Republicans stressed, "that . . . Alfred E. Smith characterized him as a demagogue." [66]

Most encouraging of all to the G.O.P. was the fact that Roosevelt, and not Smith, was the opposition candidate. Confident that thousands of Irish and New Immigrant Democrats would bolt their party's ticket or stay away from the polls altogether on election day, Republican leaders foresaw an impending breakup of the Democratic coalition that had wrested control of Massachusetts politics since 1928. The Republican national committee also considered the state "safe" for President Hoover, and concluded that a campaign appear-

ance in Boston was unnecessary. His time could be better
spent in other, doubtful, areas.[67]

Then, in mid-September, <u>Maine</u> held its state election, and
the result was astounding. While the notion that the country
goes as Maine goes is largely chimeric, it is not so when Maine
goes Democratic; and on September 12 the Democrats captured the governorship and two of the state's three congressional districts.[68] The outcome revealed the intensity of the
resentment produced by depression. It revealed, too, that
Franklin D. Roosevelt would be the next President of the
United States.

The upheaval in Maine soon influenced the conduct of the
Democratic campaign in Massachusetts. Now it behooved the
regular organization to climb on the bandwagon, and when
the state convention assembled at Lowell on October 1, ref-
erences to Roosevelt by Governor Ely and Senator Walsh
were much warmer than their previous endorsements. By then
it was also known that Al Smith himself would soon come
out strong for the national ticket and campaign in a number
of eastern cities.[69] Although most observers felt that Roosevelt
no longer needed Smith's help, the healing of the breach gave
another green light to Bay State Democrats. By the middle
of October, Governor Ely was making "red-hot" speeches
for Roosevelt not only in his own state but in such places as
Hartford, Rochester, and Cleveland.[70] The regular organization's tepidness toward the national ticket had disappeared;
for Walsh, Ely and their followers wanted to be welcome at
the White House, too, after March 4, 1933.

A mounting uneasiness regarding the certainty of Ely's re-
election also helped bring about the organization's change of
face. For one thing, registration figures indicated that traditionally Republican towns and suburban cities were outdoing

Democratic strongholds in adding new names to the lists.[71] Even more important was the change of tactics initiated by Lieutenant Governor Youngman in his own campaign during October. Reading the signs of the times, Youngman decided to abandon reliance on Hoover's coat-tails and instead struck out on his own. Determined to stir up a rumpus to attract attention, the Lieutenant Governor unleashed a barrage of charges that Ely was guilty of fraudulent land deals, selling pardons, having improper connections with banking interests, power trusts, and insurance companies, and other varieties of corruption. Finally, on October 16, in an open bid for the support of Roosevelt Democrats, the Youngman forces accused Ely and Republican National Committeeman John Richardson of arranging a trade of votes to insure a Hoover-Ely outcome in the election.[72] Confronted with Youngman's moves, the Walsh-Ely men had to wage a more energetic campaign and, in the process, remove all doubt of their allegiance to the Roosevelt cause.

By mid-October, then, the Democrats' strategy had changed in several respects. Franklin D. Roosevelt and the presidential race now occupied the center of attention. And the tempo of the campaign was accelerated beyond anything planned. Through the remaining half of October and the first week of November all the prominent men in the regular organization engaged in strenuous tours that missed no corner of the Commonwealth. Once again Wisnioski, Rainey, Brogna, and the other ethnic leaders contributed help among "their people." Also in the field was a "flying wedge" of labor leaders, who canvassed the state's industrial centers.[73] And James Michael Curley was back in Massachusetts.

Moreover, the nature of the Democrats' plea for votes changed. The outcome of the Maine election had demonstrated that easterners were not disturbed by Roosevelt's so-called "radicalism," and party spokesmen spent little time thereafter trying to remove that label. Massachusetts Democrats still referred on occasion to their candidate's "soundness" regarding fiscal policy, the tariff, and repeal of Prohibition. But now they tended to put more emphasis on other aspects of his program — on such things as the federal government's responsibility to provide direct relief; the desirability of promoting public works during hard times; the need for a federal public health and welfare program, a national employment service, and state systems of unemployment insurance. Roosevelt himself stressed those topics in his Boston speech on October 31.[74]

With new aggressiveness Bay State Democrats held the Republicans responsible for "the orgy of speculation and mergers" that produced the depression. Mayor Curley dwelled on what many considered a black spot in the Administration's record by expressing his compassion for the men of the Bonus Expeditionary Force, "shot down like dogs in our national capital." Recurring to that distrust of Europe generated in the years of postwar disillusion, Curley contrasted the President's war-debt moratorium with his alleged hardheartedness toward the sufferings of his own countrymen. "Had he but served the American people with half the zeal and half the energy and half the fidelity that he . . . served the international bankers and the nations of Europe, this contest might be a difficult one. . ."[75] Some Democratic campaigners scored another supposed shortcoming of Hoover's reconstruction program: "Republicans don't stand for human beings; they stand for railroads, banks, and corporations."[76] On the night before election Governor Ely cited figures on the immense cost of relief payments made by the impoverished city and town officials of Massachusetts in the past year. "I urge you when you go to the polls tomorrow to ask yourselves if that is a responsibility of the government — of the richest government in the world." As for the President's fear that grass would grow in the streets of a hundred cities if Roosevelt's policies were put into effect, Ely regarded it as an impossibility "with eleven million men and women walking up and down those streets looking for work." [77]

The climax of the campaign began on October 27 when Al Smith came to Boston. Again fifteen thousand people crowded the Arena. The lukewarmness of Smith's initial speeches on behalf of the ticket had disappointed Roosevelt's managers, but that night in Boston he "pulled out all the stops" for the Democratic nominee. In a moving peroration Smith reminded his audience: "There can be no bigotry and there can be no resentment in the Catholic heart. It cannot be there." [78]

On October 29 Roosevelt himself began a three-day tour of Massachusetts, passing through scores of the Commonwealth's cities and towns accompanied by Governor Ely. The high point came with the candidate's address at the Boston Arena, where his audience was smaller than Smith's, but enthusiastic. Denouncing the Republicans' "fear" campaign and their reported intimidation of employees, Roosevelt outlined his program to fight the depression, and to provide a greater measure of security for industrial workers in the future. The crowd cheered his proposals, and it cheered Roosevelt's concluding promise: "I decline to accept present conditions as inevitable or beyond control. I decline to stop at saying 'It might have been worse.' I shall do all I can to prevent it from being worse — but . . . I go on to pledge action to make things better." [79]

The G.O.P. reciprocated the new intensity of the Bay State Democratic campaign. Republican leaders still anticipated large-scale defection among Irish and New Immigrant Democrats, but events after the middle of September had undermined their confidence in that outcome. Consequently, in an effort to counteract the effects of depression resentment, Republicans stepped up their attack on the "loose" economic thinking of the Democratic candidate. The President himself set the pace. After the Maine election Hoover, who had previously confined himself to "nonpolitical" pronouncements, took to the political battlefield to defend his record against the "airy promises" of his opponent. Inauguration of Franklin Roosevelt's "new deal," he said, would not only end recovery — it would "destroy the American system of life." [80]

Massachusetts campaigners underscored the President's dire predictions. The transcending issue of the election, Congressman James Beck told a Boston audience, was Hoover conservatism versus Roosevelt radicalism. Numerous speakers cited Roosevelt's record as a spender in New York and the Democrats' record of "treasury raiding" in Congress as evidence of their essential "unsoundness." Some felt that the endorsements Roosevelt received from Senators Norris, La Follette, Johnson, and other members of the radical insurgent bloc were enough to damn him.[81] In a speech at Madison Square Garden — the last political address of his life — former President Coolidge compared the impending election to that in 1896. Defeat of the Democrats in 1932, he asserted, would promote recovery, just as the defeat of Bryan and his revolutionary proposals ended the depression of 1893.[82] To the end of the campaign the *Boston Transcript* felt confident, as it had at the outset, that although the radical Roosevelt program might have appeal in the "socialistic" West, it would be found repulsive in the "thoughtful" East.[83]

Nevertheless, despite Republican efforts, it was evident by the first week of November that the Democratic campaign in Massachusetts had made headway. Following Youngman's attack on National Committeeman Richardson, it was clearer than ever that the regular party organization would do little to help him. After the novelty of the Lieutenant Governor's sensational tactics wore off, Ely resumed his status as a "sure thing." [84]

Moreover, the presidential contest was now "admittedly close." After the Smith and Roosevelt visits some thought it advisable to bring President Hoover to the Bay State to insure his victory there. In the end it was decided that his presence was needed more elsewhere. The *Literary Digest* poll, after all, still showed Massachusetts and the other New England states, along with New Jersey, in the Hoover column by a comfortable margin — and they were the only states there.[85] So the people of Massachusetts got no chance to see the President who had worked conscientiously, against tremendous odds, to do the right thing as he saw it. On November 8 they went to the polls to confirm or deny Speaker Leverett Saltonstall's estimation of their mood earlier in 1932: "Our people, this year, desire certainty, not change."

Returns that came in from small towns on the afternoon of election day indicated that Franklin D. Roosevelt was even surpassing Al Smith's performance of 1928. Then, in the early evening, the result in New Bedford was announced. The Democratic candidate carried the city by seven thousand votes, although the party's city chairman had predicted a margin of only four thousand — Smith's margin in 1928. That made it plain Massachusetts would again be found in the Democratic presidential column.[86]

While registration had increased since 1928, the percentage of registrants who actually voted declined (from 93.5 to 89.6), and thus the total number who went to the polls in 1932 was slightly smaller than the number called out by the rousing battle four years earlier. But Roosevelt polled 7,390 votes more than Smith, while Hoover's total was 38,607 votes less than he got in 1928. Hence Roosevelt's margin of victory over Hoover was 63,189 — 800,148 to 736,959. His 52.0 per cent of the two-party vote represented an increase of 1.5 points over Smith's figure, 50.5. Only 34,305 Bay Staters voted for Socialist Norman Thomas. The Communist vote was even smaller.[87]

Analysis of the returns indicates that Republican hopes and Democratic fears of Newer American defection from Roosevelt were wholly unfounded. While the 1932 candidate's percentage of the two-party vote in the state as a whole showed an increase of 1.5 points over Smith's mark, for Boston the figure was 1.7; for the aggregate vote of the ten other Newer American cities over 25,000 (each having 70 per cent or more foreign-stock population), it was 2.1; for the aggregate vote of the eleven Newer American places of 10,000 to 25,000 (each having 70 per cent or more foreign-stock population), it was 2.9; and for the aggregate vote of the sixteen Newer American towns of 2,500 to 10,000 (each having 70 per cent or more foreign-stock population), it was 2.7.

In Boston's Irish Wards Two (Charlestown) and Six and Seven (South Boston) the Democratic nominee received 91.2, 90.3, and 87.9 per cent of the two-party vote, actually registering *increases* of 0.3, 1.1, and 1.1 points over Smith's performance in 1928. The same tendency held true for the other Irish wards of the city. In Malden's heavily Irish Ward Two, probably the most Democratic electoral district in the Commonwealth, Roosevelt got fully 95.1 per cent of the vote. In 1928 Smith received 94.3 per cent.

Roosevelt's hold on the newer ethnic groups was just as firm as his hold on the Irish. Jewish Wards Twelve and Fourteen in Boston gave him 58.9 and 71.3 per cent of their votes respectively, representing increases of 3.4 and 7.1 points over Smith's record. Chelsea's strongest Jewish ward gave Roosevelt 85.9 per cent of the vote (the same figure as for the city's heaviest Irish district), bettering Smith's mark by 5 points. In Revere's heavily Jewish Ward Two, Roosevelt increased the Democratic percentage by 6.3 points. That city's Italian-American wards, Three and Four, showed increases in the Democratic percentage of 2.9 and 2.5 points respectively over 1928. In French-Canadian wards in Chicopee, Taunton, and elsewhere the 1932 candidate bettered his party's showing. New Bedford's heaviest French districts, Wards One and Six, gave Roosevelt 78.5 and 74.8 per cent of the two-party vote; Smith's figures, by contrast, were 70.0 and 68.9. In many of the great melting-pot districts — Cambridge's East End and Haverhill's Ward Five were examples — Roosevelt also did better than the New Immigrants' hero of 1928. Martin Lomasney, a bitter foe of the Curley-Roosevelt slate in the primary, nevertheless saw to it that his polyglot Ward Three increased Roosevelt's percentage by 1.7 points over Smith's, giving him 83.4 per cent of the vote in the election — destined to be Martin's last. In sum, Roosevelt's performance among the Bay State's Newer Americans outdid even Al Smith's.

Moreover, Roosevelt, like Joseph Ely in 1930, increased the Democratic percentage of the vote in many old-stock Republican strongholds as a result of economic distress. In the thirteen old-stock cities over 25,000 (each having more than 30 per cent "native white of native parentage" population), Roosevelt's percentage of the aggregate two-party vote showed an increase of 1.1 points over Smith's proportion in 1928. For the aggregate vote of the twenty-nine old-stock towns of 2,500 to 10,000 (each having 50 per cent or more "native white of native parentage" population), the increase was 1.9 points.

In Haverhill's strongest Republican ward, for example, Roosevelt got 33.7 per cent of the vote, compared to Smith's 28.9 per cent four years earlier. Lynn's banner Republican ward increased its Democratic percentage from 26.0 for Smith, to 30.1 for Roosevelt. In Waltham's Republican Ward Six the Democratic increase was 5.5 points. Roosevelt carried each of those cities, whereas Smith carried none of them. He also carried the cities of Everett and Medford which, like the places just mentioned, were hitherto counted Republican strongholds in presidential elections. On the other hand, marked declines in Roosevelt's percentage of the vote compared to Smith's were observable in some places dominated by old-stock Republicans of the upper economic classes — Boston's Back Bay and suburban Newton, Brookline, and Belmont were examples. Here the Republican campaign against "Roosevelt radicalism," coupled with the absence of the Prohibition issue which operated in 1928, had done its work.

Governor Ely in his bid for re-election had no trouble subduing William Youngman, 825,479 to 704,576. The Governor's absolute number of votes exceeded his presidential running-mate's by more than 25,000, and his percentage of the two-party gubernatorial vote (53.9) outstripped Roosevelt's in the presidential contest (52.0). Analysis of the returns reveals, however, that Ely in most cases actually ran somewhat behind Roosevelt in Irish and New Immigrant Democratic strongholds. The fact that he did outdistance his running-mate was attributable to the greater vote he received in old-stock Republican areas. In Newton, for example, Roosevelt got only 32.3 per cent of the two-party presidential vote, but Ely got 41.0 per cent of the gubernatorial vote. In Brookline Roosevelt had 34.8 per cent and Ely 47.0 per cent. For Belmont the corresponding figures were 36.0 and 42.9. There was "cutting" in the 1932 election, but it was done by old-stock Republicans against William Youngman in the gubernatorial race, not by Newer Americans against Franklin Roosevelt in the presidential one.

In other contests the Democratic Hurleys retained office as treasurer and auditor by large votes. However, the Republican escalator's candidate for lieutenant governor, President of the Senate Gaspar Bacon, managed to beat his Democratic opponent by a slim 4,813 votes. The incumbent Republican attorney general and secretary of state were re-elected by somewhat larger margins. The Democrats acquired another seat in the state's congressional delegation — now reduced to fifteen members as a result of reapportionment following the 1930 census — by winning the heavily New Immigrant district formerly represented by Congressman Underhill; Massachusetts would send ten Republicans and five Democrats to the next session of the national legislature. As for the state legislature, the Democrats increased their representation in the Senate from ten to fourteen, though suffering a small net loss of strength in the lower house. The victory of Democratic candidates for local offices in Worcester County ended the reign of another long-entrenched Republican "county ring."

The 1932 election was fought on the purely "traditional" issue of economic conditions, and on the basis of that issue the Massachusetts Democratic coalition again remained intact. Augmented by the addition of still more recruits from among all strata of the Bay State's social structure, the coalition delivered the Commonwealth's electoral votes to the Democratic nominee even more decisively than four years earlier.

The election's outcome signified the desire of Massachusetts people to initiate a period of "experiments in men and measures" in the federal administration, just as the 1930 election signified their desire for a new departure in state administration. Aggravation of economic suffering in 1931 and 1932 directed attention to the national government, which alone seemed capable of remedying the situation. There President Hoover had already terminated the sway of normalcy, but in the end the majority in the Bay State rejected his relatively cautious program. Instead they turned to a new man who promised a bolder approach to the problems of relief, recovery, security, and reform.

Economic distress had similar effects across the nation, to Hoover's detriment, and to the advantage of Franklin Roosevelt. On election day industrial workers, farmers, small businessmen, middle-class reformers, and advanced liberals everywhere joined in the call for a new leader. Thus the depression, which enabled Roosevelt to retain the support of the Massachusetts Democratic coalition, also made it possible for him to carry those other Newer American states where the impact of the "Al Smith revolution" had increased the Democratic vote four years earlier. At the same time he was able to reconsolidate the traditionally Democratic South and to win the support of the West, old-stock areas that had been repelled by Smith.

Between 1928 and 1932, then, economic policy became the central concern of politics in all parts of the country. In the process, those ethnic and cultural tensions which divided America into two civilizations during the 1920's, and culminated in the election of 1928, receded into the background.[88] Hyphenism, one hundred per cent Americanism, Prohibition, immigration restriction, Tammanyism, religion — and the social graces of the candidates' wives — played little part as issues in the 1932 campaign, being displaced by such matters as federal relief and public works, crop-surplus controls and farm-credit facilities. From the debate over those and similar issues there emerged a new dominant alignment in control of national politics — the Roosevelt coalition. Based on the depression frustrations of Newer Americans and old-stock Americans alike, the coalition delivered its leader a vague but decisive mandate to begin a program of economic experiment. In granting Franklin Roosevelt that commission on election day, Massachusetts and Rhode Island — charter members of the new coalition since 1928 — were now joined in the Democratic column by all but six of the states that made up the nation.

Chapter Nine

Conclusion and Epilogue

THE election of 1932 began a new political era in the United States, and between election day and inauguration day Bay State politicians were already setting the stage for the fresh series of partisan encounters that would follow the installation of Franklin D. Roosevelt as President of the United States. On the Republican side came the final displacement of the Old Guard regime that rose to power with Calvin Coolidge. The Roosevelt and Hoover ballots were hardly counted when younger members of the G.O.P. began demanding a "new deal" in the handling of party affairs. State Chairman Amos Taylor's resignation was expected, and the question of party control centered around the identity of his successor. When the state committee met on January 5 two names were voted on: Charles Innes, backed by Taylor and the remainder of the Coolidge machine, and Carl Terry of Fall River, the favorite of National Committeeman John Richardson and other newcomers to leadership. Terry won by a substantial margin and then, just a day later, former President Coolidge himself died at his Northampton home. The old names — Butler, Stearns, Taylor, Allen, and the rest — receded from the limelight. Younger men like Lieutenant Governor Gaspar Bacon, Speaker Leverett Saltonstall, Christian Herter, Henry

Cabot Lodge, Jr., and Sinclair Weeks were now the ones to watch in the affairs of Massachusetts Republicanism.[1]

The high-riding Democrats also wondered what the new regime would mean in terms of their own party organization. One source of conjecture was the matter of James Michael Curley's "reward" for being the "original Roosevelt man" in Massachusetts. Speculation regarding it ranged from a cabinet position as Secretary of the Navy to an ambassadorship at Rome or one of the Latin American countries. Despite the Mayor's frequent interviews with the President-elect, however, his exact status was still unknown when inauguration day arrived. Some inferred that Roosevelt had dropped Curley from his list of appointments, but the Mayor's followers assured doubters that everything was "in the bag" for their chief.[2]

In any case, it was clear that the truce in the battle for control of the party in the Bay State, forced by the 1932 campaign, would end soon. The election's outcome promised to strengthen Curley's hand in his attempt to wrest the reins from the Walsh-Ely organization. One challenge would probably come at the next gubernatorial election in 1934, and already there was talk of drafting Ely for a third term as the only means of blocking Curley's ambitions. Even more immediate was the problem of who would control federal patronage in the Bay State. Curley's admirers hailed him as "Roosevelt's Big Gun of New England now," and saw him as the dispenser of Massachusetts' share of political plums. Others hoped that the regular organization would get at least an equal voice in such matters.[3]

While politicians occupied themselves with the details of their profession, the public's attention focused on the desperate economic situation of the state and nation, which plummeted to new lows in the four months between Roosevelt's election and inauguration. Between October 1932 and March 1933 the index of employment in the country's manufacturing industries dropped from 59.9 to 55.1, the lowest point since the stock market crash, and the index of pay roll totals declined from 39.9 to 33.4. In Massachusetts the number of industrial wage earners fell from 376,660 in October to 335,132 in March (for March 1929, by contrast, the number had been 564,381).[4]

President Hoover responded to the crisis by intensifying his efforts to reduce government expenditures and balance the nation's budget. In his annual message to Congress on December 6, 1932, the President recommended reduction of federal employees' salaries, elimination of certain veterans' benefits, a huge slash in federal public works appropriations, and abandonment of all projects not already begun. In Massachusetts, Governor Ely, too, adhered to a policy of strict economy in government in order to safeguard the state's credit. His 1933 budget called for appropriations of approximately fifty-six million dollars — nearly four million less than in 1932 — and recommended cuts in state salaries and elimination of various divisions and services in the Commonwealth's administrative system.[5]

But the attention of the country's lawmakers, like that of all Americans, now centered on the man who would become President on March 4. With private, local, and state means for providing relief all but exhausted, the nation awaited the debut of the candidate who had pledged "action to make things better." Anticipation of the new regime heightened as, in the last week of the Hoover Administration, a financial panic developed and state after state ordered banks closed. It was the darkest moment of the depression. On the very morning of inauguration day Governor Ely, in a telephone call from Washington, instructed the lieutenant governor to declare an immediate bank holiday in Massachusetts.[6]

A few hours later, Franklin Roosevelt took the oath of office and outlined in general terms his program and his hopes for the nation. Again he promised bold leadership, declaring he would not hesitate to seek broad executive power — as great as that exercised by the President in time of war — if the old balance of powers between the executive and legislative branches of government interfered with the job at hand. That afternoon the ultra-Republican *Boston Transcript* called the President's avowal "unprecedented." But, the *Transcript* continued, "such is the desperate temper of the people, it is welcome." Roosevelt's program demanded "the dictatorial authority he requests. . . He is the great reliance in this dark hour of national moratorium." [7]

Surely, then, a different epoch in American life had begun.

* * *

The period from 1919 to 1933 — the era of the flappers and the "lost generation" — witnessed a striking transformation in the political status of Massachusetts, from a rock-bound Republican stronghold to a Democratic state. The fact that the Bay State's conversion took place in 1928 made her almost unique, and a harbinger of what was to follow in the rest of the nation. As we have seen, that conversion was accomplished through the gradual evolution of a new Democratic majority coalition, displacing the Republican coalition that swept the state in 1920. The bedrock of the new alignment consisted of the Massachusetts Irish, who returned to their traditional Democratic allegiance soon after the League of Nations fiasco. But the essential element in the welding of the new coalition came with the addition of large numbers of the state's New Immigrant voters. Aroused to unaccustomed self-consciousness by the events of the First World War and its aftermath, the New Immigrants' political interest was heightened still further by the rise of issues peculiarly affecting them in the postwar decade. Prohibition, one hundred per cent Americanism, Ku Kluxism, immigration restriction, and similar considerations evoked political responses among these people which accrued to the benefit of the Democrats as the party of cultural liberalism. At the same time there emerged fresh leaders among the various groups who rejected the Republican organization's record toward them as lacking in just "recognition," and they turned to the Democrats for consolation. Finally, the failure of Massachusetts to share adequately in the benefits of "Coolidge prosperity" relieved New Immigrant voters of their formerly strong belief in the magical powers of Republican economic doctrine. Under such circumstances the various newer ethnic groups overlooked, to some extent, their mutual enmities and their common resentment against the Irish. Joined together, these Newer Americans formed the basic components of a revivified Democratic Party. With the addition of strength derived from remaining Yankee Democrats, labor leaders, advanced liberals, and disaffected old-stock Republicans attracted to the Democratic standard by the issues of Prohibition and economic depression, a new majority alliance emerged in control of the Bay State political scene.

Senator David I. Walsh was the first to mobilize the power of the new coalition and hence, as far as Massachusetts was concerned, there was a "Walsh revolution" even before there was an "Al Smith revolution." The Senator's victory over Republican National Chairman William M. Butler in 1926 was a portent of things to come. When the national convention two years later nominated Alfred E. Smith, whose special qualifications made him the idol of the emergent coalition, the process of its construction was completed. His candidacy took Massachusetts' popular vote from the Republican column in a national election for the first time in history, and began a whole era of Democratic presidential majorities in the Commonwealth.[8] The Great Depression which ensued in 1929 dashed the Republicans' hopes for a quick disintegration of the new Democratic alignment, and increased its effectiveness. By 1932 the Republicans had become the state's minority party, its basic strength limited mainly to those old-stock people of the towns and suburban cities, and of the higher economic classes, who through thick and thin saw the G.O.P. as the sole safeguard of the country's economy, or of its cultural traits and standards.

Massachusetts voted Democratic in the next four presidential elections after Franklin Roosevelt's inauguration. On the level of state politics, however, the cohesiveness of the new majority coalition was less regular. The Democrats increased their hold on the state government in 1934 and 1936, but in the 1938 election and in three of the six elections that followed it up to 1952, the Republicans gained control of the governorship.

Several developments were responsible for the G.O.P.'s resurgence in state politics.[9] One was the factionalism within the Democratic organization, which increased as the fruits of political power became more obtainable. Although James Michael Curley was denied his coveted cabinet or diplomatic post, he profited from James Farley's patronage policy of giving preference to the leaders who were with F.D.R. "before the convention." The Walsh-Ely organization, so assiduously wooed by the Roosevelt managers during the 1932 campaign, was largely left out in the cold once the New Deal began. Consequently, Senator Walsh's and Governor Ely's affection for the Administration cooled, while Curley nuzzled up to the popular President and basked in his re-flected glory. A showdown came in 1934. Under newly en-acted legislation the two parties held pre-primary conventions that year and the Democratic convention, dominated by the Walsh wing of the party, endorsed General Charles H. Cole for the gubernatorial nomination. Curley, refusing to abide by the convention's choice, challenged Cole in the primary, beat him, and subsequently won the general election in No-vember.

Curley's victory in the struggle for party control ended the sway of the relatively efficient organization built by Walsh, Ely, and Donahue between 1928 and 1932, and ex-tinguished the air of "refinement" imparted to the Bay State Democrats in those years. Ely became an ultra-conservative businessman and Senator Walsh reverted to "paddling his own canoe," while high-brow Democrats of the Jeffersonian So-ciety again dissociated themselves from formal party work, at least as far as state politics were concerned. Curley and the numerous chieftains who rose up to challenge him proved uninterested or incapable in constructing a close-knit, effec-tive organization. The party was left rudderless, except for its quadrennial mobilization behind the Democratic presidential nominee. This haphazard system of management, ridden by factional strife, sometimes produced candidates of questionable quality — men who were unable to recruit the full support of the Democratic coalition — and consequently split-ticket voting became a frequent characteristic of Bay State elections. Only after the New Deal era had ended in 1952, were there signs of the emergence of a more stable and constructive group of party leaders.

A different factor affecting the durability of the Demo-cratic coalition on the state level was the gradual reconstruc-tion of the Massachusetts Republican Party following its

chastening experience of 1928–1932. The process of reconstruction involved, among other things, a liberalization to
some degree of the party's views on economic policy, to conform more closely to the spirit of innovation that characterized all levels of government after 1932. While Democrats
at the State House continued to be the staunchest supporters
of economic, labor, and welfare reform legislation, Republican conservatism regarding such measures lessened after the
new managers of the G.O.P. took over in 1933. At the same
time, moreover, the significance of the differences between
the two parties' economic programs on the state level diminished, with the ever-increasing tendency of people to look
to Washington as the proper and most important agency of
government intervention in their economic lives.

Another phase of Republican reconstruction took place in
the field of ethnic group politics. Now the Democrats were
the ones plagued by demands for "recognition" from the Commonwealth's newer citizens, and the longer they were in power
the more insistent those demands became. Before much time
elapsed some New Immigrant leaders began to think that the
Irishmen who controlled the party were just as miserly in the
matter of patronage and recognition as the old-stock Republicans had been in their heyday, for the Irish continued to
dominate the primary and seemed to monopolize nominations
and appointments for themselves. The new Republican leadership gradually "liberalized" the G.O.P.'s ethnic attitude and
moved to capitalize on their opponents' discomfiture, hoping
to subtract the essential New Immigrant element from the
Democratic coalition.[10] After 1932, indeed, "league of nations"
politics became more important than ever in the struggle for
control of Massachusetts' state political machinery.

To sum up, then, Massachusetts Democrats in the era which
began with Roosevelt's inauguration generally enjoyed an

edge over the Republicans as far as appeals based on economic liberalism were concerned. But as time wore on, there was mounting tension within the new majority coalition as a result of two other considerations: the question of party leadership and quality of candidates — an old problem that bothered Bay State Democrats before and during the period covered in this study — and the question of accommodation and satisfaction for the coalition's junior but vital element, the "newer races" — a problem which, along with victory, came to the Democrats in the years of the "Al Smith revolution." These two factors became the major tests of the solidarity of the Democratic alliance within Massachusetts, aside, of course, from influences exerted by national and international affairs in the realm of state politics.

In the nation as a whole the years from 1919 to 1933 witnessed a process of coalition building and unbuilding similar to that in Massachusetts. After the Harding-Cox election the Republicans were clearly the country's majority party — a coalition of voting elements embracing both the industrial, urban East and the agricultural, rural West. The Democrats, their effective strength reduced to the party's traditional southern stronghold, faced the task of wooing away parts of the Republican alliance if they were to win again.

Mounting agrarian discontent seemed to offer the Democrats some hope of capturing the western wing of the G.O.P., and the movement for William G. McAdoo was predicated on that strategy. But the Democrats' own internal crisis, stemming from the issues of cultural liberalism, made McAdoo particularly unacceptable to the party's Newer Americans and led to the deadlocked convention of 1924. On the other hand, popular zeal for Al Smith in the East indicated that perhaps the Newer Americans' craving for "recognition" might be just as potent a weapon for disrupting the Republican alliance as the West's desire for economic justice. Nomination of the Happy Warrior represented an attempt to carry out this second strategy — of luring away the eastern wing of the G.O.P. — but in the end the experiment proved disappointing. Smith's candidacy made no dent at all in old-stock American parts of the country and actually alienated a considerable portion of the traditionally Democratic South. Cultural and economic factors combined to keep the nation Republican in 1928.

The clash between Smith and Franklin Roosevelt in 1932 seemed to force the Democrats to choose again between the alternative tactics of catering to the East or to the West, and with the nomination of Roosevelt it appeared that the party chose to concentrate on the West. As the campaign developed, however, it became evident that the economic issues of the Great Depression had produced a common meeting ground where the mutual cultural antagonisms of East and West and South could be overlooked or, at least, subdued. Roosevelt therefore won strong support in all sections of the country — support that added up to a new national Democratic majority coalition. The G.O.P. replaced the Democracy as the minority party, its core strength reduced mainly to those old-stock Americans who remained economically and culturally conservative.

Construction of the Roosevelt coalition also involved a confluence of the mainstreams of American economic liberalism, which had run parallel yet largely separate courses in previous years. One was the old rural tradition of agrarian protest bound up with the name of William Jennings Bryan. Concentrating on economic equality for the farmer in the face of America's rapid industrialization and urbanization, it tended to see everything connected with those two great forces as corrupt, "reactionary," and un-American. That tradition con-

tinued active during the 1920's, and its cultural ramifications were much in evidence in efforts to "uplift," or circumscribe, the influence of the Newer American civilization it despised. A second stream was the relatively newer concept of urban welfare reformism — represented by Al Smith and other spokesmen for the city masses — concentrating on economic security for those already living in the industrialized, urban-ized, Newer American society. Active during the Progressive era, this type of economic liberalism was greatly subdued during the early 1920's because of two considerations: the Newer Americans' general distrust of all "reformers," due to resentment of Prohibition and similar "uplift" measures aimed at their group preferences and traits; and their concentration on the noneconomic struggle for equal citizenship status and "recognition" — the struggle for the principles of *cultural* liberalism.

During the 1920's subscribers to the rural and urban brands of economic liberalism distrusted each other, and the cultural antagonisms bound up with the two civilizations in which they were rooted heightened mutual animosity. Meanwhile, other contributors to America's reform heritage — labor lead-ers, advanced liberals, and middle-class progressives — stood by immobilized, or dazzled, by "Republican prosperity." But when the prosperity boom ended, Franklin Roosevelt won support from followers of all these traditions, embodying in himself the attraction of Bryan for farmers, of Smith for the urban masses, and of Teddy Roosevelt and Wilson for re-formers of all types. His New Deal became a symbol of a revived, nation-wide quest for economic liberalism, embracing all the earlier versions of that term.

Economic discontent was the matrix of the Roosevelt coalition in 1932, then, and the New Deal's strides in the direction of economic reform were the main source of the coalition's solidarity in future years. At the same time, however, concentration on the nation's economic problems by both Old and Newer Americans after 1933 further diminished those cultural tensions which had occupied so much of the country's attention in the 1920's, and other factors too lessened their significance. One thing was the virtual ending of European immigration in the depression decade. Another was the general acquiescence in the fact that national Prohibition had been a failure. Moreover, with the rise abroad of totalitarian regimes based on racism and conformity, there came a growing appreciation of the value of diversity in American society. Thus after 1933 the term "reform" in the United States carried a primarily economic connotation, with little reference to personal drinking habits, sabbath laws, parochial schools, or Americanization. Indeed, with time American "liberalism" came to include, besides economic security for citizens of all classes, a large infusion of that tolerance of ethnic and cultural variety which had been so notably lacking in the 1920's.

Such was the meaning imparted to liberalism by the New Deal Administration, at any rate, for by legislation, appointments, and rhetoric Franklin Roosevelt and Harry Truman demonstrated their subscription to the ideals of cultural liberalism.[11] In the years after 1933 the people of America's "new frontier" achieved much in the way of securing the status and recognition that had been their main concern during the 1920's, and which was so instrumental in bringing them to the polls for Al Smith and the Democratic Party in 1928. Hence the allegiance of the Newer American wing of the Roosevelt coalition was made stronger by something more than economic determinism. It was largely for this reason that the Newer American Commonwealth of Massachusetts remained steadfast when, after 1936, some other members of the coalition showed signs of weakening. Not until 1952, with the rise of a new set of international and "Communist" issues peculiarly affecting her large Irish Catholic and New Immigrant populations, would the Bay State's loyalty to the national Democracy falter.

Appendix

Appendix

Election Statistics, 1916-1932

Tables 1–3: Statistics of registration and voter participation.
Tables 4–7: Democratic per cent of the vote.

Explanation of classifications used in the tables:

In Table 1, figures are presented for Massachusetts as a whole, for the state's 39 cities (including Boston), and for the state's 316 towns.

In Tables 2 and 4, Boston is segregated from the state's cities, and thus figures are presented for Massachusetts as a whole, for Boston, for the 38 other cities, and for the state's 316 towns.

Three of the 39 places listed as cities in the 1920 census were actually towns in 1916 and 1918. Their figures for those two years, however, have been included with those of the 36 places that actually were cities, in order to lend uniformity to the tables. After 1920 the number of cities in Massachusetts remained stable, at 39, for the remainder of the period covered in this study.

In Tables 3 and 5–7, figures are presented for Massachusetts as a whole, for Boston, and for the following selected categories of municipalities (based on the federal census of 1920):

Newer American cities over 25,000, excluding Boston. This category includes all cities of this population class (except Boston) having 70 per cent or more foreign-stock population (i.e., foreign born, plus native born of foreign or mixed parentage) in 1920. The ten cities were: Chelsea, Chicopee, Fall River, Fitchburg, Holyoke, Lawrence, Lowell, New Bedford, Revere, and Worcester.

Old-stock cities over 25,000. This group includes all cities of this population class having 30 per cent or more "native white of native parentage" population in 1920. The thirteen cities were: Brockton, Brookline, Haverhill, Lynn, Malden, Medford, Newton, Pittsfield, Quincy, Somerville, Springfield, Taunton, and Waltham.

Newer American places of 10,000 to 25,000. This category includes all places of this population class having 70 per cent or more foreign-stock population. The eleven places were: Adams, Clinton, Easthampton, Gardner, Methuen, Milford, Northbridge, Norwood, Peabody, Southbridge, and Webster.

Old-stock places of 10,000 to 25,000. This category includes all places of this population class having 40 per cent or more "native white of native parentage" population. The sixteen places were: Amesbury, Arlington, Belmont, Beverly, Braintree, Danvers, Framingham, Greenfield, Melrose, Natick, Newburyport, Saugus, West Springfield, Weymouth, Winchester, and Winthrop.

Newer American towns of 2,500 to 10,000. This group includes all places of this population class having 70 per cent or more foreign-stock population. The sixteen towns were: Acushnet, Blackstone, Dracut, Dudley, Hadley, Hardwick, Hatfield, Ludlow, Maynard, Montague, North Andover, Palmer, South Hadley, Ware, Westford, and Wilbraham.

Old-stock towns of 2,500 to 10,000 population. This category includes all places of this population class having 50 per cent or more "native white of native parentage" population. The twenty-nine towns were: Abington, Amherst, Athol, Barnstable, Bourne, Dalton, East Bridgewater, Foxborough, Groveland, Hanover, Harvard, Hingham, Holbrook, Holliston, Hopedale, Longmeadow, Marblehead, Middleborough, Nantucket, North Brookfield, Orange, Reading, Rockland, Scituate, Swampscott, Templeton, Whitman, Williamstown, and Wrentham.

Note that in the "old-stock" categories the percentage of "native white of native parentage" rises as the size of the municipalities included in the category declines.

For sources of registration, voter participation, and election statistics, see the Bibliography.

Table 1

Registration and Voting Statistics for Massachusetts, the 39 Cities, and the 316 Towns, 1916–1932

	1916	1918	1920	1922	1924	1926	1928	1930	1932
Registered Voters									
State	650,882	626,050	1,179,085	1,248,520	1,392,584	1,356,853	1,722,263	1,629,704	1,796,588
Cities	438,940	420,820	780,217	843,565	943,815	907,100	1,157,193	1,086,037	1,190,153
Towns	211,942	205,230	398,868	404,955	448,769	449,753	565,070	543,667	606,435
Index Numbers of Registration									
State	100.0	96.2	181.2	191.8	214.0	208.5	264.6	250.4	276.0
Cities	100.0	95.9	179.8	192.2	215.0	206.7	263.6	247.4	271.1
Towns	100.0	96.8	184.0	191.1	211.7	212.2	266.6	256.5	286.1
Actual Voters									
State	557,499	428,741	1,029,138	910,891	1,213,377	1,038,466	1,609,975	1,250,118	1,609,548
Cities	378,523	289,794	690,788	631,327	825,880	705,168	1,086,512	847,801	1,069,302
Towns	178,976	138,947	338,350	279,564	387,497	333,298	523,463	402,317	540,246

Index Numbers of Actual Voters

State	100.0	76.9	184.6	163.4	217.6	186.3	288.8	224.2	288.7
Cities	100.0	76.6	182.5	166.8	218.2	186.3	287.0	224.0	282.5
Towns	100.0	77.6	189.0	156.2	216.5	186.2	292.5	224.8	301.9

Per Cent of Registrants Who Voted

State	85.6	68.5	87.3	72.9	87.1	76.5	93.5	76.7	89.6
Cities	86.2	68.9	87.5	74.8	87.5	77.7	93.9	78.1	89.8
Towns	84.4	67.7	86.8	69.0	86.3	74.1	92.6	74.0	89.1

Table 2

Aggregate Major Party Vote for President,* and Per Cent Change from Previous Election, 1916–1932, for Massachusetts, Boston, the 38 Other Cities, and the 316 Towns

	1916	1920	1924	1928	1932
State	516,669	957,844 (+85.4%)	1,125,532 (+17.5%)	1,568,324 (+39.3%)	1,537,107 (−2.0%)
Boston	93,145	157,547 (+68.5%)	198,935 (+26.2%)	273,725 (+37.6%)	257,727 (−5.8%)
Other Cities	258,905	484,005 (+86.9%)	562,192 (+16.2%)	785,122 (+39.7%)	744,102 (−5.2%)
Towns	164,619	316,292 (+92.1%)	364,405 (+15.2%)	509,477 (+39.8%)	535,278 (+5.1%)

* Except for 1924, the figures given are the combined Democratic-Republican presidential vote. The figures for 1924 represent the combined Democratic-Republican-Progressive (La Follette) vote.

Table 3

Aggregate Major Party Vote for President,* and Per Cent Change from Previous Election, 1916–1932, for Massachusetts, Boston, and Selected Categories of Municipalities

	1916	1920	1924	1928	1932
State	516,669	957,844 (+85.4%)	1,125,532 (+17.5%)	1,568,324 (+39.3%)	1,537,107 (−2.0%)
Boston	93,145	157,547 (+68.5%)	198,935 (+26.2%)	273,725 (+37.6%)	257,727 (−5.8%)
Cities over 25,000					
Newer American	94,983	175,541 (+84.8%)	205,965 (+17.3%)	275,729 (+33.9%)	269,585 (−2.2%)
Old-stock	107,039	206,912 (+93.3%)	242,163 (+17.1%)	349,621 (+44.4%)	336,939 (−3.6%)
Places of 10,000–25,000					
Newer American	19,151	36,660 (+91.4%)	42,392 (+15.6%)	57,121 (+34.7%)	58,583 (+2.6%)
Old-stock	35,279	71,681 (+103.2%)	82,752 (+15.2%)	123,722 (+49.5%)	127,249 (+2.9%)
Towns of 2,500–10,000					
Newer American	9,607	17,737 (+84.6%)	21,206 (+19.6%)	28,215 (+33.1%)	29,053 (+3.0%)
Old-stock	23,608	43,375 (+83.7%)	48,729 (+12.3%)	65,496 (+34.4%)	65,581 (+0.1%)

* See note to Table 2.

Table 4

Democratic Per Cent of the Major Party Vote for President, 1916–1932,* for Massachusetts, Boston, the 38 Other Cities, and the 316 Towns

	1916	1920	1924	1928	1932
State	48.0	28.9	37.5	50.5	52.0
Boston	60.2	39.7	53.7	68.0	69.7
Other Cities	48.3	29.0	38.2	53.0	54.2
Towns	40.7	23.3	27.6	37.4	40.6

* Except for 1924, the figures given are the Democratic percentage of the Democratic-Republican presidential vote. The figures for 1924 represent the combined Democratic-Progressive (Davis plus La Follette) percentage of the total three-party vote (Democratic, Republican, and Progressive), since most of La Follette's votes came from people who voted for the Democratic gubernatorial and senatorial candidates that year.

Table 5

Democratic Per Cent of the Major Party Vote for President, 1916–1932,* for Massachusetts, Boston, and Selected Categories of Municipalities

	1916	1920	1924	1928	1932
State	48.0	28.9	37.5	50.5	52.0
Boston	60.2	39.7	53.7	68.0	69.7
Cities over 25,000					
Newer American	51.3	30.9	41.9	60.4	62.5
Old-stock	44.4	26.4	34.5	46.8	47.9
Places of 10,000–25,000					
Newer American	48.5	32.8	39.8	54.4	57.3
Old-stock	41.0	22.3	27.8	38.6	39.6
Towns of 2,500–10,000					
Newer American	45.7	30.6	38.1	52.9	55.6
Old-stock	40.0	21.0	23.2	29.3	31.2

* See note to Table 4.

Table 6

Democratic Per Cent of the Major Party Vote for Senator, 1922–1930,* for Massachusetts, Boston, and Selected Categories of Municipalities

	1922	1924	1926	1928	1930
State	48.1	49.2	52.8	54.1	54.7
Boston	63.8	68.1	70.7	71.5	72.6
Cities over 25,000					
Newer American	53.5	54.3	57.7	62.4	60.9
Old-stock	44.0	45.0	49.2	50.4	51.8
Places of 10,000–25,000					
Newer American	51.2	53.8	57.7	58.2	59.0
Old-stock	37.2	38.1	43.0	43.0	43.5
Towns of 2,500–10,000					
Newer American	48.4	49.5	55.5	56.2	56.7
Old-stock	32.5	31.2	34.8	34.4	36.4

* Except for 1922, the figures given are the Democratic percentage of the Democratic-Republican senatorial vote. The figures for 1922 represent the Democratic percentage of the total three-party vote (Democratic, Republican, and Progressive-Prohibition). Most of the people who voted for the Progressive-Prohibition Party candidate that year normally voted Republican.

Table 7

Democratic Per Cent of the Major Party Vote for Governor, 1920–1932, for Massachusetts, Boston, and Selected Categories of Municipalities

	1920	1922	1924	1926	1928	1930	1932
State	31.1	46.5	42.9	40.6	49.4	50.7	53.9
Boston	42.3	64.9	59.0	56.7	66.9	68.6	70.2
Cities over 25,000							
Newer American	36.4	50.2	49.6	47.7	57.4	57.0	60.8
Old-stock	27.8	42.3	38.9	36.2	45.6	47.9	51.2
Places of 10,000–25,000							
Newer American	36.7	49.8	47.9	44.3	52.2	53.2	58.4
Old-stock	22.9	35.4	32.0	29.6	38.6	39.2	42.2
Towns of 2,500–10,000							
Newer American	34.0	46.4	46.4	44.2	50.7	53.7	56.0
Old-stock	20.2	29.3	25.3	24.0	29.6	32.2	35.8

Bibliography

Notes

Index

Bibliography

ELECTION STATISTICS AND DATA

Commonwealth of Massachusetts. *Public Document No. 43: Number of . . . Registered Voters and Persons Who Voted . . . Together with the Number of Votes Received by Each Candidate.* Issued in each election year, this document gives registration figures for the state, by cities and towns, wards and precincts. It also records the official election returns in state primary and general elections, and on state referenda, for the state, and by cities and towns. Unfortunately, the document does not give returns by wards and precincts. For the latter, one must resort to newspapers, the annual reports of municipalities (distressingly few of which publish election returns), and communication with city and town clerks.

United States Department of Commerce, Bureau of the Census. *Fourteenth Census of the United States, 1920, State Compendium: Massachusetts.* Washington, 1924. Various tables in this census report give data on the ethnic composition of the state, and of cities and towns over 2,500 population. Especially valuable is Table 13, which presents statistics on the ethnic composition of the individual wards in cities with 50,000 or more inhabitants. For information on the ethnic make-up of the wards of smaller cities, one must rely on less precise sources: the national origins of ward-elected members of city governments, the response of wards to "foreign" names appearing on the ballot in state elections, newspaper reports and, in some cases, the word of knowledgeable politicians.

INTERVIEWS

Among the most valuable of sources are interviews with individuals who actually lived and experienced the things about which an historian writes. Interviewees provide, not only specific bits of information, but an excellent check on conclusions garnered from printed sources or evolved in the author's mind. Those consulted during the preparation of this study were the following: Elijah Adlow, Vincent Brogna, LaRue Brown, Channing Cox, James Michael Curley, Frank Donahue, Julian D. Rainey, Joseph Santosuosso, Amos Taylor, Stanley Wisnioski, and B. Loring Young.

NEWSPAPERS

Berkshire Evening Eagle (Pittsfield), 1920–1932.
Boston Herald, 1916–1933.
Boston Transcript, 1916–1933.
Chelsea Evening Record, 1920–1932.
Fall River Daily Globe, 1920–1922.
Fitchburg Sentinel, 1920–1932.
Gazzetta del Massachusetts (Boston), 1918–1933.
Haverhill Evening Gazette, 1920–1932.
Holyoke Daily Transcript and Telegram, 1928–1932.
Holyoke Telegram, 1920–1926.
Italian News (Boston), 1922–1933.
Jewish Advocate (Boston), 1918–1932.
Lawrence Sun American, 1920.
Lawrence Sunday Sun, 1924.
Lowell Courier Citizen, 1920–1922.
Lowell Evening Leader, 1922–1932.
Lynn Daily Evening Item, 1920–1932.
New Bedford Standard-Times, 1932.
New Bedford Times, 1920–1930.
New York Times, 1923–1924.
North Adams Transcript, 1920–1932.
Springfield Republican, 1920–1933.
The Pilot (Boston), 1919–1922.
Worcester Evening Gazette, 1920.
Worcester Telegram, 1920–1932.

CONTEMPORARY PERIODICALS

The periodical literature of a given era is useful chiefly in that it reflects the prevailing attitudes, opinions, and prejudices of the time. In addition, however, the best of contemporary magazine writers are often cognizant of deeper forces and meanings sometimes overlooked by later historians. Particularly perceptive in the 1920's were the writings of Walter Lippmann, Hendrik W. Van Loon, William Hard,

BIBLIOGRAPHY

John W. Owens, Stanley Frost and, in general, the contributors to the *Nation* and the *New Republic*. The contemporary periodicals consulted during the preparation of this study were the following: *American Mercury, Annals of the American Academy of Political and Social Science, Atlantic Monthly, Current History Magazine, Current Opinion, Congressional Digest, Forum, Good Housekeeping, Harper's Magazine, Independent, Literary Digest, Nation, New Republic, North American Review, Outlook, Review, Review of Reviews, Scribner's Magazine, Survey,* and *World's Work.*

UNPUBLISHED PAPERS, AND MANUSCRIPTS

Adlow, Elijah. Papers and scrapbooks, in Judge Adlow's possession.
Jamison, Alden. "Irish-Americans, the Irish Question, and American Diplomacy." Unpublished doctoral dissertation, Harvard University, 1943.
Massachusetts Department of Labor and Industries. In addition to the published studies made by this agency, cited elsewhere in this bibliography, the author made use of the wealth of unpublished statistical surveys and reports on the Massachusetts economic situation between 1919–1933, available at the Department's Reference Library in the State House at Boston.
Roosevelt, Franklin D. Papers, Franklin D. Roosevelt Library, Hyde Park, New York.
Walsh, David I. Papers and scrapbooks, Holy Cross College Library, Worcester, Massachusetts.
Young, B. Loring. Papers and scrapbooks, in Mr. Young's possession.

OFFICIAL PUBLICATIONS

Commonwealth of Massachusetts. *Final Report of the Special Commission on Stabilization of Employment.* Boston, 1933.
———— *Journals,* of the state Senate and House of Representatives. Boston, 1920–1932.
———— *The Decennial Census, 1915.* Boston, 1918.
Federal Reserve Bank of Boston. *Monthly Review of Business and Industrial Conditions in the New England District.* Boston, 1919–1933.
Massachusetts Department of Labor and Industries. *Massachusetts Industrial Review.* Boston, 1920–1922.
———— *Statistics of Manufactures in Massachusetts: 1920–1938.* Place and date of publication not given.

BIBLIOGRAPHY

Massachusetts State Branch, American Federation of Labor. *Proceedings of the . . . Annual Convention*. Boston, 1919–1933.

Massachusetts State Federation of Labor. *Roll Calls of the Massachusetts Legislature on Labor Measures, 1927–1928*. Place and date of publication not given.

—— *Roll Calls of the Massachusetts Legislature on Labor Measures, 1929–1930*. Place and date of publication not given.

Official Report of the Proceedings of the Democratic National Convention of 1924. Indianapolis, 1924.

United States Department of Commerce, Bureau of the Census. *Fourteenth Census of the United States, 1920, State Compendium: Massachusetts*. Washington, 1924.

United States Department of Labor, Bureau of Labor Statistics. *Monthly Labor Review*. Washington, 1920–1933.

BOOKS AND ARTICLES

Abell, A. I. "The Catholic Church and Social Problems in the World War I Era, 1910–1922," *Mid-America*, XXX (1948), 139–151.

Adams, S. H. *Incredible Era: The Life and Times of Warren Gamaliel Harding*. Boston, 1939.

Allen, F. L. *Only Yesterday*. New York, 1931.

Artman, C. E., ed. *Commercial Survey of New England*. 3 vols. United States Department of Commerce, 1929–1930.

Bates, J. L. "The Teapot Dome Scandal and the Election of 1924," *American Historical Review*, LX (1955), 303–322.

Berthoff, R. T. *British Immigrants in Industrial America, 1790–1950*. Cambridge, Mass., 1953.

Brewer, D. C. *The Conquest of New England by the Immigrant*. New York, 1926.

Burns, J. M. *Roosevelt: The Lion and the Fox*. New York, 1956.

Coolidge, Calvin. *Autobiography*. New York, 1929.

Cox, J. M. *Journey through My Years*. New York, 1946.

Dinneen, J. F. *The Purple Shamrock: James Michael Curley*. New York, 1949.

Ducharme, Jacques. *The Shadows of the Trees: The Story of French-Canadians in New England*. New York, 1943.

Ely, Joseph. *The American Dream*. Boston, 1944.

Farley, J. A. *Behind the Ballots*. New York, 1938.

Freidel, Frank. *Franklin D. Roosevelt: The Ordeal*. Boston, 1954.

—— *Franklin D. Roosevelt: The Triumph*. Boston, 1956.

Frost, Stanley. *The Challenge of the Klan*. Indianapolis, 1924.

Fuess, C. M. *Calvin Coolidge*. Boston, 1940.

Garraty, J. A. *Henry Cabot Lodge*. New York, 1953.

Handlin, Oscar. *Al Smith and His America*. Boston, 1958.

———— *Boston's Immigrants, 1790–1865*. Cambridge, Mass., 1941.

———— *The American People in the Twentieth Century*. Cambridge, Mass., 1954.

———— *The Uprooted*. Boston, 1951.

Hennessy, M. E. *Four Decades of Massachusetts Politics, 1890–1935*. Norwood, Mass., 1935.

Higham, John. *Strangers in the Land*. New Brunswick, 1955.

Hofstadter, Richard. *The Age of Reform*. New York, 1955.

Hoover, Herbert. *The Memoirs of Herbert Hoover: The Cabinet and the Presidency, 1920–1933*. New York, 1952.

Klimm, L. E. *The Relation between Certain Population Changes and the Physical Environment in Hampden, Hampshire, and Franklin Counties, Massachusetts, 1790–1925*. Philadelphia, 1933.

Lubell, Samuel. *The Future of American Politics*. New York, 1951.

McKay, K. C. *The Progressive Movement of 1924*. New York, 1947.

Mecklin, J. M. *The Ku Klux Klan: A Study in the American Mind*. New York, 1924.

Moon, H. L. *Balance of Power: The Negro Vote*. Garden City, 1948.

Nicolson, Harold. *Peacemaking, 1919*. Boston, 1933.

Peel, R. V., and T. C. Donnelly. *The 1928 Campaign: An Analysis*. New York, 1931.

———— and T. C. Donnelly. *The 1932 Campaign: An Analysis*. New York, 1935.

Perkins, Frances. *The Roosevelt I Knew*. New York, 1946.

Pringle, H. F. *Alfred E. Smith: A Critical Study*. New York, 1927.

Roosevelt, Elliott, ed. *F. D. R.: His Personal Letters, 1928–1945*. New York, 1950.

Schlesinger, A. M., Jr. *The Age of Roosevelt: The Crisis of the Old Order, 1919–1933*. New York, 1957.

Schriftgiesser, Karl. *This Was Normalcy*. Boston, 1948.

Smith, A. E. *Up To Now*. New York, 1929.

Solomon, B. M. *Ancestors and Immigrants*. Cambridge, Mass., 1956.

Warner, W. L., and others. *The Yankee City Series*. 4 vols. New Haven, 1941–1947.

Wayman, D. G. *David I. Walsh: Citizen-Patriot*. Milwaukee, 1952.

White, W. A. *A Puritan in Babylon*. New York, 1938.

Whyte, W. F. *Street Corner Society*. Chicago, 1943.

Notes

Chapter One.

A MODERN BAY STATE AND HER PEOPLE

1. See C. E. Artman, ed., *Commercial Survey of New England* (United States Department of Commerce, 1929–1930), 3 vols., *passim*; United States Department of Commerce, Bureau of the Census, *Fourteenth Census of the United States, 1920, State Compendium: Massachusetts* (Washington, 1924), *passim*.

2. *Fourteenth Census, Massachusetts Compendium*, pp. 7, 9.

3. Cf. O. Handlin, *The American People in the Twentieth Century* (Cambridge, Mass., 1954), pp. 81–82.

4. All statistics in this chapter pertaining to the ethnic composition of Massachusetts' population in 1920 are taken from *Fourteenth Census, Massachusetts Compendium*, pp. 18, 60, unless otherwise noted.

5. See R. T. Berthoff, *British Immigrants in Industrial America, 1790–1950* (Cambridge, Mass., 1953), *passim*.

6. See O. Handlin, *Boston's Immigrants, 1790–1865* (Cambridge, Mass., 1941), *passim*.

7. See Commonwealth of Massachusetts, *The Decennial Census, 1915* (Boston, 1918), pp. 536ff, for the occupations of Irish immigrants. It should be noted that the table presented there deals only with the foreign-born and not with the second and later generations of immigrant children, whose occupational status presumably would show further improvement.

8. Very few French-Canadians settled in Boston, however. See *Fourteenth Census, Massachusetts Compendium*, pp. 39–40, for a table showing the distribution of the Bay State's foreign-born population by counties and by major cities and towns.

9. See *Massachusetts Decennial Census, 1915*, pp. 536ff, for the occupations of the various New Immigrant groups. Again it should be observed that the table there concerns only foreign-born persons,

not the second and later generations. See *Fourteenth Census, Massachusetts Compendium*, pp. 62ff, for the occupations of Negroes.

10. The largest categories were: French, 303,821; Italian, 237,858; Polish, 145,822; Yiddish and Hebrew, 141,228; Portuguese, 99,096; Lithuanian and Lettish, 44,064; Russian, 32,617; and Greek, 29,044 (*Fourteenth Census, Massachusetts Compendium*, p. 60).

11. Cf. O. Handlin, *The Uprooted* (Boston, 1951), *passim*.

12. See Handlin, *The American People*, pp. 99ff; J. Higham, *Strangers in the Land* (New Brunswick, 1955), *passim*; B. M. Solomon, *Ancestors and Immigrants* (Cambridge, Mass., 1956), *passim*.

13. The author's observations in these paragraphs are based in large part on interviews with a number of Massachusetts political leaders of both parties, whose names are cited elsewhere in this work.

14. See J. Ducharme, *The Shadows of the Trees: The Story of French-Canadians in New England* (New York, 1943), pp. 75ff.

15. At that time state elections were held annually in Massachusetts. Beginning with the election of 1920, executive and legislative officers served two-year terms.

16. For fuller details and sources of election statistics see Appendix and Bibliography.

Chapter Two.

THE POLITICS OF POSTWAR DISILLUSION

1. See J. A. Garraty, *Henry Cabot Lodge* (New York, 1953), pp. 336–401.

2. *Gazzetta del Massachusetts* (Boston), December 28, 1918, January 11, 1919 (in Italian).

3. H. Nicolson, *Peacemaking, 1919* (Boston, 1933), pp. 157–184.

4. *Gazzetta del Massachusetts*, March 1, 1919 (in Italian).

5. *Ibid.*, May 3 (in Italian), 17, October 11, 1919.

6. *Ibid.*, May 12, 1919 (in Italian).

7. Quoted from a resolve adopted by the St. Anne Italian Society of Marlboro, Massachusetts, reported in the *Worcester Telegram*, May 2, 1919 (clipping in the personal scrapbooks of Senator David I. Walsh, Holy Cross College Library, Worcester, Massachusetts).

8. Quoted in *Gazzetta del Massachusetts*, May 12, 1919.

9. *Ibid.*

10. A copy of the resolution is in the Senator David I. Walsh papers, Holy Cross College Library.

11. *Boston Advertiser*, March 9, 1919 (clipping, Walsh scrapbooks).

12. *Boston Transcript*, February 10, 1920.

13. *The Pilot* (Boston), January 4, February 1, 1919; A. Jamison, "Irish-Americans, the Irish Question, and American Diplomacy" (Unpubl. doctoral dissertation, Harvard University, 1943), pp. 532ff.

14. Jamison, "Irish-Americans and American Diplomacy," pp. 626–661.

15. A copy of the resolution is in the Walsh papers.

16. *The Pilot*, March 29, April 5, 1919.

17. Jamison, "Irish-Americans and American Diplomacy," pp. 626–627, 713–714. See also E. R. Turner, "America and the Irish Question," *World's Work*, XXXVIII (October 1919), 580–589.

18. *The Pilot*, July 5, 1919. See also Jamison, "Irish-Americans and American Diplomacy," pp. 718–720.

19. Walsh papers; *Boston Post*, March 17; *Newburyport News*, March 24; *Boston Globe*, April 28; *Worcester Telegram*, April 7, 1919 (clippings, Walsh scrapbooks).

20. *The Pilot*, June 14; *Boston Transcript*, October 9; *Holyoke Telegram*, December 2, 1919 (clipping, Walsh scrapbooks).

21. *World's Work*, XXXVIII (August 1919), 349.

22. *Boston Transcript*, February 17, 1920.

23. *Ibid.*, March 20, 24, June 4, 1920.

24. *Ibid.*, March 24, April 5, 1920.

25. *Ibid.*, January 9, 1920.

26. See *ibid.*, June 28–July 7, 1920, for coverage of the convention.

27. *Current Opinion*, LXIX (August 1920), 139–148; *Review of Reviews*, LXII (August 1920), 198–199; *World's Work*, XL (September 1920), 426; *Outlook*, CXXV (July 14, 1920), 486–494.

28. *Boston Transcript*, May 3, June 19, July 12, 1920.

29. *Ibid.*, August 7, 1920; J. M. Cox, *Journey through My Years* (New York, 1946), pp. 241–244.

30. *Boston Transcript*, September 7, 10, October 5, 1920.

31. *Ibid.*, September 29, 30, 1920; *World's Work*, XLI (November 1920), 15–16; *Review*, III (October 13, 1920), 304.

32. *Boston Transcript*, August 23, 1920; Massachusetts State Branch, American Federation of Labor, *Proceedings of the . . . Annual Convention, 1920*, pp. 135–142; *Lawrence Sun American*, August 7, 1920.

33. Statements by the Rt. Rev. Michael Gallagher, Bishop of Detroit, and the national council of the Friends of Irish Freedom, quoted in the *Lawrence Sun American*, August 8, and the *Boston Transcript*, October 16, 1920.

34. *Boston Transcript*, September 23, 27, October 7, 1920.

35. *Ibid.*, November 4, 1922.

36. *Jewish Advocate* (Boston), June 19, 1919. See also *ibid.*, July 3, 1919, April 29, 1920; J. L. Magnes, "Jewry at the End of the War," *Nation*, CXII (May 4, 1921), 647–648; *Nation*, CXI (November 3, 1920), 493.

37. *Boston Transcript*, August 18, 1920.

38. *Lawrence Sun American*, September 8, 1920, quoting from resolutions adopted by a meeting of Lithuanian-Americans in Methuen, Massachusetts.

39. *Boston Transcript*, October 15, 1920.

40. Commonwealth of Massachusetts, *Public Document No. 43: Number of . . . Registered Voters and Persons Who Voted . . . Together with the Number of Votes Received by Each Candidate,* 1916, 1920.

41. *Boston Transcript*, October 4, 1920.

42. *Ibid.*, July 29, August 3, 1920.

43. *Ibid.*, September 20, October 20, 21; *Worcester Evening Gazette,* October 13, 1920.

44. *Lawrence Sun American,* September 18; *Springfield Republican,* September 19; *Fall River Daily Globe,* September 20, 1920.

45. *Worcester Evening Gazette,* October 19; *Boston Transcript,* October 20, 21, 1920.

46. *Boston Transcript,* July 12, October 18; *Springfield Republican,* October 27, 1920.

47. *Boston Herald,* October 18, 1919 (clipping, Walsh scrapbooks), June 13, 14, 1920.

48. See the *Boston Transcript,* June 8–13, 1920, for convention coverage.

49. *Ibid.*, July 22, August 28, October 7, 15, 27, 1920. See also S. H. Adams, *Incredible Era: The Life and Times of Warren Gamaliel Harding* (Boston, 1939), pp. 175–177.

50. Statement by the Rev. M. A. N. Shaw at the Republican state convention (*Springfield Republican,* September 18, 1920).

51. *Boston Transcript,* September 18, 23, 1920.

52. *Berkshire Evening Eagle* (Pittsfield), November 1; *Worcester Telegram,* October 24, 25; *Springfield Republican,* October 26, 1920.

53. *Springfield Republican,* October 26, 30, 1920.

54. *Boston Transcript,* June 11, 1920.

55. *Nation,* CXI (October 27, 1920), 466; *New Republic,* XXIV (September 22, 1920), 82–83; Massachusetts A.F. of L., *Proceedings of the Annual Convention, 1920,* p. 82.

56. *Springfield Republican,* October 26, 30; *Worcester Telegram,* October 27; *New Bedford Times,* October 23, 1920.

THE POLITICS OF POSTWAR DISILLUSION

57. *Springfield Republican*, October 26, 30; *Worcester Telegram*, October 27, 1920.

58. See Federal Reserve Bank of Boston, *Monthly Review of Business and Industrial Conditions in the New England District*, 1919–1921, *passim*; Massachusetts Department of Labor and Industries, *Massachusetts Industrial Review*, 1920–1921, *passim*.

59. The proportion of members reported as unemployed by labor union locals in Massachusetts rose from 8.7 per cent on March 31, 1920, to 31.8 per cent on December 31 (Massachusetts Department of Labor and Industries, *Industrial Review*, 1920–1921, *passim*). The economically disadvantageous position occupied by farmers in 1920 was depicted in the index numbers of wholesale prices compiled by the U.S. Bureau of Labor Statistics (United States Department of Labor, Bureau of Labor Statistics, *Monthly Labor Review*, February 1922, p. 48).

60. Federal Reserve Bank of Boston, *Review*, March 25, 1920.

61. *Worcester Telegram*, November 1, 1920, quoting Congressman Samuel Winslow of the Fourth District. See also *Worcester Telegram*, October 22, 26, 29; *New Bedford Times*, October 10; *Lawrence Sun American*, October 20, 1920.

62. *Worcester Evening Gazette*, October 29; *Worcester Telegram*, November 1, 1920.

63. *Boston Transcript*, October 27, 30; *Springfield Republican*, October 29, 1920.

64. *Boston Transcript*, October 26, 1920.

65. *Berkshire Evening Eagle*; *Lawrence Sun American*, November 1, 1920.

66. *Boston Transcript*, October 30, November 1; *Gazzetta del Massachusetts*, October 30, 1920 (in Italian).

67. For fuller details and sources of election returns, registration statistics, and data on the ethnic composition of electoral districts, see Appendix and Bibliography.

68. See, for example, F Freidel, *Franklin D. Roosevelt: The Ordeal* (Boston, 1954), p. 88.

69. *Boston Transcript*, November 27, 1920.

70. Cf. S. Lubell, *The Future of American Politics* (New York, 1951), chap. 7, "The Myth of Isolationism."

71. *Boston Transcript*, November 3, 1920.

72. *Ibid.*, November 3, 6, 1920; Cox, *Journey through My Years*, pp. 272–273.

73. *Worcester Telegram*, November 3, 1920.

Chapter Three.

NORMALCY, IN NATION AND STATE

1. For a brief account of the first two years of the Harding Administration see K. Schriftgiesser, *This Was Normalcy* (Boston, 1948), pp. 91–138.

2. Federal Reserve Bank of Boston, *Monthly Review of Business and Industrial Conditions in the New England District*, 1920–1922, *passim*; Massachusetts Department of Labor and Industries, *Massachusetts Industrial Review*, 1920–1922, *passim*.

3. L. E. Tilden, "New England Textile Strike," in United States Department of Labor, Bureau of Labor Statistics, *Monthly Labor Review*, May 1923, pp. 13–36.

4. See, for example, W. Jett Lauck, "Industrial Significance of Immigration," *Annals of the American Academy of Political and Social Science*, XCIII (January 1921), 185–190; W. M. Leiserson, "Immigration and Unemployment," *Survey*, XLV (December 11, 1920), 388.

5. Vincent Brogna, Justice of the Superior Court of Massachusetts, to the author, October 26, 1955 (interview); Joseph Santosuosso to the author, September 23, 1955 (interview).

6. A. Jamison, "Irish-Americans, the Irish Question, and American Diplomacy," (Unpubl. doctoral dissertation, Harvard University, 1943), p. 828.

7. *Boston Transcript*, March 17, 1921; *Literary Digest*, June 25, 1921, pp. 7–8.

8. *Boston Transcript*, December 12, 1921, March 13, 17, 1922; *Providence Tribune*, September 9, 1922 (clipping in the personal scrapbooks of Senator David I. Walsh, Holy Cross College Library, Worcester, Massachusetts).

9. *Boston Transcript*, August 30, October 18, 21, 1922.

10. C. M. Fuess, *Calvin Coolidge* (Boston, 1940), p. 289; *Boston News Bureau*, September 18, 1922 (clipping, personal scrapbooks of Elijah Adlow); Amos Taylor to the author, September 20, 1955 (interview); Channing Cox to the author, October 28, 1955 (interview). Taylor was chairman of the Republican state committee, 1928–1933. Cox was lieutenant governor of Massachusetts, 1919–1921, and governor, 1921–1925. Both men were closely associated with Coolidge.

11. *Boston Transcript; Springfield Republican*, January 6, 1921.

12. *Boston Transcript*, August 29, October 11; *New Bedford Times*, October 31, November 1, 6, 1922.

13. *Gazzetta del Massachusetts* (Boston), November 4, 1922 (in Italian); *Italian News* (Boston), November 4, 1922; *Boston Globe*, May 19, 1922 (clipping, personal scrapbooks of B. Loring Young); *Jewish Advocate* (Boston), November 2, 1922; *Boston Transcript*, August 5, 31, October 23, 26, November 3, 4, 1922; *Springfield Republican*, October 24, 1922.

14. *Holyoke Telegram; Lowell Evening Leader*, November 1; *Boston Transcript*, August 29, 1922.

15. *Holyoke Telegram*, November 2, 1922. See also the *Boston Transcript*, March 13, 1922.

16. *Boston Transcript*, September 13, 1922.

17. What follows is based on newspaper accounts, particularly the *Boston Transcript* of February 21, 1922, supplemented by details gained in personal interviews with Elijah Adlow (September 21, 1955) and B. Loring Young (October 10, 28, 1955). Adlow, a Republican member of the legislature in the 1920's, later became Chief Justice of the Municipal Court of Boston. Young served as Speaker of the state House of Representatives, 1921–1925, and was the Republican candidate for United States senator in 1928. See also A. Warner, "Blackmail à la Boston," *Nation*, CXIII (November 2, 1921), 499–500.

18. *Boston Transcript*, February 24, 27, 1922.

19. *Ibid.*, September 26, 27, 1922. In the November election Pelletier was defeated, 100,782 to 76,131.

20. *Springfield Republican*, November 5; *Boston Transcript*, October 20, 26–28, November 2; *Holyoke Telegram*, November 1, 1922; D. G. Wayman, *David I. Walsh: Citizen-Patriot* (Milwaukee, 1952), p. 137.

21. *Fall River Daily Globe*, November 3, 1922. For similar statements see the *Springfield Republican*, November 5, and the *Lowell Evening Leader*, November 4, 1922.

22. *Lynn Daily Evening Item*, November 6, 1922 (Republican campaign advertisement).

23. *Holyoke Telegram*, November 1, 6; *Boston Transcript*, September 27, October 18, 24, November 4; *Fall River Daily Globe*, November 3; *Berkshire Evening Eagle* (Pittsfield), November 6; *Lowell Evening Leader*, November 4; *Springfield Republican*, November 5, 1922.

24. *Springfield Republican*, November 5; *Lynn Daily Evening Item*, November 6, 1922.

25. *Springfield Republican*, September 13, 1922.

26. Commonwealth of Massachusetts, *Public Document No. 43: Number of . . . Registered Voters and Persons Who Voted . . . To-*

gether with the Number of Votes Received by Each Candidate, 1922. John Nicholls, the Progressive-Prohibition candidate, received 24,866 votes. Analysis of ward returns shows that his strength was among old-stock Republicans disaffected from Lodge because of the League, Prohibition, and other issues. He got very few votes in Irish and New Immigrant wards, indicating his platform's lack of appeal among those elements.

27. *Springfield Republican*, September 6, 1922.

28. *Boston Transcript*, January 8, 1920.

29. For an extended discussion of the effects of the First World War on the Progressive spirit see R. Hofstadter, *The Age of Reform* (New York, 1955), pp. 270–280.

30. *Boston Transcript*, October 1, 1923. See also C. M. Wright, "Labor in American Politics," *Current History Magazine*, XX (August 1924), 741–747.

31. *Boston Transcript*, February 1–3, 1922.

32. See the roll calls on labor bills recorded in the *Journals* of the state Senate and House of Representatives, in newspapers, and in Massachusetts State Federation of Labor, *Roll Calls of the Massachusetts Legislature on Labor Measures, 1927–1928, 1929–1930* (places and dates of publication not given), *passim*.

33. For an extended discussion of the "neutral state" concept in the Progressive era see Hofstadter, *The Age of Reform*, pp. 232ff.

34. During 1921 the chairwomen of fifteen women's organizations were meeting monthly in Washington to promote what became known as their "Six P's Program." It embraced Prohibition, Public school aid through the Towner-Sterling education bill, Protection of infancy through the Sheppard-Towner maternity bill, Physical education in the public schools, Protection of women in industry, and Peace through international arms reduction (*Boston Transcript*, August 22, 1921). For A.F. of L. endorsement of some of these measures see United States Bureau of Labor Statistics, *Monthly Labor Review*, August 1921, pp. 151–154, August 1922, pp. 189–193, December 1923, pp. 173–174, February 1925, pp. 186–189.

35. *Boston Transcript*, July 7, 1922.

36. *Boston Herald*, January 21, 1922.

37. *Boston Transcript*, April 26, 1924.

38. *Ibid.*, May 27, 1921.

39. *Ibid.*, May 9, 1921; *Massachusetts Public Document No. 43*, 1922.

40. See, for example, Hofstadter, *The Age of Reform*, pp. 184, 318.

41. Wayman, *David I. Walsh*, pp. 57–86; D. I. Walsh, "Labor in Politics: Its Political Influence in New England," *Forum*, LXII

(August 1919), 215–218; Vincent Brogna to the author, October 26, 1955 (interview); B. Loring Young to the author, October 10, 1955 (interview). Brogna, a Democrat, and Young, a Republican, were both members of the legislature during the Progressive era. See also A. I. Abell, "The Catholic Church and Social Problems in the World War I Era, 1910–1922," *Mid-America*, XXX (July 1948), 139–151.

42. *Massachusetts Public Document No. 43*, 1911, 1916–1918.

43. A law giving the state's Commissioner of Public Safety censorship power over films was enacted by the legislature in 1921 with Governor Cox's backing. On referendum at the 1922 election, however, the measure was rejected by the voters (*Boston Transcript*, May 25, 1921; *Massachusetts Public Document No. 43*, 1922).

44. *Boston Transcript*, June 5, 1920, May 31, 1924. The legislature passed a Prohibition enforcement act in 1922, but the voters rejected it on a referendum later in the year. Undaunted, the drys secured repassage of the same bill in 1923, and on a referendum vote at the 1924 general election it was approved by a narrow margin. The anti-Prohibitionists immediately began their campaign for repeal of the measure, however, and achieved success in 1930. Thus, the fight over the state's liquor laws spanned the entire decade (*ibid.*, April 19, 1922, May 10, 1923; *Massachusetts Public Document No. 43*, 1922, 1924, 1930).

45. For such statements by candidates in the Democratic gubernatorial and senatorial primary campaigns of 1922, for example, see the *Boston Transcript*, April 29, August 31, 1922.

46. Cf. Hofstadter, *The Age of Reform*, pp. 287–291.

47. *Boston Transcript*, May 12, 1921.

48. *Lowell Courier Citizen*, November 4, 1920; *Boston Transcript*, November 10, 1922.

49. *Boston Transcript*, April 30, 1921; United States Bureau of Labor Statistics, *Monthly Labor Review*, November 1928, pp. 104–107.

50. On the Chamberlain commission's report see C. C. Carstens, "Is Education Behind in Massachusetts?" *Survey*, XLII (June 14, 1919), 425–426; and K. Sargent, "Catholicism in Massachusetts," *Forum*, LXXIV (November 1925), 733–737.

51. Copies of such resolutions adopted during March 1919 are in the Walsh papers, Holy Cross College Library.

52. *The Pilot* (Boston), March 29, 1919; Sargent, "Catholicism in Massachusetts," pp. 734–736.

53. *Boston Transcript*, February 19, 1920; Sargent, "Catholicism in Massachusetts," p. 736.

54. *The Pilot*, June 28, 1919.

55. See statements made in testimony favoring the bill before a committee of the national House of Representatives (*Boston Transcript*, February 20, 1924).

56. *Ibid.*, December 9; *Fall River Daily Globe*, November 1, 1920. For similar criticism of the proposal see *The Pilot*, May 17, 1919.

57. *The Pilot*, June 28, 1919.

58. *Boston Transcript*, October 6, 17, 1924. Martin Lomasney seconded the Cardinal's denunciation of the amendment in his Sunday-before-election "instructions." His reasons are interesting: "If that bill is passed they may take your boy for compulsory military training at any age. Then they may try to put across the Sheppard-Towner [education] bill" (*ibid.*, November 3, 1924).

59. *Ibid.*, October 10, 1922.

60. *Ibid.*, November 4; *Fall River Daily Globe*, October 31; *Springfield Republican*, November 2, 1922.

61. *Italian News*, November 4, 1922.

62. *Boston Transcript*, September 27; *Worcester Telegram*, November 1; *Fall River Daily Globe*; *New Bedford Times*, November 3; *Lowell Evening Leader*, November 4, 1922.

63. *Boston Transcript*, April 29, 1922.

64. *Berkshire Evening Eagle*, October 28; *Fall River Daily Globe*, November 6, 1922.

65. *Springfield Republican*; *Holyoke Telegram*, November 2; *Boston Herald*, November 4, 1922.

66. For fuller details and sources of election returns, registration statistics, and data on the ethnic composition of electoral districts, see Appendix and Bibliography.

67. In 1922 William Connery, Jr., of Lynn recaptured for the Democrats the congressional seat in the Seventh District, lost to the Republicans two years earlier. The state's congressional delegation now consisted of thirteen Republicans and three Democrats. Democratic membership in the state House of Representatives increased from forty-five to seventy-two, and in the state Senate from five to seven.

68. In 1922 only 72.9 per cent of the Commonwealth's registered voters actually voted — the lowest figure for any state or national election in the period 1920–1932 inclusive.

69. *New Bedford Times*, November 2, 1922, quoting a prominent New Bedford labor leader.

Chapter Four.

KU KLUX YEARS

1. The nature of the American party system and its alleged defects were discussed extensively in the periodical literature of the early 1920's. See, for example, W. Hard, "Party Government Ebbs," *Nation*, CXIX (August 20, 1924), 189–190; H. L. Keenleyside, "The American Political Revolution of 1924," *Current History Magazine*, XXI (March 1925), 833–835; W. Hard, "The Republican Party — A Stricken Mob," *Nation*, CXVIII (February 13, 1924), 163–164; J. W. Owens, "Are the Republicans a Party," *New Republic*, XXXVIII (March 19, 1924), 89–91; S. Frost, "Democratic Dynamite," *Outlook*, CXXXVII (June 18, 1924), 265–268; *Nation*, CXI (November 24, 1920), 580–581, CXIX (July 16, 1924), 60.

2. See the *New Republic*, XL (October 8, 1924), 131–133, and H. W. Van Loon, "Maccabees of 1924," *Nation*, CXIX (July 9, 1924), 37–38, for speculation on possible patterns of factional and party realignment.

3. *Boston Transcript*, December 6, 1923. See also C. Coolidge, "Whose Country Is This?" *Good Housekeeping*, LXXII (February 1921), 13–14.

4. See, for example, M. Grant, "Racial Transformation of America," *North American Review*, CCXIX (March 1924), 343–352; F. Strother, "Immigration Peril," *World's Work*, XLVI (October 1923), 633–637; J. H. Cobb, "The Changing Conception of Government in America," *Current History Magazine*, XX (July 1924), 579–585; B. J. Hendrick, "The Jews in America," *World's Work*, XLV (December 1922, January, February, 1923), 144–161, 266–286, 366–377.

5. N. Thomas, "Progressivism at St. Louis," *Nation*, CXVIII (February 27, 1924), 224–225. On the C.P.P.A. and the La Follette candidacy in general see K. C. McKay, *The Progressive Movement of 1924* (New York, 1947), *passim*.

6. *Boston Transcript*, November 16, 1923; *Literary Digest*, December 1, 1923, pp. 18–19, December 22, 1923, pp. 8–9; J. L. Bates, "The Teapot Dome Scandal and the Election of 1924," *American Historical Review*, LX (January 1955), 303–322.

7. *Boston Transcript*, April 26, June 10–13, 1924; *Literary Digest*, June 21, 1924, pp. 6–8; *Current Opinion*, LXXVI (June 1924), 749–750; W. Hard, "Johnson Chases Coolidge," *Nation*, CXVIII (January 16, 1924), 59; A. B. Hart, "The Republican National Convention," *Current History Magazine*, XX (July 1924), 543–544; W. A. White, *A Puritan in Babylon* (New York, 1938) pp. 295–303.

8. *Boston Transcript*, June 9, 1924, September 10, 1930; White, *Puritan in Babylon*, pp. 296–298.

9. *Boston Transcript*, June 10, 1924.

10. *Ibid.*, June 12, 1924; *New Republic*, XXXIX (June 25, 1924), 116–117.

11. *Boston Transcript*, January 16, 1924; *Literary Digest*, December 1, 1923, pp. 16–17; M. Sullivan, "McAdoo's Chances for the Democratic Nomination," *World's Work*, XLVI (June 1923), 193–201; J. W. Owens, "Coolidge or McAdoo?" *New Republic*, XXXVII (January 2, 1924), 139–140; G. F. Milton, Jr., "What Mr. McAdoo Stands For," *Outlook*, CXXXV (November 21, 1923), 488–489.

12. *Nation*, CXVIII (June 25, 1924), 724. See also Sullivan, "McAdoo's Chances"; Owens, "Coolidge or McAdoo?"; Thomas, "Progressivism at St. Louis."

13. *Literary Digest*, December 1, 1923, pp. 16–17; Owens, "Coolidge or McAdoo?"

14. *Literary Digest*, August 11, 1923, p. 15.

15. *Boston Transcript*, February 1, 1924; *Literary Digest*, February 23, 1924, p. 13; *New Republic*, XXXVII (February 20, 1924), 324–325; *Nation*, CXVIII (June 25, 1924), 724; B. Stolberg, "Third Party Movement," *Independent*, CXII (March 15, 1924), 142–143; J. W. Owens, "Prospect for a Third Party," *New Republic*, XXXVII (February 20, 1924), 328–329.

16. S. Frost, "The Klan Restates Its Case," *Outlook*, CXXXVIII (October 15, 1924), 244–245. See S. Frost, *The Challenge of the Klan* (Indianapolis, 1924), *passim*, and J. M. Mecklin, *The Ku Klux Klan: A Study in the American Mind* (New York, 1924), *passim*.

17. H. W. Evans, "The Klan's Fight for Americanism," *North American Review*, CCXXIII (March 1926), 36, 52.

18. *Literary Digest*, January 20, 1923, pp. 18–19.

19. *Boston Herald*, September 28; *Boston Transcript*, September 28, 29, 1923.

20. *Boston Transcript*, April 21; *Springfield Republican*, October 20, 1924.

21. *Literary Digest*, June 10, 1922, p. 15, November 25, 1922, pp. 12–13, December 2, 1922, pp. 12–13, November 24, 1923, pp. 13–14; *Nation*, CXVII (November 21, 1923), 570.

22. *Boston Transcript*, June 6, 10, 1924; *Springfield Republican*, September 29, 1923.

23. *New York Times*, October 26, 28, 1923, January 23, 1924.

24. *Ibid.*, June 22, 1924; *Literary Digest*, April 5, 1924, p. 11, June 14, 1924, pp. 12–13; Frost, "Democratic Dynamite," p. 267.

25. *Boston Transcript*, September 9, 1921, February 3, October 18, 19, 1923; *Literary Digest*, November 25, 1922, p. 33.

26. H. M. Kallen, "Democracy Versus the Melting-Pot," *Nation*, C (February 25, 1915), 219. The changing views of Americans regarding the nature of their society and national identity are treated in O. Handlin, *The American People in the Twentieth Century* (Cambridge, Mass., 1954), *passim*.

27. *Nation*, CXVIII (June 18, 1924), 698; *New Republic*, XXXVI (November 21, 1923), 321–322; C. T. Hallinan, "The Liberal and the Jew," *Nation*, CXVIII (January 23, 1924), 81–82; Van Loon, "Maccabees of 1924," p. 38.

28. Cf. Handlin, *The American People*, pp. 158–162.

29. See, for example, *Review of Reviews*, LXX (October 1924), 426–427. For foreign-language press reaction to immigration restriction see *Congressional Digest*, II (July 1923), 316; *Literary Digest*, May 17, 1924, pp. 77–78.

30. *Boston Transcript*, April 2, 1920, June 6, 9, 1922, April 15, 1929.

31. *Literary Digest*, June 24, 1922, p. 28, July 8, 1922, pp. 28–29, February 3, 1923, pp. 32–33; *Nation*, CXIV (June 14, 1922), 708; *New Republic*, XXXI (August 16, 1922), 322–323.

32. *Boston Transcript*, August 9, 1923.

33. *Boston Post*, March 18, 1923 (clipping, personal scrapbooks of B. Loring Young).

34. *Boston Transcript*, April 15, 1924.

35. See H. F. Pringle, *Alfred E. Smith: A Critical Study* (New York, 1927), *passim;* A. E. Smith, *Up To Now* (New York, 1929), *passim;* and O. Handlin, *Al Smith and His America* (Boston, 1958), *passim*, published after the author had completed this work.

36. F. H. Simonds, "Could Al Smith Win?" *New Republic*, XXXIX (June 25, 1924), 120. See also *New Republic*, XXXIII (January 31, 1923), 241–242; *Outlook*, CXXXIII (January 17, 1923), 120–121; *World's Work*, XLVI (June 1923), 131–132.

37. J. W. Owens, "Dilemma of the Democrats," *New Republic*, XXXIX (June 4, 1924), 37. See also G. Soule, "Signs of a New Party," *New Republic*, XXXVIII (May 14, 1924), 304.

38. *Boston Transcript*, March 18; *Springfield Union*, June 23, 1924 (clipping in the personal scrapbooks of Senator David I. Walsh, Holy Cross College Library, Worcester, Massachusetts).

39. *Boston Transcript*, March 18, April 2, 22, 30, May 28, 29, 1924.

40. *Springfield Union; Springfield News*, June 23, 1924 (clippings, Walsh scrapbooks); *Boston Transcript; Springfield Republican*, June 24, 26, 1924.

41. *New York Times*, June 22, 1924.

42. *Boston Transcript*, June 19, 21, 24; *New York Times*, June 23, 1924; A. Krock "Damn Fool Democrats," *American Mercury*, IV (March 1925), 261.

43. Cf. Van Loon, "Maccabees of 1924," pp. 37–38; *Current Opinion*, LXXVII (August 1924), 140. For the proceedings of the convention see the *Boston Transcript* or *New York Times*, June 24–July 12, 1924.

44. *Official Report of the Proceedings of the Democratic National Convention of 1924* (Indianapolis, 1924), pp. 244–245, 248; S. Frost, "The Klan's One-Half of One Per Cent Victory," *Outlook*, CXXXVII (July 9, 1924), 385.

45. "As the campaign begins, it is as impossible to tell as it was during the convention whether the Democratic party is the party of the Solid South, the Klansman, and the Dry, or the party of Tammany Hall, the alien Catholic, and the Wet" (*Outlook*, CXXXVII [July 23, 1924], 458–459). See also S. Frost, "Nomination by Exhaustion," *Outlook*, CXXXVII (July 23, 1924), 464–466.

46. M. Coleman, "La Follette Day at Cleveland," *Outlook*, CXXXVII (July 16, 1924), 425–426; B. Stolberg, "La Follette Crosses the Rubicon," *Independent*, CXIII (July 19, 1924), 34.

47. *New Republic*, XXXIX (August 20, 1924), 339–341; M. D. Post, "John W. Davis," *Review of Reviews*, LXX (August 1924), 149–156; W. Hard, "Davis the Double-Edged," *Nation*, CXIX (July 23, 1924), 94–95; *Literary Digest*, July 19, 1924, p. 8, September 6, 1924, p. 10.

48. W. Hard, "That Man La Follette," *Nation*, CXIX (July 16, 1924), 65–66. See also W. Hard, "La Follette's Strategy," *Nation*, CXIX (September 10, 1924), 260–261; Keenleyside, "The American Political Revolution," p. 833.

49. *Boston Transcript*, September 20, 1924. See also *Outlook*, CXXXVIII (September 3, 1924, October 8, 1924), 12, 196.

50. S. Frost, "Our Four-Handed Political Chess Game," *Outlook*, CXXXVII (August 20, 1924), 598–599; *New Republic*, XL (November 5, 1924), 240–242; *Nation*, CXIX (October 8, 1924), 350. That La Follette's platform was "one-sided" in favor of the farmers was admitted by some of his most ardent backers. See *New Republic*, XXXIX (June 18, 1924), 88–90.

51. *Literary Digest*, September 6, 1924, p. 10, November 1, 1924, pp. 14–15. The New York state convention of the Association for Recognition of the Irish Republic officially endorsed La Follette for President in 1924 (*Boston Transcript*, July 21, 1924).

52. C. M. Fuess, *Calvin Coolidge* (Boston, 1940), p. 353.

53. Federal Reserve Bank of Boston, *Monthly Review of Business and Industrial Conditions in the New England District*, 1923–1924, *passim; Berkshire Evening Eagle* (Pittsfield), November 1; *Lawrence*

Sunday Sun, October 26; *Lowell Evening Leader*, October 30; *New Bedford Times*, October 29, 1924.

54. *New Republic*, XL (October 15, 1924), 157; *Nation*, CXIX (September 10, 1924), 250–251.

55. *Boston Transcript*, October 17, 22, 1924.

56. *Ibid.*, July 29, 1924; Fuess, *Calvin Coolidge*, p. 164; C. Coolidge, *Autobiography* (New York, 1929), p. 103.

57. *Boston Transcript*, May 2, 9, June 9, 16, 20, September 4, 1924; Channing Cox to the author, October 28, 1955 (interview).

58. *Holyoke Transcript*, May 10, 1924 (clipping, Young scrapbooks); *Boston Transcript*, May 17, 19, September 8, 1924. The primary vote, in round figures, was: Gillett, 146,000; Louis A. Coolidge, 94,000; and Dallinger, 62,000 (*Boston Transcript*, September 23, 1924).

59. *Boston Transcript*, September 15, 17, 18, 1924.

60. *Ibid.*, October 16; *Chelsea Evening Record*, October 16, November 1; *Gazzetta del Massachusetts* (Boston), October 11 (in Italian); *Lowell Evening Leader*, October 22, 1924.

61. *Boston Transcript*, September 20, 21, 1924.

62. *Ibid.*, August 22; *Holyoke Telegram*, October 23, 1924. See also J. F. Dinneen, *The Purple Shamrock: James Michael Curley* (New York, 1949), pp. 151–153.

63. *Boston Transcript*, October 18, 25, 1924.

64. *Ibid.*, October 24, 1924.

65. *Ibid.*, October 15, 1924.

66. *Ibid.*, September 20; *Springfield Republican*, October 25; *New Bedford Times*, October 30, 1924.

67. *Holyoke Telegram*, October 27, 1924.

68. *Boston Transcript*, October 7; *Chelsea Evening Record*, November 1, 1924.

69. Walsh's "difference" from Curley was invariably emphasized by interviewees with whom the author talked.

70. *Berkshire Evening Eagle*, November 1; *Lowell Evening Leader*, November 3; *Holyoke Telegram*, October 29, 1924.

71. *Boston Transcript*, August 23, 1924.

72. *Ibid.*, March 19, October 18, 31, 1924.

73. *Ibid.*, October 14, 1924.

74. *Springfield Republican*, October 24, 1924.

75. *New Bedford Times*, May 14, 1919 (clipping, Walsh scrapbooks).

76. Thomas J. Flannery to Walsh, September 27, Dan O'Connell to Walsh, October 3, 1924, Walsh papers; *Boston Transcript*, August

23, September 21; *Berkshire Evening Eagle; New Bedford Times,* November 1, 1924.

77. *Boston Transcript,* September 21; *Chelsea Evening Record,* October 29; *Holyoke Telegram,* November 1, 1924.

78. *Boston Transcript,* November 5, 1924.

79. *Ibid.,* November 1, 1924.

80. *Berkshire Evening Eagle,* October 30, 1924.

81. For fuller details and sources of election returns, registration statistics, and data on the ethnic composition of electoral districts, see Appendix and Bibliography.

82. In every Massachusetts city, La Follette's percentage of the presidential vote was highest in those wards carried by Walsh and Curley, while his vote was substantially smaller in the wards that went to Gillett and Fuller. In Boston, for example, La Follette received 18.4 per cent of the aggregate three-party presidential vote in the wards carried by Walsh, but only 10.5 per cent of the aggregate three-party presidential vote in the wards carried by Gillett.

83. Within these old-stock cities, the Newer American wards invariably showed the largest decreases in the Republican percentage of the vote.

84. *Boston Transcript,* November 13, 1924.

Chapter Five.

THE WALSH COALITION

1. See F. L. Allen, *Only Yesterday* (New York, 1931), pp. 159ff.

2. D. C. Brewer, *The Conquest of New England by the Immigrant* (New York, 1926), pp. 150, 242–243, 336, 345.

3. *Italian News* (Boston), April 22, 1922.

4. *Ibid.*

5. *Boston Transcript,* January 28, July 30, 1925.

6. Vincent Brogna to the author, October 26, 1955 (interview).

7. *Italian News,* August 26, 1922; *Gazzetta del Massachusetts* (Boston), November 4, 1922 (in Italian).

8. *Boston Transcript,* May 10, June 2, 1926; *Fall River Herald,* August 23, 1926 (clipping, personal scrapbooks of Elijah Adlow).

9. Julian D. Rainey to the author, August 8, 1955 (interview). Rainey was in charge of activities among Negro voters for the Democratic national committee in presidential elections from 1928

to 1944, and was an advisor to President Franklin D. Roosevelt on racial matters.

10. *Boston Transcript*, September 11; *Boston Herald*, September 13; *Jewish Advocate* (Boston), August 12, 1926.

11. *Italian News*, September 4, 1926. Actually, Adlow was born in Boston. He was graduated *cum laude* from Harvard in 1916, and from Harvard Law School in 1918. During the First World War he served in the navy (Adlow to the author, September 21, 1955 [interview]).

12. *Boston Telegram*, September 15, 17; *Boston American*, Sepember 15, 1926 (clippings, Adlow scrapbooks); *Chelsea Evening Record*, October 4; *Jewish Advocate*, October 21, 1926.

13. The term applied by Samuel Lubell to the ethnic "recognition" phenomenon. For an illuminating discussion of the whole matter see Lubell's *The Future of American Politics* (New York, 1951), chap. 4.

14. *Boston Transcript*, August 14, September 11, 15, 16; *Springfield Republican*, September 18, 1926.

15. *Boston Transcript*, September 21, 22, 1926.

16. Federal Reserve Bank of Boston, *Monthly Review of Business and Industrial Conditions in the New England District*, January 1, 1927.

17. *Ibid.*, 1919–1933, *passim*. See also Massachusetts Department of Labor and Industries, *Statistics of Manufactures in Massachusetts: 1920–1938* (place and date of publication not given), *passim*.

18. *Ibid.*, pp. 4, 9, 19.

19. United States Department of Labor, Bureau of Labor Statistics, *Monthly Labor Review*, July 1927, p. 133, October 1927, p. 152; D. Yorke, "Bad Business in New England," *American Mercury*, IX (October 1926), 139–140.

20. United States Bureau of Labor Statistics, *Monthly Labor Review*, May 1922, pp. 100–105, September 1922, pp. 110–114, February 1929, p. 7.

21. Yorke, "Bad Business in New England," p. 141. See also the *Boston Transcript*, June 13, 1922.

22. Quoted in Yorke, "Bad Business in New England," p. 142.

23. J. S. Lawrence, "New England — A Case of Industrial Maturity," *Independent*, CXVI (April 17, 1926), 441.

24. W. E. Freeland, "Resistance to Change: New England's Marketing Problem," *Independent*, CXVI (April 17, 1926), 445.

25. *Literary Digest*, November 28, 1925, p. 12.

26. Federal Reserve Bank of Boston, *Review*, August 1, 1926.

27. Massachusetts Department of Labor and Industries, *Statistics of Manufactures . . . 1920–1938*, pp. 20–32.

28. See Commonwealth of Massachusetts, *Final Report of the Special Commission on Stabilization of Employment* (Boston, 1933), pp. 71–78.

29. Quoted in W. Robinson, "Fall River: A Dying Industry," *New Republic*, XXXIX (June 4, 1924), 39.

30. *New Bedford Times*, October 27, 1926.

31. *Boston Transcript*, October 29, 1926.

32. *Ibid.*, October 14, 1926.

33. *Ibid.*, December 24; *Springfield Republican*, December 25, 1921.

34. *Boston Globe*, January 4, 1922 (clipping, personal scrapbooks of B. Loring Young); *Boston Transcript*, April 19, 1922. The act was rejected on a referendum at the November election that year. The Republican legislature repassed it in 1923 and finally, on a referendum at the 1924 election, the voters approved it by a narrow margin.

35. *Boston Transcript*, February 15, 19, 1924.

36. See above, p. 67. See also the *Boston Transcript*, October 9, 1926.

37. *Boston Transcript*, September 11, 15, October 7, 1926.

38. *Ibid.*, November 10, 1924.

39. *Berkshire Evening Eagle* (Pittsfield), November 3, 1926.

40. *Boston Transcript*, February 17, 20, 1926.

41. *Ibid.*, October 6, 7, November 2, 1926.

42. B. Loring Young to the author, October 10, 1955 (interview); *Springfield Republican*, October 29; *New Bedford Times*, October 27; *Boston Transcript*, February 20, 1926.

43. *Springfield Republican*, October 26; *Boston Transcript*, October 14, 19, 21, November 1, 1926.

44. *Boston Herald*, October 17, 1926. See also the *Boston Transcript*, August 14, 1926.

45. *North Adams Transcript*, November 1; *Holyoke Telegram*, October 23; *Lowell Evening Leader*, October 27, 1926.

46. *Boston Transcript*, September 23, October 21, 23, 28; *Springfield Republican*, October 29; *Jewish Advocate*, October 21, 1926.

47. *Gazzetta del Massachusetts*, October 30; *Holyoke Telegram*, October 25, 1926.

48. *Italian News*, October 30, 1926 (advertisement).

49. *Boston Transcript*, April 6, October 26, 28; *Holyoke Telegram*, October 23, 1926.

50. *Boston Transcript*, May 6, October 7, October 25, 26, 1926.

51. *Berkshire Evening Eagle*, October 23, 1926. See also the *Boston Transcript*, October 30, November 3, 1926.

52. *Boston Transcript*, October 14; *Holyoke Telegram*, October 28, November 4, 1926.

53. Walsh to George F. O'Dwyer, July 26, 1921, personal papers of Senator David I. Walsh, Holy Cross College Library, Worcester, Massachusetts.

54. *Holyoke Telegram*, October 25; *Boston Transcript*, October 29, 1926.

55. *Lowell Evening Leader*, October 21, 1926. See also the *Boston Transcript*, December 3, 1926.

56. *Boston Transcript*, October 29, 1926.

57. *New Bedford Times*, October 29, 1926.

58. *Springfield Republican*, October 22, 1926. A copy of the booklet referred to is in the personal scrapbooks of Elijah Adlow.

59. *Holyoke Telegram*, November 4, 1926.

60. William A. Howard to Walsh, April 6, 1919, Walsh papers.

61. Julian D. Rainey to the author, August 8, 1955 (interview).

62. *Boston Transcript*, August 6; *Springfield Republican*, October 28, 1926.

63. Richard Gibbons to Walsh, August 26, October 1, Joseph B. Casey to Walsh, September 20, James E. Markham to Walsh, October 10, Dan O'Connell to Walsh, October 3, Henry A. Harrison to Walsh, September 17, 1924, Walsh papers.

64. *Boston Transcript*, May 4, 1925; Stanley Wisnioski to the author, July 18, 1955 (interview). Wisnioski, as a young attorney, became active in politics in the latter half of the 1920's. Thereafter he was a recognized leader among Polish-American Democrats of Massachusetts.

65. *Italian News*, October 30, 1926.

66. *Berkshire Evening Eagle*, October 29, 1926.

67. *Boston Transcript*, September 17; *New Bedford Times*, October 29, 1926.

68. *Boston Transcript*, October 28, 29, 1926.

69. For fuller details and sources of election returns, registration statistics, and data on the ethnic composition of electoral districts, see Appendix and Bibliography of this work. Republican membership in the state Senate (40 members) increased from 34 to 35. In the House (240 members) it increased from 169 to 173. The division of the Bay State congressional delegation remained the same: 13 Republicans and 3 Democrats.

70. The figures for 1922 represent Gaston's percentage of the three-party senatorial vote that year (Democratic, Republican, and Progressive-Prohibition parties), while the 1926 figures represent Walsh's percentage of the two-party vote (Democratic and Republican). The figures are comparable, however, since the votes received by John

Nicholls, the Progessive-Prohibition candidate in 1922, came from normally Republican voters.

71. *Lowell Evening Leader*, November 3, 1926.

72. James Michael Curley to the author, June 15, 1955 (interview); Vincent Brogna to the author, October 26, 1955 (interview).

73. *Springfield Republican*, November 3, 1926.

Chapter Six.

AL SMITH'S REVOLUTION

1. *Boston Transcript*, August 2, 9, October 20, November 22, December 7, 1927, April 21, 1928.

2. H. Hoover, *The Memoirs of Herbert Hoover: The Cabinet and the Presidency, 1920–1933* (New York, 1952), p. 193.

3. *Boston Transcript*, June 12, 1928.

4. *Literary Digest*, August 28, 1926, pp. 5–7, December 4, 1926, pp. 8–9; *World's Work*, XLIX (January 1925), 234–235; F. R. Kent, "Smith in 1928?" *Nation*, CXXIV (January 19, 1927), 65–66.

5. *Boston Transcript*, January 28, August 30, 1927, March 23, April 15, August 24, September 17, 24, 1928; *Literary Digest*, February 12, 1927, pp. 5–7, October 1, 1927, pp. 8–10; F. R. Kent, "Democrats in 1928," *Scribner's Magazine*, LXXXII (November 1927), 515–520; M. Sullivan, "Al Smith's Chances," *World's Work*, LVI (July 1928), 242–249; W. Lippmann, "Sick Donkey: Democratic Prospects for 1928," *Harper's Magazine*, CLV (September 1927), 415–421.

6. *Boston Transcript*, June 26, 27, 29, 30, 1928.

7. See R. V. Peel and T. C. Donnelly, *The 1928 Campaign: An Analysis* (New York, 1931), *passim*.

8. *Boston Herald*, November 5, 1928. See also *New Republic*, LVI (November 7, 1928), 314–315.

9. S. Michelet, "Analysis of the Vote in the National Election," *Current History Magazine*, XXIX (February 1929), 781–782.

10. *New Republic*, LV (July 11, 1928), 186. Lippmann's comment is quoted in M. Sullivan, "Al Smith's Chances," p. 249.

11. Peel and Donnelly, *The 1928 Campaign*, p. 114.

12. *Boston Transcript*, August 23, 29; *Boston Herald*, September 30, 1928.

13. *Boston Transcript*, October 9, July 21, 1928.

14. *Fitchburg Sentinel*, November 5; *Lynn Daily Evening Item*, October 22; *Berkshire Evening Eagle* (Pittsfield), November 3, 1928.

15. *Boston Transcript*, August 10, 11, 14, September 19, 1928.

16. *Gazzetta del Massachusetts* (Boston), October 13, 20; *North Adams Transcript*, October 30; *Haverhill Evening Gazette*, October 30, November 2, 1928.

17. *Springfield Republican*, November 4, 1928; Amos Taylor to the author, September 20, 1955 (interview).

18. Massachusetts Department of Labor and Industries, *Statistics of Manufactures in Massachusetts: 1920–1938* (place and date of publication not given), p. 3. See also Federal Reserve Bank of Boston, *Monthly Review of Business and Industrial Conditions in the New England District*, 1927–1928, *passim*.

19. Massachusetts Department of Labor and Industries, *Statistics of Manufactures . . . 1920–1938*, pp. 22, 24, 25, 27.

20. See the *Boston Transcript*, August 3, October 6; *Springfield Republican*, October 8, 1928; *Literary Digest*, May 5, 1928, p. 16; P. Blanshard, "New Bedford Goes on Strike," *New Republic*, LV (May 23, 1928), 10–12.

21. *Springfield Republican*, October 8, 1928.

22. *Lowell Evening Leader*, November 5; *Berkshire Evening Eagle*, November 3; *North Adams Transcript*, November 6, 1928.

23. *Boston Transcript*, June 29, October 15, 1928; *Literary Digest*, July 21, 1928, pp. 5–7, October 27, 1928, pp. 7–9.

24. *Boston Transcript*, October 25, 1928.

25. *North Adams Transcript*, November 1, 1928.

26. *Ibid.*, October 30; *Haverhill Evening Gazette*, November 1; *Lynn Daily Evening Item*, October 26, November 1, 1928.

27. *Jewish Advocate* (Boston), November 1, 1928.

28. *Boston Transcript*, October 19, 23, 1928.

29. *Springfield Republican*, October 24, 1928.

30. *Ibid.*, October 6, 1928.

31. C. C. Marshall, "Open Letter to the Honorable Alfred E. Smith," and A. E. Smith, "Catholic and Patriot: Reply to C. C. Marshall," *Atlantic Monthly*, CXXXIX (April, May 1927), 540–549, 721–728.

32. *Boston Transcript*, August 21, 1928.

33. *Springfield Republican*, October 20, 1928. According to a Republican campaigner in Boston: "Al Smith was brought up in the city where he learned a lot, and also a lot which perhaps he shouldn't have learned, but for a choice to lead the country the son of the country blacksmith would make the better man" (*Boston Transcript*, October 18, 1928). Such utterances reflect the persistence of the "agrarian myth" discussed by R. Hofstadter in *The Age of Reform* (New York, 1955), pp. 23–36.

34. *Chelsea Evening Record*, November 1, 1928. See also Peel and Donnelly, *The 1928 Campaign*, p. 100.

35. *Boston Transcript*, February 14, 1928.

36. *Ibid.*, September 25; *Springfield Republican*, October 24, 1928.

37. Ellery Sedgewick, editor of the *Atlantic Monthly*, congratulated the Catholic clergy on their forbearance in a letter to the *New York Sun*, October 20, 1928, concluding that "had the Catholic clergy thrown themselves into the hurly-burly after the manner of their Methodist brothers the Republic would have rocked on its foundations" (quoted in J. A. Ryan, "A Catholic View of the Election," *Current History Magazine*, XXIX [December 1928], 380).

38. *Boston Transcript*, October 20, 1928.

39. Poem submitted by Edward Bacigalupo, a North End youth, and printed in the *Italian News* (Boston), October 20, 1928, "in view of the unpleasant religious issue raised by the Republicans," according to the editor's note.

40. *Boston Transcript*, October 29, 1928.

41. *Jewish Advocate*, October 25, 1928.

42. *Boston Transcript*, August 23, October 13, 1928; *Literary Digest*, September 22, 1928, p. 16; *Holyoke Daily Transcript and Telegram*, November 2, 1928.

43. *North Adams Transcript*, November 2, 1928.

44. *Holyoke Daily Transcript and Telegram*, October 29, 1928 (Democratic campaign advertisement).

45. *Ibid.*, November 1; *North Adams Transcript*, October 23; *Boston Transcript*, November 2; *Jewish Advocate*, November 1, 1928.

46. *New Republic*, LVI (September 19, October 10, 1928), 112, 190. See also *New Republic*, LV (July 11, 1928), 187–188.

47. Quoted in M. Sullivan, "Al Smith's Chances," p. 248.

48. Included on the Democratic slate was Joseph Santosuosso, running for the position of secretary of state. He was the first Italian-American ever to appear as a major party candidate in a state-wide election contest.

49. According to a poll conducted by the Republican national committee (*Boston Transcript*, October 18, 1928).

50. *Lynn Daily Evening Item*, November 5; *Springfield Republican*, October 26, 1928.

51. *Boston Transcript*, September 28, 1928.

52. *North Adams Transcript*, November 5; *Berkshire Evening Eagle*, October 29, 31; *Gazzetta del Massachusetts*, October 27, 1928 (in Italian).

53. *Worcester Telegram*, October 21; *Lowell Evening Leader*, October 23, 1928.

54. *Gazzetta del Massachusetts*, October 20 (in Italian), November 3; *Clinton Item*, November 1, 1928 (clipping, personal scrapbooks of B. Loring Young); *Literary Digest*, September 22, 1928, p. 16.

55. *Boston Transcript*, September 26; *North Adams Transcript*, November 6; *Lynn Daily Evening Item*, November 1, 1928.

56. *New Bedford Times*, October 24, 1928.

57. Amos Taylor to the author, September 20, 1955 (interview); *New Bedford Times*, October 24; *Berkshire Evening Eagle*, October 20, 1928.

58. *New Bedford Times*, November 5, 1928. On the Rhode Island religious controversy see J. Ducharme, *The Shadows of the Trees: The Story of French-Canadians in New England* (New York, 1943), pp. 79ff.

59. *New Bedford Times*, November 3, 1928.

60. *Springfield Republican*, November 3, 1928.

61. *Jewish Advocate*, October 25; *Springfield Republican*, October 8, November 5; *New Bedford Times*, October 24, 1928; H. L. Moon, *Balance of Power: The Negro Vote* (Garden City, 1948), p. 106.

62. *North Adams Transcript*, October 27; *Boston Transcript*, October 10; *Springfield Republican*, October 29, 1928.

63. *New Republic*, L (March 23, 1927), 128, LVI (September 5, 1928), 60.

64. *Nation*, CXXVII (October 31, 1928), 440.

65. *Ibid.*, CXXVII (November 7, 1928), 470–471; *New Republic*, LVI (October 17, 1928), 245–246.

66. LaRue Brown to the author, September 20, 1955 (interview). Brown, a prominent Boston attorney, had been an ardent supporter of Woodrow Wilson in the 1910's. He considered himself an independent in politics during the 1920's, but accepted appointment to the Democratic state committee after Smith's nomination. He and his wife, Dorothy Kirchwey Brown, have long been identified with advanced liberal causes.

67. *Berkshire Evening Eagle*, October 20; *Boston Post*, November 4, 1928 (clipping, Young scrapbooks).

68. *Boston Transcript*, August 18; *Berkshire Evening Eagle*, October 20, 1928.

69. Frank Donahue, Justice of the Superior Court of Massachusetts, to the author, October 26, 1955 (interview); LaRue Brown to the author, September 20, 1955 (interview); *Boston Transcript*, July 14, October 2; *Springfield Republican*, September 16; *Fitchburg Sentinel*, November 3, 1928.

70. *Boston Transcript*, October 27, 1928. Curley also believed that Walsh and his organization were interested primarily in the Senator's

re-election and were not rendering full support to Al Smith's cause (James Michael Curley to the author, June 15, 1955 [interview]).

71. *Boston Transcript*, October 13, 18, 1928.

72. Author's interviews with Vincent Brogna (October 26, 1955), Stanley Wisnioski (July 18, 1955), Julian D. Rainey (August 8, 1955), and Frank Donahue (October 26, 1955).

73. *Berkshire Evening Eagle*, October 24; *Boston Transcript*; *Springfield Republican*, October 25, 1928.

74. *Boston Transcript*, October 25, 1928.

75. *Ibid.*, June 13, 14; *Springfield Republican*, June 12, 14; *New Bedford Times*, October 24, 1928.

76. *Boston Transcript*, July 19, October 17; *New Bedford Times*, October 24, 1928.

77. *Boston Advertiser*, November 2, 1928 (clipping, Young scrapbooks).

78. *New Bedford Times*, October 24, 1928.

79. For fuller details and sources of election returns, registration statistics, and data on the ethnic composition of electoral districts, see Appendix and Bibliography.

80. *Boston Transcript; Holyoke Daily Transcript and Telegram; Berkshire Evening Eagle*, November 7, 1928.

81. *Boston Transcript*, November 9, 1928.

82. L. E. Klimm, *The Relation between Certain Population Changes and the Physical Environment in Hampden, Hampshire, and Franklin Counties, Massachusetts, 1790–1925* (Philadelphia, 1933), pp. 37, 87–89.

83. Massachusetts Department of Labor and Industries, *Statistics of Manufactures . . . 1920–1938*, p. 22.

84. *Boston Transcript*, November 9, 1928.

85. *Ibid.*, October 24, 25, November 1, 2; *North Adams Transcript*, October 23; *Springfield Republican*, October 25; *Holyoke Daily Transcript and Telegram*, October 30; *Boston Herald*, September 30; *Boston Post*, November 4, 1928 (clipping, Young scrapbooks).

86. *Boston Transcript*, December 5, 1928.

87. *Ibid.*, October 29; *Lowell Evening Leader*, October 29; *Chelsea Evening Record*, November 5, 1928.

88. See S. Lubell, *The Future of American Politics* (New York, 1951), pp. 34ff.

89. *St. Paul Pioneer Press*, quoted in Peel and Donnelly, *The 1928 Campaign*, p. 121.

90. *Boston Herald*, November 7, 1928. The *Boston Transcript*, too, believed that "Massachusetts is still essentially Republican. . ." (*Boston Transcript*, November 7, 1928).

91. The culminating battle between Older Americans and Newer Americans at the polls in 1928 re-aroused the political interest of a nation that had tired of "traditional" issues like the tariff, and brought into active political participation millions of old and new citizens who had been apathetic toward national politics before. Certainly considerations capable of producing such momentous results in the political life of a democracy can hardly be classed as "nonpolitical factors." On this matter of "issues" in the 1920's see W. Lippmann, "The Causes of Political Indifference Today," *Atlantic Monthly*, CXXXIX (February 1927), 261–268.

92. *Boston Herald*, November 7, 1928.

Chapter Seven.

BREAD, BEER, AND BEACON HILL

1. Federal Reserve Bank of Boston, *Monthly Review of Business and Industrial Conditions in the New England District*, 1929, *passim*; Massachusetts Department of Labor and Industries, *Statistics of Manufactures in Massachusetts: 1920–1938* (place and date of publication not given), *passim*.

2. Quoted in the *Boston Transcript*, August 9, 1929.

3. *Ibid.*, October 31, 1929. See also President Hoover's State of the Union message to Congress (*ibid.*, December 3, 1929).

4. *Ibid.*, December 18, 1929.

5. Massachusetts Department of Labor and Industries, *Statistics of Manufactures . . . 1920–1938*, p. 49.

6. *Boston Transcript*, February 3, 1930.

7. *Ibid.*, November 30, December 5, 1929, January 18, 1930.

8. *Ibid.*, February 3, 1930.

9. *Ibid.*, December 3, 1929.

10. *Ibid.*, July 20, December 5, 7, 1929, January 13, 1930.

11. *Ibid.*, June 14, August 15, 1929.

12. *Ibid.*, June 14, 15, August 19, 21, 26, 1929.

13. *Ibid.*, January 2, 1930.

14. *Ibid.*, February 12; *Springfield Republican*, February 8, 10, 1930.

15. *Springfield Republican*, February 9; *Boston Transcript*, February 12, 1930.

16. *Boston Transcript*, February 12, 15, 1930.

17. Amos Taylor to the author, September 20, 1955 (interview); *Boston Transcript*, March 14, 26, 1930.

18. *Boston Transcript*, August 12, 20, 22, 26, September 12; *Springfield Republican*, September 11, 14, 1930; Commonwealth of Massachusetts, *Public Document No. 43: Number of . . . Registered Voters and Persons Who Voted . . . Together with the Number of Votes Received by Each Candidate*, 1930.

19. The initiative measure was defeated in the House by a vote of 123 (all Republicans) to 110 (83 Democrats and 27 Republicans). In the Senate the adverse vote was 26 (all Republicans) to 11 (8 Democrats and 3 Republicans) (*Boston Transcript*, April 2, 3, 1930).

20. *Ibid.*, March 7, April 4, 23, May 8, June 10, 1929, March 3, 5, 18, April 16, May 28, 1930. See also Massachusetts State Federation of Labor, *Roll Calls of the Massachusetts Legislature on Labor Measures, 1929–1930* (place and date of publication not given), *passim*.

21. *Boston Transcript*, April 13, August 16, September 9, 14, 1929; Frank Donahue to the author, October 26, 1955 (interview).

22. *Boston Transcript*, May 25, June 10, 21, 1929; LaRue Brown to the author, September 20, 1955 (interview).

23. *Boston Transcript*, November 6, December 4, 1929.

24. *Ibid.*, July 26, 1930; Frank Donahue to the author, October 26, 1955 (interview).

25. *Boston Transcript*, June 7, July 1, August 6, 1930; Dorothy Kirchwey Brown to Franklin D. Roosevelt, June 6, 1930, personal papers of Franklin D. Roosevelt, Franklin D. Roosevelt Library, Hyde Park, New York.

26. *Boston Transcript*, July 9, 26; *Springfield Republican*, November 2, 7, 1930; Julian D. Rainey to the author, August 8, 1955 (interview). See also J. F. Dinneen, *The Purple Shamrock: James Michael Curley* (New York, 1949), pp. 166–167.

27. *Boston Transcript*, August 7, September 13, 1930.

28. *Ibid.*, September 9, 11, 13, 1930.

29. *Ibid.*, September 15, 16; *Springfield Republican*, September 16, 1930.

30. *Massachusetts Public Document No. 43*, 1930.

31. *Boston Herald*, September 28, 1930.

32. *Springfield Republican*, November 2; *Boston Transcript*, October 15, 29, 1930.

33. *Springfield Republican*, September 11; *Holyoke Daily Transcript and Telegram*, November 1, 3, 1930.

34. *Holyoke Daily Transcript and Telegram*, October 30, November 3; *Springfield Republican*, October 31, 1930. The Republicans took their cue from the Democrats who in 1928 mixed sports and politics by having Leo Durocher, a native of West Springfield and then playing with the New York Yankees, campaign for Al Smith before

French-Canadian audiences in the Second Congressional District (*Holyoke Daily Transcript and Telegram*, November 1, 1928).

35. *Springfield Republican*, October 23, 29; *Fitchburg Sentinel*, October 23, 1930.

36. *Boston Transcript*, October 10, 18, 1930.

37. *Ibid.*, September 27, October 10, 28; *Boston Herald*, September 28; *New Bedford Times*, October 30, 1930.

38. *Boston Transcript*, September 27, 1930.

39. *Ibid.*, October 3; *Boston Herald*, September 28; *Holyoke Daily Transcript and Telegram*, October 31, 1930.

40. *Springfield Republican*, September 28, 1930.

41. *Boston Transcript*, September 29, 1930.

42. *Ibid.*, November 1, 1930.

43. *Ibid.*, March 8, 1930. See United States Department of Labor, Bureau of Labor Statistics, *Monthly Labor Review*, June 1933, p. 1419, for monthly indexes of industrial employment and pay rolls covering January 1926 through April 1933, with the twelve-month average for 1926 equaling 100.

44. *Boston Transcript*, February 24, October 18, 1930.

45. *Ibid.*, October 16, 23, 28; *Springfield Republican*, October 30, 1930.

46. *Boston Transcript*, October 10; *Lowell Evening Leader*, October 29; *New Bedford Times*, October 30, 1930.

47. *Holyoke Daily Transcript and Telegram*, October 31; *Boston Transcript*, October 17, 1930.

48. Federal Reserve Bank of Boston, *Review*, February 1, 1931; Massachusetts Department of Labor and Industries, *Statistics of Manufactures . . . 1920–1938*, p. 49.

49. Federal Reserve Bank of Boston, *Review*, December 1, 1930.

50. *Boston Transcript*, February 15, March 17, August 4, October 27, November 3, 1930.

51. *Ibid.*, October 10, 18, 25, November 3; *Springfield Republican*, November 4, 1930.

52. *Holyoke Daily Transcript and Telegram*, October 31; *Boston Transcript*, November 1, 1930.

53. *Holyoke Daily Transcript and Telegram*, October 30, 1930.

54. *Boston Transcript*, October 31, 1930.

55. For fuller details and sources of election returns and of data on the ethnic composition of electoral districts, see Appendix and Bibliography.

56. *Holyoke Daily Transcript and Telegram*, November 5, 1930.

57. *Boston Transcript*, November 5, 1930.

58. *Lowell Evening Leader*, November 5, 1930.

59. *Boston Transcript*, November 5, 6; *Springfield Republican*, November 9, 1930.

60. *Boston Transcript*, November 5, 1930.

Chapter Eight.

ACTION TO MAKE THINGS BETTER

1. For a description of the American scene in the early years of the Great Depression see A. M. Schlesinger, Jr., *The Age of Roosevelt: The Crisis of the Old Order, 1919–1933* (New York, 1957), *passim*, published after the author had completed work on this study.

2. *Boston Transcript*, December 2, 3, 23, 1930.

3. *Ibid.*, December 3, 9, 1930.

4. *Ibid.*, September 10, 1931.

5. United States Department of Labor, Bureau of Labor Statistics, *Monthly Labor Review*, June 1933, p. 1419. In these indexes the twelve-month average for the year 1926 equals 100. See also the *Boston Transcript*, August 12, September 22, 23, 1931.

6. *Boston Transcript*, September 10, 1931.

7. *Ibid.*, December 4, 1931.

8. *Ibid.*, December 8, 9, 1931.

9. *Ibid.*, January 8, 1931.

10. *Ibid.*, January 14, February 9, March 16, 25, June 23, November 13, 1931.

11. *Ibid.*, March 18, 1931.

12. *Ibid.*, February 11, March 25, April 28, 1931.

13. Massachusetts Department of Labor and Industries, *Statistics of Manufactures in Massachusetts: 1920–1938* (place and date of publication not given), p. 49; Federal Reserve Bank of Boston, *Monthly Review of Business and Industrial Conditions in the New England District*, December 1, 1931.

14. *Boston Transcript*, October 23, 1931, January 6, 1932.

15. *Ibid.*, January 6, 1932.

16. United States Bureau of Labor Statistics, *Monthly Labor Review*, June 1933, p. 1419.

17. *Boston Transcript*, December 29, 1931, June 4, 1932.

18. *Literary Digest*, March 19, 1932, p. 12, May 7, 1932, p. 18; *Boston Transcript*, April 13, May 26, June 6, 16, 18, July 2, 29, 1932.

19. *Boston Transcript*, January 23, 1932.

20. *Ibid.*, May 13, July 22, 1932.

21. *Ibid.*, January 9, 1931.

22. *Ibid.*, June 14; *Springfield Republican*, June 14, 15, 1932.

23. *Boston Transcript*, October 27, 1931, April 22, June 13, 1932.

24. H. Hoover, *The Memoirs of Herbert Hoover: The Cabinet and the Presidency, 1920–1933* (New York, 1952), pp. 275–276; *Boston Transcript*, June 16, 1932.

25. *Boston Transcript*, April 30, May 2, 1932.

26. *Ibid.*, November 26, December 6, 1930. For discussions of the Democratic and national political situations in the early years of the Great Depression see the appropriate sections in Schlesinger, Jr., *The Age of Roosevelt: The Crisis of the Old Order*; F. Freidel, *Franklin D. Roosevelt: The Triumph* (Boston, 1956); J. M. Burns, *Roosevelt: The Lion and the Fox* (New York, 1956); and J. A. Farley, *Behind the Ballots* (New York, 1938). These books, with the exception of Farley's, were published after the author had completed work on this study.

27. *Boston Transcript*, April 22, 1931.

28. *Ibid.*, November 26, 1930.

29. *Ibid.*, March 3, 1931.

30. *Ibid.*, March 4, 1931.

31. *Ibid.*, January 14, March 4, 1931, January 9, 1932.

32. *Ibid.*, July 27, August 1, 1931; Farley, *Behind the Ballots*, pp. 76ff; F. Perkins, *The Roosevelt I Knew* (New York, 1946), pp. 48–53.

33. *Boston Transcript*, March 4, October 21, 1931; *Literary Digest*, March 21, 1931, pp. 8–9.

34. *Boston Transcript*, May 6; *Boston Herald*, June 14, 1931; Frank Donahue to the author, October 26, 1955 (interview).

35. *Boston Transcript*, June 12, 19, 1931. For Curley's version of his relations with Roosevelt see J. F. Dinneen, *The Purple Shamrock: James Michael Curley* (New York, 1949), pp. 178–210.

36. *Boston Transcript*, June 12, 1931; Frank Donahue to the author, October 26, 1955 (interview).

37. *Boston Transcript*, September 19, November 12, 14, 1931, January 29, 30, February 4, 1932.

38. *Ibid.*, January 30, 1932; LaRue Brown to Franklin D. Roosevelt, December 6, 1931, personal papers of Franklin D. Roosevelt, Franklin D. Roosevelt Library, Hyde Park, New York; LaRue Brown to the author, September 20, 1955 (interview). See also Elliott Roosevelt, ed., *F. D. R.: His Personal Letters, 1928–1945* (New York, 1950), pp. 274–275.

39. *Boston Transcript*, February 8, 16, 20, 1932; *Literary Digest*, February 20, 1932, pp. 8–9.

40. *Boston Transcript*, February 23, March 1, 1932; Frank Donahue

to the author, October 26, 1955 (interview); J. Ely, *The American Dream* (Boston, 1944), pp. 56–57.

41. *Boston Transcript*, March 10, 11, 1932; LaRue Brown to the author, September 20, 1955 (interview).

42. *Boston Transcript*, March 12, 16, 17, 1932; LaRue Brown to the author, September 20, 1955 (interview).

43. *Boston Transcript*, March 21, April 16, 1932.

44. *Springfield Republican*, April 24, 1932.

45. *Boston Transcript*, April 14, 1932. See also *Literary Digest*, April 23, 1932, p. 11.

46. *Boston Transcript*, April 27, 1932.

47. LaRue Brown to the author, September 20, 1955 (interview); Frank Donahue to the author, October 26, 1955 (interview).

48. *Springfield Republican; Boston Transcript*, July 1, 1932.

49. *Boston Transcript*, July 2; *Boston Herald*, July 3, 1932.

50. *Boston Herald*, July 2, 1932.

51. *Ibid.*, July 2; *Italian News* (Boston), October 21; *Springfield Republican*, June 28, 1932.

52. *Boston Herald*, July 4; *Boston Transcript*, July 23, 27, 1932.

53. *Boston Transcript*, July 5, 1932.

54. *Ibid.*, July 18, 22, 27, August 1, 1932.

55. *Ibid.*, July 19, August 4, 1932; Curley to Roosevelt, July 15, 1932, Roosevelt papers.

56. *Springfield Republican*, November 6; *Boston Transcript*, July 30, September 3, 1932.

57. *Boston Herald*, July 31, September 4; *Boston Transcript*, August 1, 27, 1932. See also R. V. Peel and T. C. Donnelly, *The 1932 Campaign: An Analysis* (New York, 1935), *passim*.

58. *Boston Transcript*, August 19, 1932.

59. Quoted in the *Boston Herald*, September 4, 1932. In a letter dated September 7, 1932, LaRue Brown warned Roosevelt that "Massachusetts needs prayerful attention from the high command" (Roosevelt papers).

60. *Boston Transcript*, June 29, July 15, September 17, 1932.

61. *Worcester Telegram*, September 9, 1928 (clipping, personal scrapbooks of B. Loring Young).

62. *Boston Transcript*, October 3; *Springfield Republican*, October 24, November 6, 1932.

63. Elijah Adlow to the author, September 21, 1955 (interview); Amos Taylor to the author, September 20, 1955 (interview).

64. *Boston Transcript*, August 12, September 30; *New Bedford Standard-Times*, October 21; *Springfield Republican*, October 24, 1932.

65. United States Bureau of Labor Statistics, *Monthly Labor Review*, June 1933, p. 1419; Federal Reserve Bank of Boston, *Review*, October 1, November 1, 1932; Massachusetts Department of Labor and Industries, *Statistics of Manufactures . . . 1920–1938*, p. 49.

66. *Boston Transcript*, July 2, 5, August 12, 1932.

67. *Ibid.*, August 12, 23; *Berkshire Evening Eagle* (Pittsfield), November 1, 1932.

68. *Boston Transcript*, September 13, 1932.

69. *Boston Herald*, October 1, 2; *Boston Transcript*, October 5, 8, 1932.

70. *Boston Transcript*, October 15, 1932.

71. *Ibid.* Aggregate registration in the thirty-nine cities showed an increase of only 2.8 per cent over 1928, while for the towns of the Commonwealth the figure was 7.3 per cent (Commonwealth of Massachusetts, *Public Document No. 43: Number of . . . Registered Voters and Persons Who Voted . . . Together with the Number of Votes Received by Each Candidate*, 1932).

72. *New Bedford Standard-Times*, October 21; *Boston Transcript*, October 16, 22; *Chelsea Evening Record*, November 8, 1932.

73. *Boston Transcript*, October 29, 1932.

74. *Ibid.*, November 1; *Boston Herald*, October 14, 1932.

75. *Boston Transcript*, September 13; *Springfield Republican*, October 28, 1932.

76. *New Bedford Standard-Times*, November 5, 1932.

77. *Chelsea Evening Record*, November 8, 1932.

78. *Boston Transcript*, October 28, 1932.

79. *Ibid.*, November 1, 1932.

80. *Ibid.*, October 5, 24, 29, November 1, 1932.

81. *Ibid.*, October 13, 22, 27, 28; *Berkshire Evening Eagle*, November 4; *Springfield Republican*, October 24, 29; *Gazzetta del Massachusetts* (Boston), November 5, 1932.

82. *Boston Transcript*, October 13, 1932.

83. *Ibid.*, August 22, 1932.

84. *Ibid.*, November 7; *Springfield Republican*, November 6, 1932.

85. *Boston Transcript*, October 22, 26, November 1, 4, 1932.

86. *Ibid.*, November 9; *New Bedford Standard-Times*, November 9, 1932.

87. For fuller details and sources of election returns, registration statistics, and data on the ethnic composition of electoral districts, see Appendix and Bibliography.

88. Cf. *Literary Digest*, December 10, 1932, p. 16.

Chapter Nine.

CONCLUSION AND EPILOGUE

1. *Boston Transcript*, November 26, December 7, 10, 1932, January 4, 5, 1933.

2. *Ibid.*, November 12, 1932, February 25, March 3, 1933.

3. *Ibid.*, November 19; *Italian News* (Boston), November 11, 1932.

4. United States Department of Labor, Bureau of Labor Statistics, *Monthly Labor Review*, June 1933, p. 1419; Massachusetts Department of Labor and Industries, *Statistics of Manufactures in Massachusetts: 1920–1938* (place and date of publication not given), p. 49.

5. *Boston Transcript*, December 6, 1932, January 5, 24, 1933.

6. *Ibid.*, March 4, 1933.

7. *Ibid.*

8. Wilson in 1912 got the Bay State's electoral votes, but the Republicans Taft and Theodore Roosevelt together got a large majority of the popular vote.

9. The author's observations in these paragraphs are based in large part on interviews with the Massachusetts political leaders of both parties whose names are cited elsewhere in this work.

10. The state ticket endorsed by a G.O.P. pre-primary convention in 1956, for example, consisted of two old-stock Americans, an Irishman, a Jew, a French-Canadian, and an Italian-American.

11. Lubell points out that under Harding, Coolidge, and Hoover only one out of every twenty-five judicial appointments went to a Catholic, while under Roosevelt and Truman the proportion was one out of four (S. Lubell, *The Future of American Politics* [New York, 1951], pp. 78–79). See also O. Handlin, *The American People in the Twentieth Century* (Cambridge, Mass., 1954), pp. 183–184, 203.

Index

grants, 94; gubernatorial campaign of *1924*, 102–7, 111–14; Smith campaign, 165–66, 176–78; re-election as mayor, 199–200; role in *1930* gubernatorial election, 201–4, 216; in conflict with Walsh-Ely coalition, 218, 233–38, 258, 262–63; and public works projects, 222, 225; role in Mass. Democratic primary of *1932*, 233–38; role in Democratic campaign of *1932*, 239–42, 246–47

Daignault, Elphege, 172–73
Dallinger, Frederick, 103, 133
Danes, 6. *See also* Ethnic groups
Davis, Arthur, 216
Davis, John W.: presidential campaign of *1924*, 98–99, 102; election results, 111–13, 151, 182, 184–85; and Al Smith, 229, 232
Deficit financing, 220–25
Demobilization, 48
Democratic Party, of Massachusetts: its composition, 14–18; and League of Nations, 19–28; campaign of *1920*, 32–34, 40–42; election returns *1920*, 42–47; disunity in *1922*, 54; platform in *1922*, 72–76; campaign of *1924*, 102–11; election results *1924*, 111–16; and "recognition" politics, 123; campaign of *1926*, 145–49; casts majority vote in *1928*, 154; and Prohibition, 155–56; campaign of *1928*, 159–60, 164–70, 174–76; election returns *1928*, 180–85, 187–88; campaign of *1930*, 198–212; election returns *1930*, 212–18; campaign of *1932*, 238–42, 245–50; election returns *1932*, 250–56; position after *1932* election, 257–58, 260–65

of United States, 265–69; composition in the *1920's*, 77–78; convention of *1924*, 84–86, 94–99; shift in control *1928*, 151–52; internal struggle in *1932*, 228–32; convention of *1932*, 38–39
Denby, Edwin, 51

Depression, of *1921–22*, 49. *See* Great Depression (1929)
De Valera, Eamonn, his U.S. tour, 25–26
Dewey, John, 175
Discrimination among ethnic groups, *see* Cultural liberalism, Ethnic groups
Doheny, E. L., 86
Donahue, Frank: becomes Democratic state chairman, 176; role in gubernatorial campaign of *1930*, 199–203; role in Mass. Democratic primary of *1932*, 232–38
Dooley, Harry, 124–25
Draper, Eben, 193, 197, 207, 217
Dyer federal anti-lynching bill, 142

Economic liberalism, 266–68
Edwards, Clarence, 39
Eighteenth Amendment, *see* Prohibition
Eisner, Michael, 104
Eliot, Charles, 27, 34
Elliott, William Yandell, 199
Ely, Joseph: supports Smith in *1924*, 96; in *1926* primary, 124–25; and Jeffersonian Society, 199; in *1930* primary, 200–3; gubernatorial campaign of *1930*, 204, 211–16, 252; policies as governor, 222–24, 228; in primary of *1932*, 232–38; supports Roosevelt, 239–42; campaign of *1932*, 245–48, 250, 253; and Curley, 258; depression measures, 259–60; after *1932* election, 262–63
Emergency Immigration Quota Law, 49, 53
Emergency Reconstruction Corporation, 222
England, Daniel, 124
English immigrants, in Massachusetts, 5–6. *See also* Ethnic groups
Ethnic groups: and assimilation, 10–14; and discrimination, 7, 9–10, 13, 27–28, 93; form pressure groups, 92–94; and reform legislation, 63–64; and Al Smith, 95–96; as voter

INDEX

13
21 Italians — Fiume
24, 33 Irish oppose League
*42 Irish + NIs desert Demos, 1920
45 NI self-consciousness increases
63
*65-7 "Reform" = uplift; Americanize
*70 NIs' suspicion of "reform"
78-9 3 major elements
*79 NIs' dualism
*88 Klan in Mass. — unites NIs. (93)
100 La Follette
116
*139-41 Discontent — ethnic, economic, Prohibition
148 Walsh coalition
*164-6 Reaction to anti-Cathol.
168 Smith's reform — not "uplift" type
169 "Recognition" (119)
173
182-3 NIs desert GOP
*188 Smith attracts NI voters ("A.S. Revolution")
190
215-16 1930: NIs stay with Demos; Yankee ticket
230 FDR vs. Raskob
237 Smith wins Mass. primary
251-2 FDR surpasses Smith; keeps NI vote.
*254-5 1932 issue is economics, but coalition intact.
**261 Conclusion
265
**266-8 Economic issues — common meeting ground, joining urban + rural reform

Lubell
41
49
83
144

328